Economic Controversies

Innovative and thought-provoking, the Economic Controversies series strips back the often impenetrable facade of economic jargon to present bold new ways of looking at pressing issues, while explaining the hidden mechanics behind them. Concise and accessible, the books bring a fresh, unorthodox approach to a variety of controversial subjects.

Also available in the Economic Controversies series:

Yanis Varoufakis, *The Global Minotaur: America, Europe and the Future of the World Economy*

Robert R. Locke and J.-C. Spender, *Confronting Managerialism: How the Business Elite and Their Schools Threw Our Lives Out of Balance*

Lorenzo Fioramonti, *Gross Domestic Problem: The Politics Behind the World's Most Powerful Number*

Heikki Patomäki, *The Great Eurozone Disaster: From Crisis to Global New Deal*

Lorenzo Fioramonti, *How Numbers Rule the World: The Use and Abuse of Statistics in Global Politics*

About the author

Richard Javad Heydarian is a lecturer (political science and international relations) at Ateneo De Manila University (ADMU), the Philippines, and consultant to a number of institutions, including the House of Representatives and Friedrich Ebert Stiftung (Manila office). As an expert on geopolitics and development issues in the Asia-Pacific and MENA regions, he has written for or been interviewed by *Asia Times*, *New York Times*, *Huffington Post*, *Bloomberg*, *The Diplomat* and *Tehran Times*, among other publications. He has participated in and/or presented papers at varying regional and international academic and track II conferences, focusing on regional integration, economic development and international security. Currently, he is the editor of the newly launched *Socdem Asia Quarterly*, which seeks to bring together views and analyses by leading regional and international experts and policy-makers on latest developments in the Asia-Pacific region and beyond.

HOW CAPITALISM FAILED THE ARAB WORLD

THE ECONOMIC ROOTS AND PRECARIOUS FUTURE OF THE MIDDLE EAST UPRISINGS

Richard Javad Heydarian

Zed Books
LONDON | NEW YORK

How Capitalism Failed the Arab World: the economic roots and precarious future of the Middle East uprisings was first published in 2014 by Zed Books Ltd, 7 Cynthia Street, London N1 9JF, UK and Room 400, 175 Fifth Avenue, New York, NY 10010, USA

www.zedbooks.co.uk

Set in Monotype Plantin and FFKievit by Ewan Smith, London NW5
Index: ed.emery@thefreeuniversity.net
Cover designed by www.roguefour.co.uk
Printed and bound by TJ International, Padstow, Cornwall

Distributed in the USA exclusively by Palgrave Macmillan, a division of St Martin's Press, LLC, 175 Fifth Avenue, New York, NY 10010, USA

A catalogue record for this book is available from the British Library
Library of Congress Cataloging in Publication Data available

ISBN 978 1 78032 958 1 hb
ISBN 978 1 78032 957 4 pb

MIX
Paper from responsible sources
FSC® C013056
FSC www.fsc.org

CONTENTS

FIGURES AND TABLES

Figures

Tables

ACKNOWLEDGEMENTS

I would like to thank all of those who helped me throughout the years to hone my analysis of globalization and development, as well as the dynamics of Arab politics. While the following people are only a handful of the many individuals who aided the crafting of this book, I would like most especially to express my deep gratitude to my mentors and former academic advisers, starting with Dr Noel Morada, Executive Director of the Asia-Pacific Centre for Responsibility to Protect (R2P) at the University of Queensland (UQ), who, since my undergraduate years, has rigorously assessed my writings on international affairs and development, and generously encouraged me to present the initial contents of my book in the paper entitled 'The economics of the Arab Spring' at the 2011 ISA International Conference in Brisbane, Australia. I would also like to thank my long-time adviser Dr Clarita Carlos of the University of the Philippines (Diliman) for her invaluable critiques and suggestions upon patiently reviewing my writings on Middle East politics and international affairs. Her intellectual guidance was indispensable to my eventual plan to write a full-blown book on the Arab uprisings.

I would also like to thank John Feffer, co-director of *Foreign Policy in Focus* at the Institute for Policy Studies (IPS) in Washington, for being such a helpful and patient editor, who allowed me to gradually build a body of writings on Middle East affairs, especially the Arab uprisings. Above all, I would like to thank Dr Walden Bello, my long-time mentor, employer and friend, who has been pivotal to my intellectual development, especially in terms of understanding the dynamics of economic globalization and its impact on the developing world. His works on global poverty, food insecurity and developmental states played a key role in my analysis of the impact of economic liberalization on Arab societies. It was his initial suggestion of co-authoring a new book on globalization amid the Arab uprisings which paved the way for our eventual decision – after months of evaluating the merits of authoring separate individual works with common themes as opposed to a joint work – to write our own books, looking at the dynamics of the 2008 Great Recession, on the one hand, and the economic roots of the Arab uprisings, on the other.

ABBREVIATIONS

AHDR	Arab Human Development Report
AKP	Justice and Development Party (Turkey)
AQ	Al-Qaeda
ATCs	Arab transition countries
BWS	Bretton Woods System
FAO	Food and Agriculture Organization of the United Nations
FDI	foreign direct investment
FJP	Freedom and Justice Party
FSA	Free Syrian Army
GCC	Gulf Cooperation Council
GDP	gross domestic product
IFI	international financial institution
IMF	International Monetary Fund
ISI	import-substitution industrialization
MB	Muslim Brotherhood
MENA	Middle East and North Africa
NATO	North Atlantic Treaty Organization
NIC	newly industrialized country
NSF	National Salvation Front
OECD	Organisation for Economic Co-operation and Development
OPEC	Organization of the Petroleum Exporting Countries
PJD	Justice and Development Party (Morocco)
SME	small or medium-sized enterprise
SWF	sovereign wealth fund
UAE	United Arab Emirates
UN	United Nations
UNDP	United Nations Development Programme
UNSC	United Nations Security Council
WTO	World Trade Organization

FOREWORD BY WALDEN BELLO

The Arab Spring took the world by surprise in 2011. In this book, Richard Heydarian unravels the mystery behind the most significant political phenomenon of the last few years, showing how it stemmed from the impact of the gale of economic globalization on the creaky political structures of crony dictatorships.

With the same analytical acumen he displayed as my student and later as my associate, Heydarian digs beneath the surface of dramatic events to show us that what has taken place in the Middle East is not a simple case of political contagion but the overdue combustion of a mix of elements awaiting the fateful spark that was provided by the self-immolation of a young Tunisian vendor, Mohammed Bouazizi.

In this brief foreword, I do not wish to repeat Heydarian's insightful exploration of the reasons why but to ask the hard question of where, over two years after it broke out, the Arab Spring is headed. With the assassination of key opposition leaders in Tunisia, the collapse of the central state in Libya, the unending civil war in Syria, the cost of which has now exceeded 100,000 lives, and, more recently, the overthrow of the democratically elected Morsi government in Egypt, it would not be surprising if some who were initially enthused by the televised revolution in Tahrir Square are having second thoughts.

One may wonder whether, with all the violence, sufferings and interventions it has unleashed, the Arab democratic uprising is worth it. Has it not opened a Pandora's box, the bad things from which outweigh the good? That neoconservatives and Zionists answer in the affirmative is not surprising since they believe that owing to their being a Western outpost, only Israelis are capable of democratic rule. But often, when confronted with this question, many Western liberals and even progressives are paralysed.

I think when addressing this question and related issues, it is useful for us to take a comparative perspective and the long view.

With respect to violence and human rights violations, democratic transitions that are bloody far outnumber those that are peaceful. As Barrington Moore reminds us (1966), the English transition to democracy, which is often mistakenly presented as a case of peaceful evolution, was a violent one that involved numerous deaths in a civil war and ended with the beheading of a king, Charles I, in the seventeenth century. And as Arno Mayer so vividly documents in his book *The Furies* (2002), the French Revolution, the classic democratic transition, saw the interplay between revolutionary terror and counter-revolutionary terror that took thousands of lives over a chaotic five-year period. Closer to our time, democracy in Guatemala was eventually won and consolidated, but only at the cost of some 200,000 lives over a twenty-five-year period.[1] To borrow religious imagery, to which I am usually allergic, the soil of democracy is watered with the blood of thousands of martyrs.

But after the violence, after the bloodshed, will democracy ultimately prevail? Revolutions have their ebbs and flows, and it does seem that the solidity of the institutions that emerge is founded on the inevitable struggles that the democratic revolution unleashes. In this regard, the French revolutionary process that began in 1789 can only be said to have been firmly consolidated with the Third Republic from 1870 to 1940. In between the country saw counter-revolution, Napoleon's imperial government, the revolution of 1830, the revolution of 1848, the Second Empire and the Paris Commune. Much like France's experience, many democratic transitions are like a dance with several movements, consisting of two steps forward and one step back, but the overall direction is forward.

Closer to our time, the Latin American experience is instructive. The democratic struggles of the eighties were subverted and set back by democratic regimes dominated by elites that imposed structural adjustment programmes in the 1990s. But by the first decade of the twenty-first century, people throughout Latin America had had enough. People's movements produced new populist and more participatory democracies that supplanted elite democracies in Venezuela, Bolivia and Ecuador, and neoliberal economic regimes were dismantled in these countries as well as in Brazil and Argentina. The democratic revolution had its advances and retreats, but the strategic thrust of the process was forward, towards democratic deepening and consolidation. Indeed, the sharper and more protracted the struggle, the more firm, it seems, are the foundations of the democracy that emerges.

The Arab democratic revolution will have its ebbs and flows, but I am reasonably confident that the omega point of the Arab Spring will be institutionalization and consolidation of democratic forms and practices that will have their own unique features and dynamics.

Note

1 The dictator of Guatemala in 1982–83 was recently convicted of genocide inflicted on indigenous Guatemalans, but the verdict of the three-person court was overturned by the Constitutional Court, the country's highest.

To my loving parents Nasser and Evangeline, and my sister Justine

1 | A BRAVE NEW MIDDLE EAST: THE BIRTH OF A NEW ERA

> There are very few moments in our lives where we have the privilege to witness history taking place. This is one of those moments. This is one of those times. (US president Barack Obama)[1]

It was a classic Black Swan: a rare, low-probability but ultimately high-impact event, which upended our most cherished notions – based on long-held conventional (but ultimately mistaken) thinking – about the Arab world. Dubbed the 'Arab Spring', or Arab awakening/revolts by others, it marked a paradigm shift in our whole conception of the world's last autocratic fortress (Diamond 2010) which had plagued the (once proud and mighty) civilizations along the Fertile Crescent for decades. Few could deny its prowess: like a tidal wave, unleashed by centuries of pent-up social discontent, the Arab Spring swept across the whole region.

The popular protests' largely secular and democratic character, bereft of all the anti-Western slogans that embellished earlier regional uprisings, such as the 1979 revolution in Iran, (seemingly) heralded the end of history: the ineluctable triumph of liberal-democratic ideology over all rivals, including Islamic fundamentalism – a Hegelian antithesis to secular, Arab autocracies that supplanted centuries-old European colonialism in the post-Second World War era. For Western pundits, focusing especially on the role of the 'information revolution' in galvanizing the teeming youth protesters, the Arab world seemed to have finally succumbed to the forces of globalization – the powerful, largely market-driven force behind universal integration of diverse civilizations. Mainstream global media, quite naively, went so far as to term these massive expressions of popular revulsion at Arab autocracies as 'Facebook/Twitter revolutions', ignoring the sustained, passionate and methodical on-the-ground mobilization efforts of a vast network of civil society organizations, labour unions and even politico-religious forces such as the Muslim Brotherhood (*al-Ikhwan al-Muslimun*) and its many offshoots across the Arab world. Not all observers, however, concurred with this (myopic) Western reading.

Tehran's ayatollahs, viewing their own theocratic regime as the Arab world's ideational inspiration, begged to disagree: they claimed, instead, that the Arab world was following in the footsteps of the 1979 revolution – and that the 'clash of civilizations' was far from over. In their view, a more potent region-wide resistance against Western hegemony was in the offing. What the Iranian leadership – along with their radical-revisionist sympathizers across the region – saw was diametrically opposed to triumphant Western pundits. For Tehran, the Arab Spring spelled the defeat of globalization in the Arab world. In short, they saw a popular backlash against the secular, quasi-capitalist autocrats serving Western interests in the Middle East. The Iranian leadership, instead, saw an 'Islamic Awakening' – the 1979 revolution writ large.

One thing, though, was undeniable: a whole new era was born. Francis Fukuyama (1983), author of the seminal book *The End of History*, talked about the necessity to distinguish 'between what is essential and what is contingent or accidental in world history'. Following this logic, it is important to assess the historical significance of the Arab Spring.

For the Turkish academic-turned-foreign minister Ahmet Davutoglu (2011), the Arab Spring is part of a broader, trans-historical march of history. In an almost Hegelian sense, he described the uprisings as 'naturalizing the flow of history', since 'They were ... a delayed process that should have happened in the late 80s and 90s as in eastern Europe. It did not because some argued that Arab societies did not deserve democracy, and needed authoritarian regimes to preserve the status quo and prevent Islamist radicalism ...'

For British historian Perry Anderson, what occurred in the Arab world was similar to the Hispanic American Wars of Liberation that began in 1810 and ended in 1825, the European revolutions of 1848–49 that reconfigured the monarchical order in the continent, and the fall of the communist regimes in the Soviet bloc, 1989–91. The Arab Spring, he argues, was a genuine world-historical event – a region-wide response to a long period of imperial interventions and predatory autocracies, which have haunted the Arab world for centuries. The protests, he continues, were unified by a distinct characteristic: they shared one language, Arabic, and one religion, Islam (Anderson 2011).

Other scholars, such as Jack A. Goldstone (2011: 9), an expert on revolutions at George Mason University, see the continuation of another modern historical pattern: the downfall of so-called 'Sultanistic' regimes, but not all autocratic Arab regimes per se. Such regimes, Goldstone argues, emerge when a 'national leader expands his personal power at the expense of formal institutions ... [and] appeal to no ideology and have no purpose other than maintaining their personal authority'. In historical terms, Goldstone notes, these Arab autocrats are following the fate of their earlier counterparts in Asia, Africa and Latin America, notably Mohammad Reza, Shah of Iran, Ferdinand Marcos of the Philippines, Suharto in Indonesia, Mexico's Porfirio Díaz, Nicaragua's and Haiti's Somoza and Duvalier dynasties (ibid.: 9).

Yet, beyond the debate on the historical significance and core features of the uprisings, one would tend to ask a more basic question: why they were – and still continue to be – celebrated/described as a 'spring'? Perhaps because the uprisings have opened up a floodgate of discontent, putting an end to a prolonged winter of political passivity in the face of unspeakable oppression, as they proclaimed in symphonic unison: 'People Want the Downfall of the Regime'. Just like the 'Prague Spring' in 1968, the Arab uprisings spelled the death of fear and the triumph of hope against all odds, as hundreds of thousands of protesters took on autocratic behemoths and their sprawling, brutal apparatus of oppression. With this in mind, the Syrian intellectual Burhan Ghalyoun (in Lynch 2011) described the uprisings as part of 'an awakening of the people who have been crushed by despotic regimes'. The Arab Spring was also a call to restore dignity, with protesters invoking 'freedom, social justice, and bread' as the moral and revolutionary equivalence of the French people's *liberté, égalité, fraternité* in 1789. The Arab spring was also a culmination of a broad-based 'civilian jihad' – the long, non-violent democratic struggles by a vast coalition of moderate forces across the Muslim world, previously overshadowed by a constant global obsession with extremist ideologies and their violent agenda. After all, labour unions and civil society organizations played a crucial role in deposing autocrats in Egypt and Tunisia by buttressing the ranks of non-violent mass protests, and organizing civil disobedience campaigns, which threatened to bring the country to its knees, sparking fear of national economic disintegration among the military and power elite – eventually forcing regime allies to choose between siding with the people and saving the nation, on one hand, or risking prolonged national crisis and brutal confrontation by siding with the autocrats. Far from superfluous, the Arab women, long confined to the sidelines of their societies, were also at the centre of the protests across the Arab world, from Tunisia to Egypt and Yemen.

The British newspaper the *Guardian* best captured this much-welcomed phenomenon by describing women's ubiquitous role during the protests as a 'sea of female faces' across the Middle East, 'marching for regime change, an end to repression, the release of loved ones', while others were 'delivering speeches to the crowd, treating the injured, feeding the sit-ins ...' (Guardian 2011). Yet, looking at the role of women in previous protest movements across the region, including the 1979 Iranian revolution, there is nothing surprising about women's widespread participation in galvanizing peaceful, non-violent mass protests against oppressive regimes. Their battle for gender equality, however, was set to intensify after the collapse of old secular regimes.

While the protesters shared a common desire to topple brutal tyrannies, they were, however, divided over what to replace them with. Some cried foul, claiming the Arab Spring – and its overtly secular underpinnings – was 'engineered' by outside forces, perhaps just a conspiracy by major financial and political actors in the West, which, earlier, surreptitiously sponsored 'coloured revolutions' in the post-Soviet space, stretching from Georgia in the Caucasus to Ukraine in eastern Europe. Wary of Western designs, some critics called for control to be wrested from Western interests by instead giving support to other groups, notably the socialists, nationalists and Islamists, at the expense of liberals/secular democrats. A few months into the Arab Spring, Ron Nixon, writing for the *New York*

Times, described how 'the United States' democracy-building campaigns played a bigger role in fomenting protests than was previously known, with key leaders of the [Arab Spring] movements having been trained by the Americans in campaigning, organizing through new media tools and monitoring elections' (Nixon 2011). The article mentioned the role of US-based organizations (as well as the US State Department) in training and financing 'a number of the groups and individuals directly involved in the revolts and reforms sweeping the region', ranging from the much-famed Egyptian April 6 youth movement in Egypt to Yemeni grassroots youth leader Entsar Qadhi and the Bahrain Centre for Human Rights. Based on interviews with American diplomats and Wikileaks cables, the article specified the active and sustained role of the International Republican Institute, the National Democratic Institute and the Freedom House, with Facebook, Google, MTV, Columbia Law School and the State Department providing seminars for Egyptian youth leaders about ways to utilize social networking to circumvent autocratic restrictions (ibid.). In an interview with CNN's Wolf Blitzer, Wael Ghonim, the Google executive and charismatic youth leader during the Egyptian revolution, went so far as to personally thank Facebook CEO Mark Zuckerberg for enabling the Arab Spring, expressing his intent on writing a book, *Revolution: 2.0*, about the revolutionary role of the internet and social networking (Smith 2011).

Others, with a more nuanced observation, had a different take on the issue, calling into question whether the uprisings were exogenously engineered – as opposed to a genuine and spontaneous popular upheaval. Writing for the *Washington Post*, Stanford scholar Fouad Ajami (2012a) argued that, despite the powerful role played by technology in facilitating communication and bypassing state censorship, it was 'the Friday prayers in the embattled cities of Syria; the test of wills between brutal regimes and those brave enough to challenge them; and young people in Daraa, Homs and Hama conquering the culture of fear and taking on despotism' which spelled the essence of the Arab Spring. After all, as he states correctly, Mohammed Bouazizi, the Tunisian vendor whose self-immolation inspired the uprisings, didn't have a Facebook page, but instead exemplified a collective sense of anger and despair among the Arab peoples. 'Technophilia',

Ajami argued, makes little sense in explaining revolution in a region with a relatively low internet penetration.

Depending on their ideological bent, observers had a different take on the uprisings. The Arab Spring – just like any major social phenomenon or concept – represented different things to different people. For some, it was a chance to establish accountable, democratic systems anchored in a secular-rationalist ethos such as those which had given birth to earlier revolutions in the Western world, while others, with a more pious bent, saw things quite differently. The latter group, instead, anticipated the inexorable emergence of Islamic states, reflecting the religious fervour of the wider population. Thus began not only a popular battle against autocracy, but also a wider contention for the soul of the Middle East. In this sense, the Arab people laid down the foundations of a new era, defined around the themes of *vox dei* and *vox populi.* Soon, people realized that the latter battle was more contentious than they initially thought. Two years into democratic transition, even Tunisia, the Arab world's most hopeful post-revolutionary state, would be plunged into chaos when one of the country's leading secular leaders and critics of the Islamist-led government, Shokri Belaid, was assassinated. Meanwhile, a rural–urban divide meant that there was to be divergence in how the course, intensity and meaning of the revolutions were perceived and internalized by the masses.

Yet the revolutions were far from confined to the Arab world, as they sent shock waves across the globe – inspiring popular mobilization and massive protests (as in the 'Occupy movement') against financial corruption, austerity programmes and social inequality among struggling industrialized economies. Soon, autocratic Asian regimes such as Myanmar and China also had to contend with a new wave of popular pressure for political opening, accountability and economic reforms to redress massive corruption and social inequality.

For instance, Freedom House's research director, Arch Puddington (in Kurlantzick 2013), has talked about how major authoritarian states have 'especially since the Arab Spring' stepped up their instruments of repression, because 'they are nervous, which accounts for their intensified persecution of popular movements for change'.

After all, the Arab Spring captivated the global audience, witnessing a surreal succession of revolutions unfolding before their eyes. The uprisings were a powerful reminder of 'people power' – a spontaneous, wholesale expression of popular will – and autocratic ossification. The visible power of the Arab Spring lay in the way it swiftly shattered seemingly invincible autocracies, one after the other.

As late as mid-2010, many of the toppled autocrats seemed firmly in control of their mini-empires: Tunisia's Ben Ali was ruling one of the most modern, liberal Arab countries, and Libya's Mu'ammer Gaddafi supervised a vast, oppressive apparatus greased by booming oil revenues and an expanding network of foreign partners/clients across the Mediterranean Sea and the Sahara desert, while Yemen's Ali Abdullah Salleh cleverly played into Western fears of extremism by soliciting huge strategic rents to nourish his tribal henchmen. In Egypt, Hosni Mubarak, confident in the foundations of his neo-paternalistic regime, was primarily concerned with cementing his legacy: he oscillated between running for the next presidential elections in 2011, on one hand, and building his son, Gamal Mubarak, as the next ruler of Egypt, on the other. Yet, one after the other, like dominoes, these autocrats fell in the face of the Arab Spring. In a span of a few months, beginning in late 2010, much of North Africa changed, while the rest of the Middle East, notably in the Levant and the Arabian peninsula, woke up from a prolonged stupor. These fairy-tale revolutions filled with picturesque expressions of freedom and steeped in triumphant rhetoric set off a chain reaction across the greater Middle East.

Witnessing the swift and irreversible downfall of North African strongmen, besieged autocrats in Yemen, Bahrain and Syria bitterly confronted an existential battle against forces of change. Shifting their instruments of coercion into full gear, they tirelessly courted better-endowed patrons across the region for logistical and financial support. The Gulf Cooperation Council (GCC), composed of petro-monarchies in the Persian Gulf, jumped to the aid of not only Bahrain, going as far as sending troops to quash a burgeoning democratic revolution, but also extended support to vulnerable monarchies such as Oman, Jordan and Morocco. Saudi Arabia even provided asylum to fallen allies such as Ben Ali, while incessantly dissuading Washington from abandoning the likes of Mubarak. Facing the possibility of losing its sole state ally in the world, Iran also extended its largesse to the Baathist regime in Damascus.

Patrons lavished funds and arms on their troubled clients to quell and smash all forms of opposition. Wary of the prospects of a failed state on the southern shores of the Arabian peninsula, the GCC also engaged in a series of damage-control efforts in Yemen to facilitate a peaceful political – as opposed to democratic – transition. Determined to stand their ground, these monarchies banded together, pushing back popular pressure and shaping the course of revolutions all across the Middle East. They gave birth to a counter-revolutionary winter, sniffing out opposition at home, while influencing democratic struggles without. Pooling together their vast resources, they used their multiple levers of influence – including a large network of influential GCC-based Arabic news outlets – to the fullest extent (see Chapter 6).

The monarchies also launched a massive public relations campaign to ward off external scrutiny and demoralize internal agitations. In attempting to differentiate themselves from their increasingly discredited republican counterparts, Arab monarchies shrewdly highlighted their deep roots in their respective societies, redirecting domestic resentments against their pliable parliaments and/or (real and imagined) foreign conspiracies. Aside from beefing up their security-intelligence apparatuses and throwing money at popular discontent, the Arab monarchies were further aided by the horror and violence seen in neighbouring states in the throes of revolution. (The decades-long civil war and conflict in Afghanistan and Iraq did little to calm widespread fears of regime change.) The spectre of civil war and chaos, as in Libya and Syria, and conservative Islamist takeover, as in Egypt, also provoked a serious reassessment by increasingly sobered liberal reformers calling for change within Arab monarchies (see Chapter 7).

Soon, even Western powers, citing the perils of direct intervention, abandoned any pretence of supporting political change in the region, reiterating the imperative to contain Iran, and their long-standing commitment to ensure the steady and secure supply of hydrocarbon resources, especially in trying economic times for centre economies. When Syria, Yemen and Libya became new havens for extremism, empowering Al-Qaeda branches in Iraq, the Arabian peninsula and North Africa, Western powers had to contend with a complex 'hubs-and-spokes' of terror, a hydra now reaching deep into places such as sub-Saharan Mali. Aside from the renewed threat of extremism, various forms of separatist sentiment raised the prospects of 'balkanization' – the formation of new enclaves and federations along sectarian, ethnic lines – in the Levant, southern portions of the Arabian peninsula and North Africa.

On the other hand, as the post-revolutionary states moved towards an Arab Summer, putting behind a transient moment of broad-based consensus against derided autocrats, they faced even deeper challenges. Amid a power vacuum, the new civilian governments wrestled hard against competing factions, whether remnants of the previous regime or contestants for the future of the revolution, to secure control over vital state institutions, while struggling hard to kick-start flailing economies, as public unrest and insecurity plagued commercial hubs as well as key tourist spots and industrial zones. To make matters worse, the Arab Summer had to contend with a stubborn global economic downturn, rising competition from emerging economies elsewhere, persistently high oil prices, and precarious fluctuations in basic commodity prices. But the main bone of contention among competing factions was the crucial and consequential issue of drafting new constitutions: should they be along the liberal-democratic lines of more established Western constitutions, or instead documents inspired by – or entirely based on – the principles of sharia, the Islamic jurisprudence.

Reflecting on the Arab world's post-revolutionary predicament, and the tortuous inter-factional battle for a new era, the Oxford historian Mark Almond aptly described the initial uprisings as 'an inverted fairy story with a happy ending in the beginning' (Almond 2011). Unlike the relatively peaceful post-revolutionary transitions in East Asia in the 1980s and eastern Europe in the 1990s, the Arab Spring became a prequel to greater chaos, as a spectre of unending civil war, post-revolutionary instability and external military interventions gripped the region.

Keeping all the vagaries of the Arab Spring in mind, one still discovers more fundamental issues in need of deeper exposition.

For instance, we need to understand the Arab Spring in historical terms, within the context of earlier democratic struggles throughout the nineteenth and twentieth centuries, while exploring the factors that may explain why so many governments, experts and Middle East scholars failed to see the uprisings coming.

We also need to analyse factors which have contributed to the emergence as well as the divergence of revolutionary outcomes across the region. More importantly, we should examine whether the Arab Spring is a reflection of the 'end of history' and the triumph of globalization: 'The end point of mankind's ideological evolution and the universalization of Western liberal democracy as the final form of human government', as Francis Fukuyama described the post-Cold War era (Fukuyama 1983). Or, alternatively, are we instead looking at an en masse rejection of globalization in the region, portending a renewed clash of civilizations in a reconfigured Middle Eastern political landscape? If so, we must explore how the inexorable forces of globalization have failed the Arab world. We should also understand how the forces of economic globalization – the incessant push for economic opening and political stability by international organizations and major powers, as well as multinational companies – continue to affect the Arab world and the evolution of the uprisings, whether they have been empowered or shackled by globalization. Only then will we be able to capture the essence of the Arab Spring, providing us with some preliminary framework to credibly trace its trajectory and understand its significance.

Thus, the book aims to provide a much more specific understanding of globalization, focusing on a unique episode in recent history, whereby banks, investors, and international financial institutions – aided by the retreat of regulators, and innovations in the realm of trade and finance – have come to dominate the global system after a long period of state-directed capitalism (and failed experimentations with command economy elsewhere). The intention here is to understand the nexus between the uprisings in the Middle East, on one hand, and the broader systemic developments driven by a distinct form of globalization in recent decades, on the other. Therefore, the book looks at 'economic globalization', taking off in the mid-1970s and directly impacting the Arab world in the succeeding decades.

Here, economic globalization is not understood as some 'impersonal force', which has inexorably reshaped societies across the world,[2] and the relations among people, states and markets. To the contrary, the book looks at economic globalization as a consciously driven policy paradigm, espousing the transformation of the state from a 'social state' into a 'regulatory state'.[3] The book argues that the Arab world's structural deficiencies (e.g. high unemployment, rising income inequality, a youth bulge, etc.) were a product of how economic globalization reinforced the combustible fusion of fragile, unaccountable political institutions with aggressive pro-market policies, leading to the emergence of a predatory form of capitalism.

Briefly put, the book looks at the interplay of varying elements giving birth to the Arab uprisings. It analyses how the uprisings emerged as the result of a distinct interaction among agents (i.e. the state and opposition forces), structural factors (i.e. crony capitalism), aggravating elements (i.e. global financial and commodity crises) and shock/triggering factors. It looks at how underlying structural vulnerabilities among Arab states provided the fertile grounds for growing political discontent and high vulnerability to external shocks. In the absence of democratic channels through which to constructively air their grievances, people had little choice but to confront a weak and unaccountable state, which failed to fulfil its basic obligations to provide minimum political and economic rights for common citizens. The trigger was set by the self-immolation of Mohammed Bouazizi, filmed on mobile phones, and spread instantaneously through social networking and other media outlets, proving to be an important factor in rallying the public against uncompromising autocrats.

While crony capitalism is not unique to the Arab world, many countries were able to overcome public unrest and structural economic challenges, because they adopted appropriate developmental policy reforms – coupled, in some cases, with a transition to a more democratic system. In contrast, the Arab world has suffered from not only remarkable levels of economic stagnation, but also the absence of functional electoral institutions to encourage better governance and constructively channel public grievances in the event of crisis. But a dynamic understanding of the trajectory of the Arab Spring should also consider the ability of certain states to better cope with short-term shocks, despite the lack of genuine democratic reforms. For instance, the petro-states in the Persian Gulf (despite being even more repressive than many post-revolutionary Arab states) have been, so far, able to prevent a collapse, cashing in on their huge commodity-based rents to prop up their security apparatus and placate criticisms and social pressure.

By bringing together insights from a whole range of scholars, authors and analysts, across the ideological spectrum, the book aims to provide a deeper understanding of not only the structural roots of the Arab Spring, but its trajectory across time and space, as we enter the Arab Summer. Overall, the book is a brief account of how economic globalization has failed the Arab people, blocking the emergence of genuine democracies with functional economies; but also how the reigning global order is turning a blind eye to an ongoing counter-revolutionary wave in order to preserve an increasingly unsustainable status quo.

Arab exceptionalism

While the term 'exceptionalism' tends to denote a positive attribute, the same cannot be said when it is applied to the modern Arab world. What makes the Arab Spring so special is the fact that there have been practically no established democracies in the Arab world – precisely what the uprisings are trying to upend. For years, scholars and policy-makers obsessively pondered on what was dubbed a 'democratic deficit' in the Arab world. Historically, despite several attempts at establishing constitutional monarchies and democratic republics, post-colonial Arab states, whether monarchies or republics, morphed into Orwellian states, sustained by systematic repression, strategic rents and social welfare (and other forms of dole-outs aimed at appeasing restive citizens). Prior to the Arab Spring, the most visible form of (undemocratic) opposition came from extremist elements, which provoked the ire of Western powers and their Arab clients after the 9/11 attacks. Meanwhile, the quiet sociocultural revolutions and democratic struggles, led by a burgeoning middle class, scores of high-profile liberal reformers and a loose but vibrant network of civil society organizations, were overshadowed by the focus on a multifarious violent jihad against Western interests. In this sense, democracy was hardly on top of the autocrats' and their patrons' agenda, despite the continual discourse about political reforms and 'good governance' – primarily to sustain the status quo, while cutting down on red tape and increasing market predictability in order to integrate Arab economies into the global chains of production.

Democracy was shrouded in mystery and obfuscation. Around the world, especially in the Middle East, democracy was often (and somehow continues to be) dismissed – especially by undemocratic rulers – as a fuzzy term, bereft of any defined universal essence, thus better understood within the specific structures and aspirations of individual societies and civilizations. It has also been constantly adulterated, often expressed in polemical terms and couched in cosmetic political reforms, serving the interests of undemocratic regimes; strangely, it is an idea that is even reflected in the rhetoric and title of most repressive regimes such as the *Democratic* People's Republic of Korea – the world's most hermetic nation-state, (barely surviving) under the iron fist of the Kim dynasty.

Even the Western world's greatest minds had their reservations about democracy. In *The Republic*, Plato described democracy as 'a charming form of government, full of variety and disorder, and dispensing a sort of equality to equals and unequals alike' (Plato 1973: 6). In *Politics*, Plato's stellar protégé, Aristotle, talked about an extreme form of democracy, 'analogous to tyranny, where law has ceased to be sovereign and the notion of a constitution has practically disappeared' (Aristotle 1946: 163). He defined democracy as 'a constitution in which the free-born and poor control the government – being at the same time the majority', in contrast to oligarchy, 'in which the rich and better-born control the government – being at the same time the minority' (ibid.: 164). For Aristotle, democracy was a perversion of the polity: the ideal mixed type of rule. Ancient thinkers, mainly Plato and Aristotle, were disconcerted by democracy, arguing its tendency to deteriorate into 'demagoguery', which, in turn, erodes merit-based politics and the preservation of the 'rule of law'. Modern scholars, reflecting on the experiences of post-revolutionary France and Russia as well as pre-Second World War fascist European states, had their own reservations about democracy too, arguing that high (manipulated) mass participation during tough economic times tends to favour a more 'authoritarian' system. Today there is, however, a robust and rigorous literature on democracy – capturing the universal essence of the idea in its varying forms and degrees, across time and space. The modern literature on democracy is less about normative contemplation, but instead anchored in more measurable and empirically driven analysis. Perhaps the simplest definition of democracy is the one provided by the Austrian economist Joseph Schumpeter (1962), in *Capitalism, Socialism, and Democracy*, whereby he described it as simply a method by which top political leaders are selected. For succeeding generations of scholars, notably Robert Dahl, Samuel Huntington and Adam Przeworski, democracy (in a minimalist fashion) equated to political contestation open to broadly based participation by the citizenry. Thus, the elections – the method by which top political positions are contested – must fulfil three basic criteria. First, they must be competitive, meaning electoral rules are supposed to be fair to both the incumbent (and its allies) as well as the opposition elements, accompanied by legal rights to form political parties, supervised by an independent electoral commission, and fair access to media. Also, there should be no exclusive 'state subsidy' to the incumbent, nor any for harassment of opposition forces and their supporters. Secondly, elections must be popular, meaning almost all adults (from age sixteen to eighteen, as defined by the constitution of the host country) must be allowed to vote regardless of their ethnicity, social class, colour, sex, religion, etc. Lastly, elections should embrace the choice of top political leaders; if they embrace only lower-level officials, then this is merely a form of 'political liberalization', but not democratic practice (see Przeworski et al. 2000: 1–36).

For Przeworski, democracy is about 'organized uncertainty', wherein the constitutional rules guarantee the possibility of the incumbent party losing. This, for him, differentiates democracies from authoritarian regimes, which engage in 'demonstration elections', where it is almost impossible for the incumbent and his allies to lose elections (and by extension power) (ibid.). In *Democracy and Its Critics*, Robert Dahl (1989) talked about a polyarchy (rule of many), whereby the government reflects an equal opportunity for individuals and varying interests to be considered in the process of decision-making and political freedom is matched with social justice and national independence. In *Developing Democracy*, Larry Diamond (1999) discussed the process by which a country develops through several stages of democratic transition – and how democratization is an open-ended process. Democratic transition, Diamond argues, pertains to the initial process by which top leaders are sworn in through elections. After a democratic transition, he states, the next stage is 'democratic consolidation', whereby democratic rules are diligently followed by relevant political forces: politically organized groups, which have the capacity to end the democratic system (i.e. the military, opposition political parties, incumbents, revolutionary movements/terrorist groups, and social groups such as business chambers and labour unions). In Diamond's view, one can say that a democracy has deepened when electoral rules become fairer, and are accepted by more political forces, and there is a deeper commitment from relevant political forces to democratic values (normative compliance). Moreover, the procedures of a democratic regime should go beyond the electoral process, to become more accountable, representative, liberal and accessible: rigorous checks and balances among varying branches of the state, extended civil and political liberties for citizens, and the provision of basic welfare and social rights for the majority of citizens. Once the democratic consolidation process is complete, we can talk about mature democracies, where all relevant actors have internalized systemic values to become unconditional democrats and the political system is less likely to give in to authoritarian temptations and break down in the face of pressure.

Now, looking at the Middle East one discovers that even from a minimalist perspective there is hardly any country in the Arab region that has engaged in regular cycles of competitive, popular and fair elections. Almost all major regions of the world, with the exception of the Middle East, underwent waves of democratization in the previous century, with the collapse of the Soviet Union (1989–91) coinciding with the renewed wave of democratization in eastern Europe (and later in the post-Soviet space). For almost two decades, scholars wondered whether the Arab world would follow suit, or, instead, represent a distinct fourth wave of democratization in the early twenty-first century (Schlumberger 2008; Diamond 2010).

TABLE 1.1 The Arab world's dismal political record

Country	Ruler	Date of accession	2010 world ranking for: Democracy[1]	Corruption[2]	Press freedom[3]
Algeria	Abdelaziz Bouteflika	1999	125	105	141
Bahrain	King Hamad bin Isa al-Khalifa	1999	122	48	153
Comoros	Ahmed Sambi	2006	127	154	102
Djibouti	Ismael Omar Guelleh	1999	154	91	159
Egypt	Hosni Mubarak	1981	138	98	130

Notes: 1. Of 167 countries; 2. of 178 countries; 3. of 196 countries and territories

Using the data and indices compiled by leading institutions focusing on measuring indicators of democracy, corruption and freedom around the world, the UK-based *The Economist* compiled a telling graph, which underscored the depth of democratic deficit in the Arab world. With the exception of Lebanon, and to a certain degree the Occupied Territories (i.e. Palestine), practically all Arab countries were (and continue to be) at the bottom of international rankings, compiled by Freedom House, the Economist Intelligence Unit and Transparency International, that are relevant to the measurement of democracy (see Table 1.1). As a result, one begins to ask whether the Arab Spring was inevitable; or why did it come so late, given how corruption, autocratic rule and unaccountability have been so entrenched for so long?

The new awakening

When one puts the Arab uprisings in a historical context, their novelty becomes questionable. After all, the twentieth century actually witnessed a series of democratic protests and revolts across the Middle East. Thus, what is under question is a new Arab Spring – or awakening, for that matter. Moreover, one must note how protests and upheavals in the non-Arab countries of Turkey and Iran, the two fulcrums of the region, have also played a critical role in pushing the boundaries of democratic struggles in the Middle East, especially when one considers how they have been intertwined and interactive with broader developments in the Arab world.

In an essay for *Foreign Affairs*, Fouad Ajami (2012b) contextualized the Arab Spring within a centuries-old struggle for democracy and enlightenment, describing it as the 'third awakening'. The first one, he argues, was a '*political*-cultural renaissance' in the nineteenth century, whereby a host of Arab intellectuals, hailing from the petty bourgeoisie and the professional classes, called for modernity, secularism and liberal reforms out of the 'debris of the Ottoman Empire'. The second awakening came in the immediate post-Second World War period, whereby nationalist leaders, hailing from middle and working classes, dreamed of rescuing the Arab world from the ashes of the Ottoman Empire's collapse. While autocratic in their governance paradigm, these new leaders, notably Egypt's Gamal Abdel

Nasser and Tunisia's Habib Bourguiba, followed by early leaders of the Baath Party in Syria and Iraq, saw the salvation of their countries in industrialization and modern technology. These two eras of socio-political awakening, as Ajami mentioned, provided the intellectual and cultural fuel for decades-long democratic struggles in the post-colonial Arab regimes. Each era of awakening sparked a new series of popular upheavals across the Arab world (ibid.).

The first wave of protests and democratic uprisings, inspired by the first Arab awakening, had two distinct features: (1) they were against unaccountable and/or absolute monarchies; and (2) they were anti-colonial, mainly in response to the British and French empires. The 1906 Iranian constitutional revolution and the 1908 Young Ottomans revolution represent the region's first attempts at introducing a more accountable monarchy, where rule of law, popular sovereignty, and constitutionalism could reign.[4] The year 1919 was also a crucial one in the region's history. Thanks to telegraph technology, President Woodrow Wilson's Fourteen Points speech, underscoring the centrality of nationalist self-determination, inspired popular protests across the Arab world. Civil disobedience and nationwide strikes paralysed the government, eventually toppling the Egyptian state. In Tunisia, popular protests called for the restoration of the country's constitution, while Libya's tribal and provincial leaders spared no time and energy in consolidating the newly found republic (see Anderson 2011: 2–7).

In 1923, Kemal Atatürk abolished the Ottoman Empire by establishing the Turkish republic (Zurcher 1993). From 1951 to 1953, the nationalist movement led to the rise of Prime Minister Muhammad Mossadegh as the duly elected democratic leader of Iran, almost ending the reign of Muhammad Reza Shah (Kinzer 2003; Ansari 2006). But there was also a parallel nationalist movement across the Arab world, combining a strong sense of pan-Arabism with Turkey's Kemalist notions of modernity and secularism. The 1950s would witness a series of pan-Arabist 'revolutions', some springing from the 'Baathist' ideology, originating in Syria, whereby a group of fiercely nationalist and secular officers would topple corrupt, pliable and inept monarchies: in 1952, Gamal Abdel Nasser led a revolution which toppled the Egyptian monarchy. By 1958, the Iraqi Hashemite monarchy had also fallen (Anderson 2011). However, hardly any of these protests and revolutions led to a democratic government. Instead, a new generation of autocrats emerged in the region, each following in the footsteps of the Turkish strongman Kemal Atatürk, and to a certain degree Iran's nationalist monarch Reza Pahlavi, who saw the redemption of his country – and by extension the Near East – in mimicking Western modernity and shelving traditional Islamic roots. This brand of assertive and nationalist republicanism would be termed 'Kemalism', crediting modern Turkey's founding father as the trailblazer of a new post-colonial political system/ideology in the Middle East (Nasr 2009: 85–115).

The second wave of popular uprisings and mobilizations, emerging in the post-colonial era of secular strongmen, had three distinct characteristics: (1) they were directed against brutal and unaccountable autocratic republics, which supplanted preceding monarchies; (2) they were either inspired by the Iranian Islamic Revolution or had a generally Islamist agenda; and (3) they generally emphasized the importance of popular elections and democratic politics. By the late twentieth century, the Iranian revolution marked the first popular democratic uprising to successfully dislodge a powerful and well-entrenched regime, the Pahlavi dynasty. After the Iranian revolution, a series of popular movements – with Islamist agendas – led to the rise of the Islamic Salvation Front in Algeria, Hamas in Palestine, Hezbollah in Lebanon, and most notably the Justice and Development Party (AKP) in Turkey. But there were no functioning liberal democracies to emerge out of these uprisings and movements, specifically in the Arab world (see Chapter 5).

Nevertheless, the last decade has witnessed remarkable changes in the political landscape of the region's more vibrant and influential countries, namely Iran and Turkey. In the aftermath of the Iran–Iraq war, Iran's politics took a 'pragmatic turn', with economic liberalization and normalized foreign relations at the top of President Rafsanjani's political agenda. By emphasizing political moderation and economic prosperity, his administration paved the way for the rise of a consumer society and a cadre of influential, moderate and reformist thinkers. The election of President Khatami in 1997 was a watershed in Iran's post-revolutionary history. His so-called

'Islamic democracy' thesis resonated with huge sections of Iran's youthful and highly educated population. Drawing insights from Tocqueville's *Democracy in America*, Khatami argued that religion and democratic politics are not only compatible, but are in fact mutually supportive. Drawing parallels between Iran and America, he explained how religion inspires a vibrant civic culture that is conducive to democratic exercise (Ansari 2006). Under his leadership, the 'reformist movement' gradually pushed for democratization, political liberalization and respect for the constitution's 'republican' spirit. To be sure, his agenda was eventually sidelined by a conservative backlash, culminating in the election of the hawkish President Mahmoud Ahmadinejad in 2005 (Nasr 2009; Takeyh 2006; Ansari 2006; Abrahamian 2011). However, the reformist movement experienced a revival with the rise of Mir Hossein Mousavi – the main opposition leader – during the 2009 elections. Mousavi and his core supporters were the main architects of the so-called 'Green Movement' in Iran, which eventually became the greatest source of challenge to the conservative regime since the bloody conflict between Marxist and Islamist factions in the aftermath of the 1979 revolution. The 2009 elections was followed by massive protests – initially peaceful and widespread – across the country as opposition supporters accused the government of manipulating the electoral process to favour the conservative incumbent. The opposition supporters used the latest developments in information technology to organize rallies, build momentum ahead of protests, broadcast events to the international audience, and circumvent state regulations. The Iranian Green Movement in 2009, just as in the previous 1979 revolution, proved to be a source of ideational inspiration and rich tactical lessons. In succeeding months, prominent bloggers and cyber activists, across the Arab world, utilized similar tactics and strategies – initially used by their Iranian counterparts – to challenge less adept and more vulnerable Arab autocracies, which lacked the technological sophistication and bureaucratic prowess of the Iranian state.

But Turkey would prove to be a greater inspiration. In the last decade, the country has experienced the rise of the moderate Islamist AK Party. While Atatürk is revered for his vision of a secular and modern state in the Middle East, the AKP gained international praise – especially among Arab countries – for its impeccable success in pushing the democratic agenda in Turkey. The party's rise was followed by an unprecedented era of economic dynamism, political stability, pluralism and sustained democratization and liberalization. Unlike its Iranian counterpart, the AKP brilliantly balanced its domestic Islamist political agenda with the necessity for friendly and stable foreign relations with the West, especially the USA. As a result, Turkey has avoided the kind of international isolation that Iran has suffered. Moreover, the AKP's astute mixture of modern political beliefs, market economics and conservative social policies has allowed it to increase its support among domestic constituencies and international audiences, enabling it to gradually weaken its main nemesis: the laics and ultranationalists, who would rather launch a coup and disrupt Turkey's democratic institutions than accept an Islamist party governing Turkey. Yet the AKP has proved that it is possible to reform a system from within, no matter how it has been historically dominated by the military and other hardliner elements (Nasr 2009: 232–51; Heydarian 2011).

Owing to growing domestic and international support, the AKP – under the charismatic leadership of Prime Minister Tayyip Erdogan – successfully pushed for a series of constitutional reforms and legislation, which allowed the Islamists to consolidate domestic support, establish civilian supremacy over the military, and steer the country towards greater international and regional economic integration. Of course, the AKP sagaciously used the 'European Union card' to push for democratic reforms, which in effect weakened the military and judiciary (the laics' stronghold), while strengthening the executive and parliament (the AKP's stronghold). As a result, some analysts went so far as to praise Turkey as the region's most successful and influential Muslim country. The Turkish experience also drew a lot of attention across the Arab world, with influential leaders and youth activists occasionally mentioning Turkey as a possible inspiration, if not a model, for post-autocratic politics among Arab nations. In fact, both Islamists and liberal democrats have underscored the significance of the Turkish model for Arab uprisings and the prospects for democratic politics in the Arab world. The struggles and social movements in major non-Arab neighbouring countries should be factored into the momentum, which pushed the Arab world to the brink and dramatically changed the Middle East (Heydarian 2011).

In her *Time* magazine article 'A quiet revolution grows in the Muslim world', veteran journalist Robin Wright (2009) discussed how 'a quieter and more profound revolution' was transforming the Muslim world, three decades after Iran's revolution established clerical rule. She looked at the post-9/11 Middle East, and how millions of young and modern Muslims took up the reins of a non-violent revolution, demanding change within secular autocracies, while discrediting extremism and reactionary politics. In short, she saw a 'soft revolution' that reflected more a search 'for identity and direction than expressing piety'. In *Forces of Fortune*, Iranian-American scholar V. Nasr (2009), echoing Wright's arguments, also talked about seismic shifts in the cultural and political landscape of the Muslim world, largely brought about by the emergence of a new, vibrant and self-confident middle class, or what he calls the 'critical middle', which has demanded more openness, stability and moderation in their respective countries – more successful in places such as Dubai and Anatolia, but also gaining pace in Iran, Egypt and Pakistan.

What one gathers from these works is the impression that in the first decade of the twenty-first century there were already widespread expressions of 'civilian jihad' – a non-violent struggle for self-mastery, dignity and respect – across the Arab world, signalling a broader secular transformation within the regional political landscape. Such trends towards a popular revolution were already plainly evident in major Arab countries such as Egypt, with civil society organizations and political movements constantly agitating against autocratic rule.

Looking at various non-violent movements in the Middle East, notably the 1997 Citizen Initiative for Constant Light in Turkey as well as Shayfeen.com and the Egyptians Against Corruption movements, Hassan and Beyerle (2009: 266) analysed how civil society pushed the boundaries of political action by 'harnessing civic power to fight corruption by reaching out to and engaging ordinary citizens'. By tapping into broad-based social discontent at the state of economic disarray and underdevelopment in the region, they argue, the region is reinventing notions of 'people power' and expanding the horizons of civil resistance against oppressive regimes.

Beyond the issue of corruption, there were to be even greater non-violent movements against autocratic regimes across the Arab world. For instance, in the run-up to the 2005 presidential elections, the Egyptian people formed the multi-sectoral, cross-ideological Kefaya ('*enough*' in Arabic) movement, which brought together all major elements within civil society, from secularist and Nasserite groups to the Muslim Brotherhood – collectively calling for an end to Mubarak's presidency and his bid for re-election. However, the regime – in an attempt to intimidate the opposition – ended up rigging the elections and imprisoning Ayman Nour, the main opposition challenger. But the popular yearning for change was far from silenced, and there were more popular mobilizations in store. In 2008, an increasing incidence of protests across the country, from industrial strikes to pro-democracy rallies, encouraged a number of savvy and sophisticated Egyptian youths to form the April 6 movement on Facebook. In 2010, Egypt's major cities, especially Alexandria, were engulfed in massive protests, when the dreaded police were directly implicated in the brutal murder of the twenty-eight-year-old Khaled Said. Protesters in Cairo chanted for the end of the Mubarak-military rule and the prosecution of the interior minister, to end the cycle of impunity and continuing police brutality. Instead of addressing the legitimate demands of the protesters, the Mubarak regime responded with heavy-handed repression, followed by the flagrant rigging of the 2011 parliamentary elections – signalling more state-sponsored shenanigans ahead of the fateful presidential elections the same year. At this point, Egypt was on the brink: inspired by the Jasmine Revolution in Tunisia, Egyptian activists chose 25 January, the 'National Police Day', as the day of reckoning. In this sense, one could argue that the momentum for Arab uprisings was always there, indicating the inevitability of the revolutions (Shehata 2011: 26–32). As Nasr (2009: 253) argued shortly before the Arab Spring, 'The irony is that the idea of democracy is not alien to the Middle East; it is just that the practice has never taken root.' But this was about to change.

The age of the unthinkable

In retrospect, the Arab autocracies may always have been in a state of 'self-organized criticality', an inch away from collapse, where the addition of a small input pushes the whole system off the cliff. The opaque nature of autocratic politics plus the visible entrenchment of the police state – buttressed by an army of security and intelligence forces – tends to give an impression of 'regime invincibility'. One discovers the fragility of such systems when they fail to introduce crucial reforms, manage shocks, adopt coping mechanisms, and contain mounting opposition – eventually collapsing in the face of internal defection, bureaucratic paralysis and mushrooming protests.

No wonder many analysts – presuming stability and a high degree of certainty – were dazzled by the intensity and direction of the Arab uprisings. It was the abrupt collapse of seemingly 'solid' and 'stable' autocratic regimes which perplexed even the most astute minds. Looking at the downfall of many North African autocrats, it was clear that there was no gradual and predictable transition from homoeostasis to decline and eventual collapse. The transition came almost overnight.

Shortly before the Arab Spring, the leading China-based geostrategist Joshua Cooper-Ramo published a thought-provoking book, *The Age of the Unthinkable*, which focused on how conventional wisdom tends to dodge the evolving physics of power in a new revolutionary era, where the 'world is not becoming more stable or easier to comprehend' (Ramo 2009: 8), but instead is fraught with unpredictability and complexity. Lamenting hard-nosed leaders and experts for their outdated thinking, he argued, 'We've left our future, in other words, largely in the hands of people whose single greatest characteristic is that they are bewildered by the present' (ibid.: 9). The advent of the 2008 Great Recession vindicated Ramo's premises by revealing the paucity of a whole body of theories and methods which underpinned the Western financial and economic system (see Chapter 4). Three years later, as the world moved into the second decade of the new century, the Arab Spring presented another shocking reaffirmation of Ramo's arguments: while the Great Recession undermined a long-held belief in (erroneous) conventional accounting and financial models dominating the greatest minds in Wall Street and Western governments, the Arab Spring revealed the depth of bewilderment among leading policy-making bodies as well as scholastic centres; Ramo (ibid.: 10–11) succinctly captures this cognitive gap among the elite:

> There is now hope and even the first hints of substantial changes in policy, but the basic architecture of ideas and theories necessary to back up such difficult work remains profoundly underdeveloped ... It would be nice if we lived in a time when technology or capitalism or democracy was erasing unpredictability, when shifts could be carefully mapped and planned for using logic that originated centuries ago. This is the world that many politicians or foreign and financial policy experts have been trying to peddle to us ...

He is not alone in his lamentations, for leading financial experts as well as Middle Eastern scholars do share such doubts with respect to the elite's ability to comprehend uncertainty and imagine the unimaginable. The seismic shifts in the global economic and geostrategic landscape have unsettled top decision-makers, threatening even psychological dissonance.

In *When Markets Collide*, Mohammad El-Erian (2008: 2), one of the world's leading economic experts and hedge fund managers, underscores the difficulties of even recognizing deep secular transformations which dramatically unsettle the status quo: 'Transformations are not easy to recognize or navigate, especially when they are initially unanticipated and evolve rapidly.' Reflecting on the huge cognitive debacle that prefaced the 2008 Great Recession, he argued: 'By challenging conventional wisdom and historic entitlements, transformations feed a dynamic that is inevitably uneven and, at times, unpredictable' (ibid.). In particular, El-Erian looks at how human beings are inclined to treat 'noise' – anomalous challenges to long-standing beliefs – as temporary and reversible indicators, bereft of meaningful information. Thus, he argues, participants miss 'signals of fundamental changes that, as yet, are not captured by conventional monitoring tools' (ibid.: 6). Arguably, El-Erian's analysis equally applies to the Arab Spring – a revolutionary upheaval that turned the political status quo (and its underlying paradigmatic presuppositions) in the Middle East on its head.

This is precisely the point taken by risk engineer Nassim Nicholas Taleb and Professor of International Political Economy Mark Blyth in their *Foreign Affairs* essay 'The Black Swan of Cairo'. For them, whether we are looking at the 2008 Great Recession or the Arab Spring, 'The critical issue in both cases is the artificial suppression of volatility – the ups and downs of life – in the name of stability' (Taleb and Blyth 2011: 33). For them, the Arab uprisings are 'simply what happens when highly constrained systems explode' (ibid.). Treating Arab regimes as complex systems, they identify a crucial vulnerability: autocrats tend to artificially suppress volatility (e.g. opposition demands for democratic opening) by utilizing instruments of coercion and appeasement, but their fragility lies in how silent risks accumulate beneath the surface, only to emerge later in an explosive form of systemic breakdown and/or revolutionary transition once a specific threshold is reached. In short, the Arab uprisings were a 'black swan', representing a high-impact, low-probability event, which always rested on the statistical tailspin of probability distribution of outcomes (ibid.: 33–9).

Yet, in fairness to the conventional wisdom among elites, the Arab regimes have been punching beyond their weight and constantly defying expectations in the face of challenges for many decades – creating an aura of invincibility in the eyes of even the most astute observers. Despite their colossal failures to bring about sustained development and nationalist glory, most Arab regimes, especially prior to the uprisings, aptly dealt with opposition forces of secular and Islamist persuasions as well as external threats and pressure from revolutionary regimes, transnational non-state actors and pro-market global institutions.

Against all odds, Arab regimes suavely transformed into police states, resembling George Orwell's dystopian totalitarian regimes. Dubbed 'Mukhabarat' regimes, because of their constant reliance on intelligence agents and a wide network of spies, Arab autocracies somehow optimized Jeremy Bentham's notion of the 'panopticon'. In *Discipline and Punish*, Michel Foucault, the twentieth-century post-structuralist thinker, looked at this concept by analysing modern states' so-called 'biopower': the seemingly innocuous but pervasive capacity to shape discourse (of pleasure and pain) as well as systematically survey, objectify and mould citizens into dormant subjects of control. Reflecting on Bentham's panopticon, Foucault argued, '... Bentham laid down the principle that power should be visible and unverifiable ... the inmate must never know whether he is being looked at any one moment; but he must be sure that he may always be so ... [while] in the central tower, one sees everything without ever being seen' (Foucault 1995: 201). Arab autocrats, from Syria's Assad to Libya's Gaddafi and Egypt's Mubarak, established a formidable apparatus akin to the Benthamite panopticon, constantly intimidating opponents in the hope of quashing any form of dissent, aiming to nip revolution in the bud. In the run-up to the Arab Spring, it was this constant state of terror – inspiring deep-seated mistrust and paranoia among people and even in the most intimate circles – which largely explained not only the sustained passivity of many opposition elements, but also the extremist forces' desperate use of violence to express grievances. Arab autocrats not only denied their populations genuine channels through which to formally express their legitimate demands and frustrations, they also sought to check any form of dissent before it even began. As a result, many sections of the secular opposition were stuck in a state of hibernation and co-optation, while extremist elements sought havens in failed and failing states on the peripheries, from Afghanistan, Pakistan and Somalia to the southern Philippines and Yemen.

Back in 2007, Oliver Schlumberger, a senior researcher in the German Development Institute, analysed the distinct endurance of Arab autocracies and how, despite many pro-democratic initiatives, reforms and popular mobilizations in the 2000s, there was no 'structurally enhanced quality of governance (in the sense of guaranteed basic freedoms that Arab citizens enjoy), let alone any instances of democratization' (Schlumberger 2007: 5.) The panopticon of Arab regimes rested on two important strategies: (i) an elaborate system of patronage to ensure the armed forces' as well as the bourgeoisie's continual dependence and loyalty, and (ii) securing external support and amassing strategic rents by creating a state of perpetual insecurity (see Chapters 2 and 6).

The Arab Spring came as a shock, because it ran counter to an established paradigm. For decades, academics and policy-makers focused on the 'endurance' of Arab regimes, rather than the dynamic yearnings of the wider population – just as orthodox economists, enthralled by the so-called era of 'great moderation', focused on the 'stability' and 'predictability' of markets prior to the Great Recession. This is not to say that there have not been 'minority reports' or heterodox opinions, radically departing from the established wisdom. In his essay for *Foreign Affairs* entitled 'Why Middle Eastern Studies missed the Arab Spring', Middle East scholar Gregory Gause (2011) puts forward a persuasive case for how a 'myth of authoritarian stability' blinded leading scholars to the tectonic shifts in the Arab political landscape. He opened up his analysis by lamenting how 'The vast majority of academic specialists on the Arab world were as surprised as everyone else by the upheavals ... [since] many academics focused on ... the persistence of undemocratic rulers.' Middle East specialists' scant interest in studying the role of Arab militaries in politics, Gause continued, contributed to their failure to 'predict or appreciate the variable ways in which Arab armies would react to the massive, peaceful protests'. More importantly, he argues, scholars also failed to see how economic reforms, especially in non-petro-states, alienated many people, including sections of the bourgeoisie and military, by creating a 'new class of superwealthy entrepreneurs, including members of the presidents' families in both countries' (ibid.).

The Arab revolutions simply shattered a whole body of literature on the Middle East and Islam, which, as luminaries such as Palestinian-American intellectual Edward Said have always argued, was suffused with varying forms of the so-called 'Orientalism': the artificial, self-serving construct of the Arab people and Islam through the eyes of an imperial West, anchored on the latter's interests, biases and self-designation as the agent of history.

In his groundbreaking book *Orientalism*, Said (1979: 300) talked about how, despite earlier attempts at modernizing the social sciences and tempering colonially rooted racist misconceptions about non-Western nations, Orientalism continues to exercise a hegemonic role, serving as a powerful meta-narrative that continues to shape the Western world's understanding of the Arab Middle East. For Said, Orientalism rests on a number of principal dogmas:

> One is the absolute and systematic difference between the West, which is rational, developed, humane, superior, and the Orient, which is aberrant, undeveloped, and inferior. Another

> dogma is that abstractions about the Orient, particularly those based on texts representing a 'classical' Oriental civilization, are always preferable to direct evidence drawn from modern Oriental realities. A third dogma is that the Orient is eternal, uniform, and incapable of defining itself; therefore it is assumed that a highly generalized and systematic vocabulary for describing the Orient from a Western standpoint is inevitable and even scientifically 'objective'. A fourth dogma is that the Orient is at bottom something either to be feared (the Yellow Peril, the Mongol hordes, the brown dominions) or to be controlled (by pacification, research and development, outright occupation whenever possible). The extraordinary thing is that these notions persist without significant challenge from the academic and governmental study of the modern Near Orient.

To be sure, decades have passed since *Orientalism* was written, and scholars such as Gregory Gause (2011) have argued that 'few, if any, political scientists working on the Middle East explained the peculiar stability of Arab regimes in cultural terms' (ibid.). Yet one cannot resist the temptation to suspect that Orientalism of some sort may have played a role in colouring the views of not only the most astute analysts and pundits, but also top policy-makers in Washington, Brussels and London on the imminent eruption in the Arab world.

Beyond misunderstanding the cultural nuances of and identifying the seismic political changes in the Arab and Islamic landscape, the global elite also glossed over fundamental structural changes in the make-up of Arab economies – factors which largely explain the broad-based, spontaneous and cross-/post-ideological nature of the uprisings (see Chapters 3 and 4).

Revolutions and economic crises

Revolutions rarely happen in stagnant, destitute countries. Revolutions are a product of a dynamic process of simultaneous socio-economic change and political decay. Recent history shows that revolutions are most likely to occur in countries that either experience a long period of unprecedented economic growth not accompanied by political reform, or which undergo a sudden economic crisis following a sustained period of economic expansion and liberalization. In the context of rising expectations and relative deprivation, the masses – mobilized by opposition forces – gradually withdraw their support for the regime, step outside their comfort zones, and increasingly embrace the opportunities and challenges of revolutionary upheavals.

The cases of Chile and Turkey are illuminating. Both countries experienced a period of sustained economic growth under autocratic regimes. Turkey and Chile were also among the most aggressive in pushing economic liberalization schemes. But once the economic underpinnings of the regime deteriorated, popular uprisings surfaced. In Chile, mass mobilizations against the regime gained momentum in the aftermath of the 1982 economic crisis, when the gross domestic product (GDP) contracted by 14 per cent. This was followed by the '1983 banking crisis', which forced the government to engage in an astronomical bailout, equivalent to 35 per cent of GDP. Faced with political repression and economic turmoil, workers, students and increasingly the masses joined anti-Pinochet protests, which culminated in a transition to civilian rule in March 1990 (Carlos 2009: 197–212).

In Turkey, a combination of autocratic governance, in the shadow of four military coups against different democratic governments, and multiple economic crises, reaching its apogee in 2001, marked the country's transition, beginning in 2002, to a more pluralistic and democratic system. In both cases, the autocratic-bureaucratic system lost its power and legitimacy when its economic performance ebbed, reaching a crisis point. However, democratization was a result of a gradual or 'pacted' transition to civilian rule rather than a total revolution (Heydarian 2011). What Turkey and Chile experienced could be termed as 'refolution': the introduction of a set of peaceful, decisive and gradual reforms, which precipitated systemic change.

The more classic examples on the nexus between economic shocks and political unrest are of course the French and Russian revolutions. Chronic fiscal crisis, widespread poverty, destructive and expensive military expeditions, absence of a viable arrangement between opposing sides, and the overall but gradual decline in the social legitimacy of the monarchy played a crucial role in the collapse of the Czarist and Bourbon monarchies. What spelled their doom was the combination of tottering economic conditions and the inability and/or unwillingness of the regime to make much-needed political reforms to appease the opposition. In *Civilization*, British historian Niall Ferguson (2011: 200) underscored the depth of economic challenges that prefaced the French Revolution:

> Since the traumatic financial crisis of 1719–20 – the Mississippi Bubble – the French fiscal system had lagged woefully behind the English. There was no central note-issuing bank. There was no liquid bond market where government debt could be bought and sold. The tax system had in large measure been privatized. Instead of selling bonds, the French Crown sold offices, creating a bloated public payroll of parasites ...

The 1848 revolutions, sweeping across the European continent, were also a response to deteriorating economic conditions – from rising food costs to growing unemployment and income inequality – and the endemic political disenfranchisement of the masses under the rule of post-Napoleonic monarchies. As Ferguson (ibid.: 267) argues, a combination of deepening economic imbalances and rising political demands gave birth to the 1848 European revolutions:

> [In economic terms] inequality did increase as a result of the Industrial Revolution. Between 1780 and 1830 output per labourer in the UK grew over 25 per cent but wages rose barely 5 per cent. The proportion of national income going to the top percentile of the population rose from 25 per cent in 1801 to 35 per cent in 1848. In Paris in 1820, around 9 per cent of the population were classified as 'proprietors and rentiers' ... [politically] mid-nineteenth-century liberals wanted constitutional government, the freedoms of speech, press and assembly, wider political representation through electoral reform, free trade and, where it was lacking, national self-determination ...

Then, more recently, the collapse of the Eastern Bloc in 1989 was also a result of severe economic stagnation – as the Soviet Union experienced dismal economic conditions with falling oil prices and internal economic crisis – and decades of repressive politics.

The case of Indonesia and Iran, both Muslim-majority countries, is also interesting. After two decades of impressive economic growth, Muhammad Reza Shah's unwillingness to introduce meaningful political reforms – including changing the country's government to a constitutional monarchy by establishing an independent legislature – caught up with him. Coupled with growing economic inequality, an urban–rural schism and unprecedented inflationary pressures – as a result of massive injections of petrodollar revenues into the domestic economy – this pushed a restive population to the brink (Sick 2001). After the 1997 East Asian financial crisis, food riots and anti-government protests hit a number of autocratic regimes in the region. In Indonesia, the worst-hit economy during the crisis, the economy shrank by as much as 20 per cent and the Indonesian rupiah lost 80 per cent of its value, severely compromising the legitimacy of the Suharto regime – prompting massive riots and constant protests across the country, especially in main commercial hubs (Sharma 2011: 131). Tenuously holding on to a restive country fed up with the repressive regime, the autocratic ruler's inability to provide economic security eroded his main base of legitimacy, precipitating the collapse of the thirty-year-old 'New Order' (Carothers 2011).

The Arab Spring is arguably running along similar patterns. The uprisings came after decades of aggressive economic liberalization – with huge social implications – and repressive political rule by autocratic cliques. A modest level of economic growth allowed the autocratic leaders to maintain an effective system of patronage, while giving the masses a small slice of the growing economic pie. However, growing volatility in global financial and commodity markets gradually undermined service-oriented and commodities-import-dependent Arab economies. This external shock accentuated structural maladies: endemic corruption; lack of significant improvement in state services; dismal levels of income inequality; and constant state repression. Faced with autocrats who were unwilling to compromise and introduce a crucial set of reforms, protests transformed into outright revolutionary movements. In all cases, it was a combination of economic mismanagement and lack of political opening which led to popular revolts.

Looking at the economic roots of the Arab Spring, Lynch (2011) intelligently observed how in many ways the Arab Spring was a rejection of neoliberal policies, especially for leftist activists. Looking at the crux of the economic problems plaguing much of the Arab world, he highlighted how 'the previous decade saw neoliberal economic reforms that privatized industries to the benefit of a small number of well-connected elites and produced impressive rates of GDP growth. But … the chasm between the rich and poor grew and few meaningful jobs awaited a massive youth bulge.'

The Arab Spring, beyond questioning untenable domestic economic regimes, carried in its bosom a message of even greater significance. Interestingly, it struck just as the stubborn Great Recession of 2008 – threatening a double-dip recession at the turn of the second decade of the twenty-first century – placed the principles and wisdom of economic globalization under the spotlight. Thus, to understand the Arab Spring, we must explore the impact of globalization on the Arab world and the structural economic underpinnings of the uprisings. This will also guide us in understanding a related question: why have not all Arab countries, especially the most autocratic ones, gone through regime transitions, while much of North Africa – and increasingly the Levant – has gone through tremendous change, despite the relative (social and political) openness of pre-revolutionary regimes?

2 | THE ANTI-DEVELOPMENT STATE: ECONOMIC ORIGINS OF ARAB UPHEAVALS

The quickest way of ending a war is to lose it. (George Orwell)[1]

The Arab Spring may have represented a singular expression of popular discontent across the region, but – reflecting the unique circumstances and structural attributes of each Arab state – it has assumed varying forms, moving with sundry intensity along divergent trajectories across time and space. At the same time, we shouldn't discount the fact that the uprisings have represented a transnational, collective attempt at reconfiguring the Arab political landscape. Perhaps no document better captures the depth of common maladies plaguing the entire Arab world than the Arab Human Development Report (AHDR).

Recognizing the unique challenges facing the Arab nations, the United Nations Development Programme (UNDP), beginning in 2000, sponsored a series of independent reports, which brought together leading Arab scholars, researchers and intellectuals, providing them with a platform from which to analyse perennial challenges, and identify solutions and opportunities with respect to human development in the Arab world. After a full-spectrum diagnostic of multiple factors contributing to the Arab world's dismal human development record, the first report, from 2002, *Creating Opportunities for Future Generations*, suggested that the region is 'richer than it is developed', and that the 'Arab world is largely depriving itself of the creativity and productivity of half its citizens' (Crossette 2002). At the heart of the report lay a key finding. What makes the Arab world unique is that it simultaneously suffers from three main 'deficits': democracy, knowledge and womanpower.

In response to the first AHDR, *The Economist* (2002) provocatively wrote: 'WHAT went wrong with the Arab world? Why is it so stuck behind the times? It is not an obviously unlucky region.' True, as the

AHDR itself suggested, the Arab world has had one of the lowest rates of extreme poverty, and one of the highest levels of per capita income and education spending as a percentage of GDP in the developing world, while life expectancy increased by fifteen years and infant mortality dropped by two-thirds within three decades. However, the Arab states, as the report suggests, have failed to introduce the kind of reforms that could deal with a toxic mixture of declining productivity, extremely low per capita income growth (comparable with sub-Saharan Africa), ballooning population (among the worst in the world), and a weak scientific record (even when compared to neighbouring non-Arab states), which, in turn, explains why the Arab world, among other things, suffers from one of the highest rates of unemployment, struggles to attract sufficient investments to move up the production chain, and continues to be a laggard in science and technology, even as its Asian neighbours pull ahead in global rankings. According to the 2002 report, the Arab world's R&D investment was less than one seventh of the world average, while only 1.2 per cent had a personal computer and 0.6 per cent of the population had access to (or used) the internet (ibid.). No wonder the second AHDR, from 2003, *Building a Knowledge Society*, aptly focused on the development of human capital in the Arab world.

Despite the mind-boggling implications of the AHDR, Arab regimes were demure, to say the least, in their reactions. Instead of focusing on fundamental reforms to deal with the three basic deficits, they instead unleashed a flurry of conferences, initiatives and forums on reforms, prompting the famous *New York Times* columnist Thomas Friedman (2004) to sarcastically opine, 'There is a new industry ... in the Middle East, and that is the "reform industry." Every month there seems to be a new conference on reform in the Arab world.' In general, Arab regimes paid scant attention to less controversial issues such as education reform, vehemently rejecting the core findings and recommendations of the reports. Meanwhile, the neoconservatives in Washington abused and skewed the AHDR to push for – and legitimize – their 'democratization' agenda in Afghanistan, Iraq and elsewhere in the Middle East. When the third AHDR, *Towards Freedom in the Arab World*, also from 2003, proved to be too critical of the USA's unilateral policies and its impact in the region, the

Bush administration forced the UNDP to withhold its release, until some modifications were introduced. Fraught with criticisms of Arab autocracies and their Western patrons, the AHDR series became a highly politicized dossier, undergoing several revisions, allegedly without consultation with and the approval of some lead authors – prompting, in turn, uproar and even resignation by some notable contributors (Friedman 2004; Abdel Fatah 2009).

Analysing the fifth and last AHDR, *Challenges to Human Security in the Arab Countries*, from 2009, which focused on reimagining the notion of citizenship, security and the obligations of the state towards the citizenry, Lynch (2009) bemoaned, 'Seven years later, a fifth AHDR has been released. But it suggests that despite all the public attention devoted to the question of reform since 2002, the deficiencies outlined in the original report have only become deeper and more complex.' For Lynch, what the report emphasized was how Arab autocracies and the chaos emanating from foreign military interventions in Iraq and elsewhere led 'to the failure to achieve acceptable levels of human development'.

In short, the AHDR series reaffirmed and substantiated a core narrative, which has always been on people's minds: the Arab world has remained a unique fortress of autocratic despondency, with practically all regimes unwilling to move towards genuine democratic reform, failing to integrate women into society, and falling short of significantly uplifting the living standards of hundreds of millions of Arab citizens – precisely what the Arab Spring has attempted to change for better and for good.

An ocean of broken vows

While autocracies and hybrid regimes in other regions of the world, notably Singapore, have managed to move up the ladder of development, integrate women as productive members of the working population (and even elite sciences), and establish a formidable infrastructure for an advanced, knowledge-based economy, the whole Arab world, in comparison, suffers from a dearth of democracy, gender equality and genuine economic development.

In the Middle East alone, the non-Arab states of Turkey, Israel and Iran dominate the industrial and technological landscape, as they have swiftly pulled away from their Arab neighbours in recent decades. In this sense, the Arab world has represented a desert of discontent surrounded by oases of growth and dynamism. Time and again, Arab autocracies have promised prosperity and welfare with the implicit demand for political passivity and compliance. This was the bargain that held many regimes intact for decades. Over time, many Arab societies, however, witnessed the erosion of their national pride and basic entitlements. First came the series of military reversals at the hands of non-Arab neighbours. The Arab coalition forces suffered defeats at the hands of Israel in the 1948, 1967 and 1973 wars. Later, Saddam Hussein's invasion – supported by almost all Arab countries, with the exception of Syria – of Iran (1980–88) would end in a stalemate and no territorial gains for a devastated Iraq, while the new regime in Iran – despite the tremendous costs of the prolonged military campaign – would use the war experience to consolidate domestic power, build a potent cadre of war veterans, and gradually re-emerge as a regional powerhouse after a sustained period of reconstruction. (Despite the support of many Arab and Western countries, it was only in the first two years of the eight-year war that Iraq was on the offensive. Afterwards, Iran – emerging out of the ashes of revolutionary chaos – took the war to its enemy, threatening to annex south and eastern parts of its Arab neighbour, and spread the Islamic revolution across the region.) (Fisk 2005).

The huge costs of the military adventures would be exacerbated by the global economic downturn and a devastating oil crisis in the 1980s. Soon, many Arab countries were forced to introduce draconian belt-tightening measures to stave off an outright economic collapse, while the larger population had to contend with a dramatic decline in their living standards. Aside from caving in to Western and international financial institution (IFI) pressures for reforms, Egypt and Jordan went so far as to sign peace treaties with Israel, marking the end of their pan-Arabist campaigns. The latter decades of the twentieth century were dark moments in Arab history, with a toxic combination of humiliation and economic uncertainty facing once proud and hopeful societies. By the 1990s, the Arab world was at war with itself. Across the region, the autocrats had to contend with a new wave of extremist elements and Islamic radicals, mostly inspired by the earlier pan-Islamic jihad in Afghanistan, which led to the withdrawal – and gradual collapse – of the Soviet Union. As a result, the powerful Arab armies in Egypt and Syria were in retreat. The 1979 peace treaty with Israel pushed Egypt out of the regional picture, while Syria gradually moved into the shadows of a resurgent Tehran. Iraq, the last Baathist powerhouse, would provoke the wrath of Arab monarchies and Western powers by invading Kuwait in 1991. Soon, Algeria would be engulfed in an all-out civil war between Islamist forces and the military regime. Towards the end of the twentieth century, Arab regimes had to contend with a rising Iran, Islamic fundamentalism and all forms of economic and political challenge (ibid.; Yergin 2009).

The twenty-first century commenced with the bang of the 9/11 attacks, which, in turn, led to the invasion of Afghanistan and Iraq. Soon, it became clear that the first decade of the new century was not about reversing decades of decline in the latter half of the twentieth century, but instead the reassertion of Western hegemony in the region, which, in turn, allowed Arab autocracies to use the 'Global War on Terror' (GWOT) as a pretext to further crack down on dissent and opposition forces. The economic boom and relative stability in places such as Dubai and Doha represented tiny green shoots in a forest of rising unemployment, gender inequality, widespread poverty and economic underperformance in most Arab countries. Cosmopolitan cities such as Beirut would barely escape Lebanon's tortuous destiny of almost perpetual interference by neighbouring countries, internal ethnic-factional strife, and confrontation with Israel.

The democratic elections in the Occupied Territories, placing (Palestinian Muslim Brotherhood offshoot) Hamas in power, simply revealed the hypocrisy of the West and its so-called moderate Arab clients, especially after the latter refused to recognize the popular mandate bestowed upon the Islamist government. What followed was a prolonged split in the Palestinian leadership and further isolation for large numbers of Hamas supporters, mostly in the Gaza Strip. Meanwhile, the non-Arab powers in the region continued to surge ahead. The downfall of the Taliban in Afghanistan and the Baathist regime in Baghdad left a resurgent Iran unchecked, allowing the latter to expand its sphere of influence across the region and extend its largesse – beefed up by ballooning petrodollars – to clients across the greater Middle East. Far from remaining the 'Sick Man of Europe', Turkey would also emerge as a major regional force, with the newly Islamist leadership of the AKP reviving memories of Ottoman domination across the Arab world. Meanwhile, an increasingly hawkish leadership in Israel would continue to exploit fissures within the Palestinian leadership and the broader Arab world to torpedo any hopes of a two-state solution. Only Iran and Turkey would vigorously stand up to Israel, while the last bastion of Arab nationalism, Syria, focused its gaze on regaining the disputed Golan Heights and rescuing whatever levers of influence remained within the contested Lebanese political landscape.

Against such a backdrop of national humiliation and economic disarray, one could argue that the Arab world has suffered from a classic case of rising expectations and relative deprivation – precipitating the volcanic eruption of the Arab Spring.

The Arab Spring was by no means the first and sole expression of popular discontent with autocratic regimes across the region. In many ways, it was, instead, a culmination of decades of democratic-nationalist struggles, dating as far back as the colonial era. Beyond the issues of political freedom and accountability, economics, however, has played a pivotal role in galvanizing the people of all walks of life – the 'Arab street' – against morally bankrupt and politically frail dictators. A closer look at the Arab political landscape in recent years reveals that, beginning with the 2007/08 global financial crisis, there were already significant outbursts of popular discontent across the Arab countries, especially among the middle-income states of Egypt, Tunisia, Morocco and Jordan. What is ironic is that many of these Arab economies were actually less affected – in absolute terms – than their counterparts in the Persian Gulf and other developing regions in Asia and Latin America, given their relatively low levels of exposure to and integration with global financial markets and production chains (see Chapters 3 and 4).

Moreover, prior to the crisis, many of these economies underwent a long series of reform and macroeconomic adjustments, under the auspices of IFIs, in order to balance their budgets, stabilize inflation and interest rates, streamline financial markets, minimize systemic risk, and improve overall resilience. Yet it was precisely this group of nations, especially Tunisia and Egypt, which would be engulfed by a storm of popular revolts. Another irony is that the Arab Spring proved to be most potent and fearsome in countries with relatively higher levels of political and social freedom, while the more repressive and enclosed monarchies in the Persian Gulf managed to stand their ground, at least in the short to medium run. In light of the sudden collapse of oil prices after the global financial crisis, the third irony is that the more diversified economies – suffering less from the so-called 'resource curse' – proved to be more vulnerable, while the petro-states, with the exception of Libya, managed to survive and even help each other by coordinating their efforts and sharing funds, troops and logistics with more vulnerable peers (see Chapter 6).

Since there has been hardly a single electoral democracy in the Arab world, this triple irony underscores the importance of *identifying specific factors which contributed to the fragilities of specific types of Arab autocracies*. After all, not all dictators have succumbed, nor have all Arab regimes been forced to initiate major (genuine) reforms to placate restive masses.

At this point, it is necessary to analyse how a confluence of varying factors, both structural and agential, gave rise to the Arab Spring. In order to do this, one must first understand the specific and unique attributes of modern Arab states – and how they have brought the revolutions upon themselves. As Lisa Anderson (2011: 2), president of the American University in Cairo, puts it: 'The important story about the 2011 Arab revolts ... is not how the globalization of the norms of civic engagement shaped the protesters' aspirations. Nor is it about how activists used technology to share ideas and tactics. Instead, the critical issue is how and why these ambitions and techniques resonated in their various local contexts.' Thus, we have to look at the common tragedy of the Arab regimes, and their inability to provide freedom, sustained development and social equity.

Kemalism and its discontents

Historically, the problem in the Arab world has not been the lack of strong state intervention in social and economic affairs, nor has it been the absence of popular leaders with genuine and lofty goals of national redemption and prosperity. Therefore, one would be mistaken in assuming that the tragedy of Arab regimes is a by-product of unpatriotic leadership and weak states per se. It is also a big mistake to assume that the problems of the Arab world stem from religion (or its mixture with politics), since secularism was a core aspect of many Arab regimes in the previous century.

At the beginning of the twentieth century, after a long period of humiliation at the hands of colonial powers, Middle Eastern leaders, beginning with Kemal Atatürk in Turkey and Reza Shah in Iran, embarked on an ambitious project of modernization, which combined fierce secularism with technological and infrastructural development. Reflecting on earlier liberal and constitutional reforms in their respective nations, specifically the Tanzimat (1839–76) in Ottoman Turkey and constitutional revolution (1905/06) in Qajar Iran, they arrived at a realization that the main problem was external meddling and lack of national independence. As Nasr (2009: 91) put it, 'Those pushing for change weren't looking first and foremost for liberalism; they were intent on liberation from European control.'

More than the lofty ideals of establishing cosmopolitan, liberal democratic regimes in their respective countries, these leaders were more focused on the immediate question of state-building and ensuring national sovereignty. After all, they were heirs to once mighty kingdoms, which ruled over large swathes of land across the Eurasian landmass for centuries. The glorious days of Ottoman and Iranian Safavid empires – ruling over the remnants of the once sprawling and powerful Islamic empire stretching across three continents – were punctuated by repeated defeats at the hands of increasingly expansionist European powers – a trend which accelerated at the advent of European colonialism in the eighteenth to nineteenth centuries (ibid.: 85–115).

Atatürk, a stellar and highly distinguished soldier during the First World War, was keen on reconsolidating the flailing Ottoman Empire against the onslaught of European incursions into its territories and spheres of influence. Between the fourteenth and seventeenth centuries, the Ottomans were able to establish a formidable empire, stretching from the Arabian peninsula all the way to eastern Europe and North Africa. However, European monarchies, facing the common Ottoman threat, managed to put their continental squabbling aside, albeit temporarily, and unite against the common Eastern threat – similar to how varying Greek city-states, constantly divided by internal differences, united against the mighty Persian Empire under Darius the Great (490 BC) and Xerxes (486 BC) almost two thousand years before. In both 1529 and 1683, Europe's Christendom was able to withstand the expansion of Ottoman Muslims into the heart of western Europe, specifically at the gates of Vienna. Soon after these costly military adventures, the Ottoman Empire began to show signs of internal decay, just as Europe started to benefit from the productive fruits of scientific revolution. As historian Niall Ferguson (2011: 108–9) argues:

> In the West, science and government had gone into partnership ... In Istanbul Sultan Osman III presided indolently over a decadent Ottoman Empire, while in Potsdam Frederick the Great enacted reforms that made the Kingdom of Prussia a byword for military efficiency and administrative rationality. [There were] intra-familial wars over succession, so the primogeniture became the rule. Henceforth, the younger sons were merely confined to the harem – literally. 'the forbidden' – inhabited by the sultan's wives, concubines and offspring.

By the eighteenth century, the European kingdoms – aided by a lethal combination of unabated state-building and a prolific scientific revolution – held a decisive edge over their Muslim counterparts – a trend that peaked as the Industrial Revolution kicked in. While Napoleon's ambitious forays into the Orient saw the swift occupation of Egypt (an Ottoman province at the time) in 1798, with revolutionary France's well-trained but compact army easily outmanoeuvring their larger Muslim counterparts, the Safavid Empire (among the once-powerful 'gunpowder' eastern kingdoms) and their feckless successor, namely the Qajar dynasty, found themselves increasingly squeezed between European powers to the north and south. By 1828, Tsarist Russia had expelled Iranian forces from the Caucasus, followed by Britain's decisive elimination of Iran's footprint in Afghanistan (1856). Later, Britain would also wrest control of Bahrain (1868), gradually undermining Iran's sphere of influence in the Persian Gulf. By now, it was increasingly clear to the Muslim kingdoms that European colonialism had arrived with a vengeance, after centuries of Muslim expansion into the European lands, especially in southern Spain and south-eastern Europe (Nasr 2009; Ferguson 2011).

From the nineteenth to early twentieth century, Muslim powers, from Turkey to Iran and the Mughal empire in India, were either completely occupied (as in India by Britain) or quasi-vassal states (as in Iran during the British-Russian 'Great Game' in south-west Asia), or painfully dismembered (as in Turkey after the notorious Franco-British Sykes-Picot agreement). The Tanzimat in Turkey and constitutional reforms in Iran hardly reversed the onslaught of European incursion into the region. It was precisely this painful episode of humiliation at the hands of European powers which gave birth to a new generation of ultra-nationalist and secular leaders across the Middle East. Soon, these leaders – with varying levels of success – were able to transform their countries in profound ways, leaving a strong impression on their future counterparts in the Arab world, who would, in turn, shape the Arab landscape in the post-Second World War era (Nasr 2009).

Taking on the West

Atatürk and Reza Shah's ambitious national projects rested on one fundamental premise: that you can defeat – or at least match – the West, and prevent further humiliation and defeat at their hands, by beating them at their own game, or simply joining them – precisely what modern Turkey's rulers had in mind. This meant copying the infrastructural and technological foundations of Europe and America, with a selective adoption of Western institutions. After all, imperial Japan's impeccable rise as an industrial powerhouse and military force – propelling it into the elite club of world powers, especially after its defeat of Tsarist Russia in 1905 – could be traced back to the Meiji Restoration (1868–1912). Reflecting on the urgency to match the Western powers and protect their national patrimony, especially after the fateful visit of American commodore Matthew Perry to Japan in 1853, Ferguson (2011: 282) described Tokyo's wholesale effort to match the West through direct mimicking and embrace of its institutions and even culture:

> The Japanese decided to take no chances. They copied everything. From the Prussian-style constitution of 1889 to the adoption of the British gold standard in 1897, Japan's institutions were refashioned on Western models. The army drilled like Germans; the navy sailed like Britons. An American-style system of state elementary and middle schools was also introduced. The Japanese even started eating beef, hitherto taboo, and some reformers went so far as to propose abandoning Japanese in favour of English.

From Egypt's charismatic leader Gamal Abdel Nasser to Tunisia's Habib Bourguiba (and to a certain degree Gaddafi in Libya and a string of Baathist leaders in Syria and Iraq), a new generation of nationalist leaders – mostly with a military background, similar to Atatürk and Reza Shah – deposed feckless monarchies and regimes (garbed in traditional roots and a subservient relationship with Western powers) in favour of a modern republican state. What all these men, a new generation of Arab leaders, shared was an antipathy towards Western-style liberal democracies and market economies. Similar to the soviets in Russia, which supplanted the Tsarist regime with a centralized political system and a command economy, these new leaders built a quasi-socialist state, combining social welfare, secular politics and political patronage. These modern Arab states reflected the image of their leaders, whose shadow loomed large over huge sections of the Arab world, and played a decisive role in shaping almost all aspects of Arab societies.

The modern Arab state acted like an Orwellian 'Big Brother', stretching its long arms deep into all aspects of society. Reflecting on what they saw as the failure of earlier sociocultural and constitutional reforms in the nineteenth and early twentieth centuries, these up-and-coming leaders heeded the advice of notable intellectuals like Moshfeq Kazemi (in Nasr 2009: 94), who called for the production of a 'knowledgeable dictator … an ideal despot who could take the path of evolution many years with each of his steps'. Soon, a paternalistic state emerged, determined to propel the Arab world into a Westernized future by introducing a wholescale refurbishment of state institutions, monopolizing the national economy, and secularizing all relevant aspects of sociocultural life. What these new regimes represented were more or less replicas of what Kemal Atatürk had built in earlier decades in Turkey. All these Arab states were founded upon the so-called ideology of Kemalism. This new generation of Arab leaders had a lot of hope and goodwill at their disposal. Almost all came into power through coups against monarchies, but they – monopolizing media and steering a propaganda machine – still enjoyed considerable popularity among the masses. Of course, the most famous of all was Egypt's Nasser, who would inspire generations of Arab leaders with his message of Arab salvation and unity, sending shock waves across the region by unleashing an ambitious pan-Arabist campaign against Israel, Western powers and corrupt monarchies in the Middle East. Tapping into popular aspirations of Arab revival, these new leaders amassed a huge cachet of public trust and compliance. They were also equally brutal in silencing any signs of opposition, tirelessly sniffing out any threats to their rule.

The advent of 'black gold', following massive oil discoveries across the region and related technological breakthroughs, provided (direct and indirect) sources of rent for many of these leaders. While those in places like Iraq and Libya pushed very hard to extract maximum benefit from their gigantic hydrocarbon reserves, specifically through renegotiating earlier energy agreements with Western companies and states, others like Nasser cashed in on oil transport through the Suez Canal – which he nationalized after a risky military campaign in 1956 – and cultivated strong ties with oil-rich Arab brethren like Saudi Arabia.

Benefiting from considerable political capital and resource rents, these new autocratic states were in a particularly strong position to drag huge populations along the 'valley of tears': the painful transition from traditional, rural-based agricultural societies to an era of massive industrial, sociocultural and technological transformations brought about by their modernization programmes. On the other hand, Tunisia's Bourguiba, coming into power through peaceful means, presided over a strong office and a relatively modern nation-state with strong cultural and trade links with a prosperous Europe.

All these leaders pushed ahead with large-scale top-to-bottom reforms aimed at overhauling the society. Under their watch, literacy rates and overall infrastructure improved, with the state intent on reducing infant mortality and large-scale outbreak of endemic diseases. Egypt and Syria built formidable armies, even forming a new state together, the United Arab Republic (UAR). These new regimes were based on an implicit bargain between the populist autocrats and the citizenry: social welfare and national glory in exchange for political compliance and passivity. Soon, Arab peoples discovered the paucity of this bargain. The first decades were hopeful, at least symbolically. Arab nations were able to join their arms and blood in a common struggle against Israel, beginning in 1948. Later, in 1956, Nasserite Egypt was able to nationalize the Suez Canal, eliminating another European foothold in the region. On a more practical level, Nasser wanted an equitable rise in Egypt's proceeds from the British-controlled canal, in line with a broader trend of renegotiations of oil agreements between Arab states and Western companies.

In 1967 and 1973, the Arab world was even able to coordinate a collective oil embargo against the West. While the first embargo was concurrent with the 'Six-Day War' between Israel and Arab coalition forces, the second embargo came on the heels of a surprise joint Egyptian–Syrian military manoeuvre against Israel, jolting the latter out of a deepening strategic complacency after decades of military success. The embargo – designed to support the Egyptian–Syrian war against Israel – came as a big surprise to the industrialized world, especially with the new global swing producer, Saudi Arabia, entering the game in full force after a Cairo–Riyadh agreement to punish the West for its support for Israel. The impact on Western economies was devastating, with major European powers such as France and Germany tirelessly seeking to distance themselves from the US–Israeli dyad in order to avoid an energy crisis at home. Soon, there was a scramble for oil and a worldwide panic at the pump, forcing world powers to contemplate emergency countermeasures, while Washington embarked on a ceaseless effort to bring the embargo to an end. The whole episode underscored the Arab world's growing international influence and its ability to quite effectively unify against an external enemy (Yergin 1991: 461–80).

In the succeeding years, the Arab countries – through the Organization of Petroleum Exporting Countries (OPEC) – began to inflate oil prices, despite vehement Western opposition. The industrialized countries were already grappling with a vicious downturn, as a combination of anaemic growth and high inflation ravaged their economies. Beginning in 1971, during the so-called Tehran Agreement and a parallel gathering in Tripoli, Arab oil-producing countries were able to radically renegotiate the terms of their oil agreements with Western companies. In the same year, when Iran seized some tiny islands in the Persian Gulf claimed by the Arab neighbours, Libya and Iraq began expropriating Western oil interests as a punishment for the latter's supposed collusion with Tehran. The 1970s became increasingly a decade of Arab assertiveness and booming oil revenues. No wonder the years 1974 to 1978 were called the 'OPEC Golden Age', especially for Arabs (ibid.: 545–634).

In his Pulitzer-winning book *The Prize*, Daniel Yergin (ibid.: 616) discussed the emergence of an 'OPEC Imperium', whereby oil-exporting countries, mostly Arab states, were able to amass tremendous wealth and wield unprecedented influence in the global economy:

> The quadrupling of [oil] prices triggered by the Arab oil embargo and the exporters' assumption of complete control in setting those prices [as a result of fierce negotiations with Western oil companies] brought massive changes to every corner of the world. The combined petroleum earnings of the oil exporters rose from $23 billion in 1972 to $140 billion by 1977 ... [subsequently the exporters] embarked on a dizzying program of spending: industrialization, infrastructure, subsidies, services, necessities, luxuries, weapons, waste, and corruption.

Thus began a huge spending spree on weaponry and imports of Western durable goods such as Japanese cars. All Arab regimes, directly or indirectly, benefited from this oil bonanza. Interestingly, the Arab world was also able to benefit from the patronage of both the Soviet Union and the USA. While Moscow's strategic and economic relations with Arab powers such as Egypt, Syria and Iraq is well known, an important historical fact lost on many people is how postwar Washington, especially under President Eisenhower, played a crucial role in rolling back Anglo-French neocolonial presence in the region. In fact, during the 1956 Suez Crisis, the USA – as the Western world's pre-eminent power – played a central role in helping Nasser to nationalize the Suez Canal and prevent outright occupation by the Anglo-French–Israeli trio. Intent on projecting himself as a man of peace ahead of his re-election bid, and increasingly concerned with Nasser's strategic flirtations with the Soviet Union, Eisenhower went so far as to threaten the European powers and Israel with oil sanctions and economic reprisals, while emphasizing the threat of a Soviet nuclear intervention on behalf of the Arabs – potentially followed by a communist cascade across the region. Washington – concerned with a prolonged energy crisis and a geopolitical meltdown in the Middle East – helped Nasser to win the Suez battle. After pressuring the IMF to deny London emergency financial aid, Eisenhower also indicated that the Middle East Emergency Committee – a mechanism designed to address the impending oil shortage in Europe – would shun Paris and London, unless they completely withdrew their troops from Egypt. A ceasefire was not enough. Summing up Washington's uncharacteristic chastisement of European powers in the whole Suez Canal drama, Yergin (ibid.: 473) states, 'The Americans had carried the day. They also added to the burden of defeat and humiliation the British and French had already suffered at Nasser's hands. In the whole messy business, Nasser was the only clear winner.' Other experts such as Steve Cook (2013), Senior Fellow at the Council on Foreign Relations, have looked at how, as early as the 1950s, American diplomats, notably American ambassador to Cairo Jefferson Caffery, tirelessly sought a strategic alliance with Egypt.

While oil-rich regimes such as Saudi Arabia (along with the Persian Pahlavi monarchy) were a pillar of American interest in the Persian Gulf, other Arab states such as Egypt astutely explored patronage from both superpowers to build up their national capacity – not to mention receiving subsidies, flexible oil deals and all kinds of support from oil-rich brethren. In this sense, one could argue that the Arab regimes were in a tremendously favourable situation to solicit external support, negotiate for technology transfer, benefit from enabling trading agreements, and receive significant aid packages to pursue national development – something that other 'front-line' states such as Taiwan and South Korea were able to astutely accomplish in the Cold War era.

The grand disappointment

Yet time and again Arab armies suffered defeats at the hands of determined and highly disciplined Israeli armed forces, failed to bring the West to its knees through their collective oil embargo, and managed to alienate the USA because of a de facto alliance with the Soviet Union, the refusal to come to terms with Israel's existence, coupled with opportunistic jacking-up of oil prices, and threats to undermine global oil supply to the detriment of the industrialized West.

Even their combined collective oil embargoes failed to achieve the goal of cajoling the West to change its position on Israel. The 1967 embargo was a complete failure, with Arab producers bearing the brunt of the cutback in exports, since the West was able to institute sufficient countermeasures, while non-participating producers were able to fill in the gap and reap tremendous benefits. The 1973 embargo was a potent reminder of the growing 'oil weapon' of the Arab world. Yet, after tireless shuttle diplomacy by the Nixon administration, the end result was hardly more than Egypt's prevention of a total defeat by Israel and a modus vivendi between Damascus and Tel Aviv over the Golan Heights. Egypt's President Sadat was cheered by the masses for jolting the overconfident Israelis with a lightning military manoeuvre in coordination with Syria, and also getting Washington's attention, but there was hardly any change in the Palestine–Israel equation – the primary source of the Arab–Israeli conflicts (Yergin 1991: 570–634). Despite the oil bonanza of the 1970s, wasteful spending and mismanagement among OPEC countries transformed a $67 billion surplus in 1974 into a $2 billion deficit in 1978. The Arab region kept on importing technology, armaments and luxuries that it couldn't use and absorb for long-term development (ibid.: 617). Then came the crunch.

The 1980s was a particularly destabilizing period, as a global oil crisis – leading to a dramatic collapse in oil prices – ravaged the coffers of Arab regimes, already illiquid and battered by costly, devastating military campaigns against Israel. Refusing to learn a lesson from other Arab states, Iraq's new strongman, Saddam Hussein, followed a 'tradition of excesses', jumping into a series of misguided military adventurism, notably against Iran (1980) and Kuwait (1991).

This brought tremendous destruction upon his country – supposedly a bulwark of Arab nationalism – by taking on a nascent Iranian revolutionary regime. Soon, the Arab world was plunged back into despair and agitation. Decisive military defeats considerably undermined the credibility and sustainability of many Arab regimes, as they had previous regional monarchies in the eighteenth to early twentieth centuries.

All of a sudden, after a decade of ecstasy in the 1970s, Arab leaders were begging for foreign aid, while forced to either normalize ties with Israel or abandon any prospects of a full-scale military adventure altogether. By taking on Iran and later Kuwait, Saddam's Iraq would be severely punished and devastated, reversing arguably decades of impressive social and economic advancement. However, beyond crashing disappointments on the war front, these Arab regimes also failed on a more important front: development. As a result, Arab autocrats gave the people, under the auspices of secular opposition elements and newly energized Islamist forces, growing reasons to revolt for change. Only a combination of brute force, strategic patronage and a dizzying 'reform game' – introduction of timely but cosmetic political changes aimed at appeasing critics, weakening and dividing the opposition, and projecting a façade of democracy – kept the regimes in place, at least for some time. The autocrats, however, lost their political hegemony and ideological appeal. It was a pyrrhic victory, at best. No longer did these Arab regimes enjoy the kind of popularity and political capital they possessed in the early decades of independence and republic.

The development debacle

So what went so wrong in these Arab countries, necessitating a region-wide revolt to shake off the status quo? Many pondered whether it was the lack of democracy and freedom causing the bankruptcy of these Arab regimes and the relative backwardness of the whole region.

The book *Democracy and Development* by Przeworski et al. (2000: 1–2) represents an outstanding work of scholarship, which simultaneously combines a qualitative as well as a quantitative analysis of the correlation between two variables: democracy and development. In many ways, the authors embark on a hugely demanding task, whereby they set to 'resolve' a conceptual riddle, which has dominated political discourse and social sciences for quite some time: 'Is economic development conducive to political democracy? Does democracy foster or hinder material welfare?' Deciphering the 'exact' nature of the relationship between democracy and development has been an eternal preoccupation for many disciplines, including but not limited to political science, economics and sociology. The book stands as a seminal contribution to development and democracy studies, for it provides a comprehensive account of all major earlier works by leading scholars on this particular subject matter, an in-depth account of philosophical and theoretical undercurrents that have shaped the conceptualization of democracy, and, perhaps most importantly, a substantial quantitative-statistical analysis of democracy. The book represents an ambitious undertaking, with the authors gathering, surveying and analysing historical and economic data derived from 135 countries between 1950 and 1990. Transcending the generic, if not ambiguous, debate over democracy and development, the authors chose to analyse, in more precise terms, the impact of certain aspects of democracy – or a political regime – on a society across several key dimensions: demographics, political stability and economic growth.

Looking at the strength and wealth of data and analysis supporting the book's main arguments, one could argue that it 'conclusively' settles the debate over the exact impact of various types of political regimes on the economic performance of a specific nation. The most interesting conclusion drawn by the book – after conducting a series of careful and multifaceted statistical analyses – is that there seems to be no 'trade-off' between democracy and development. In fact, in the first four chapters of the book, it becomes increasingly evident that the debate should be more nuanced and focused by tackling the 'more specific issues concerning the particular features of political regimes on various aspects of economic performance' (ibid.: 2).

At the heart of the authors' contentions lie several key arguments: first, historically all the studies which tried to analyse the possible trade-off between political democracy and economic development adopted 'faulty methodologies'. According to the authors, the appropriate methodology is the use of 'counterfactual' analysis, whereby in order to isolate the independent impact of a political regime, one must compare countries that have adopted different regime types under similar conditions. The problem with preceding (and also future) studies is that they did not take into consideration the fact that democracies are more likely to survive in already rich countries; poor democracies tend to collapse into authoritarian regimes; and a country may have initially grown under a democratic regime then suddenly collapsed into authoritarianism owing to a period of 'severe crisis'. Secondly, the impact of political regimes on the economic performance of a country varies across different levels of income. For instance, extremely poor countries tend to be trapped in a cycle of poverty regardless of their type of political regime, while the intermediate level of income regimes tend to have divergent patterns of growth. Thirdly, in order to understand and correctly analyse the correlation between democracy and development, one needs to include other influential variables that can affect a country's level of development. Thus, the authors adopted a multi-variable framework of analysis, which incorporates other potentially independent variables such as the political legacy of a country and its past history, as well as its social structure, cultural traditions, specific institutional framework and international political environment. Fourthly, the exogenous theory of democratization – as compared to the endogenous theory of democratization – is more palatable, since there seems to be no 'income threshold' beyond which an initially authoritarian country transforms into a democracy – as argued by the proponents of 'modernization theory'. Moreover, given a specific level of income – $6,055 per capita in current prices – democracies tend to gain almost absolute immunity from democratic breakdown. Meaning democracies tend to survive in richer countries. Based on their conclusions, political legacy – the history of political instability within a nation – stands as the second-most important variable in ensuring the survival and longevity of a democracy. Fifthly, the type of political regime matters less in terms of average rates of growth in the long run; however, democracies and autocracies utilize divergent patterns of capital and wealth accumulation. Democracies tend to benefit from a rise in labour productivity, while autocracies prosper on labour exploitation – appropriating lower rates of labour share in value-added manufacturing – and more aggressive rates of capital accumulation and capital-intensive production. Lastly, political regimes tend to have a strong impact on the demographics of a particular country – authoritarian nations tend to have higher rates of population growth. This explains the abundance of surplus labour, which can be linked to the comparatively lower rates of income in authoritarian regimes. Not surprisingly, labour productivity is a secondary concern for autocracies, even if they enter higher levels of economic development.

The most enduring contribution of this book is how it persuasively dispels the common notion of a 'trade-off' between democracy and development. The immediate political implication of such outstanding conclusions is that it undermines the often-used 'rhetoric' by autocrats in the South, who argue that democracy is a 'luxury' that could not be afforded by poor countries. Another important conclusion drawn by the book is that authoritarian regimes have on average proved to be more erratic in terms of prosperity and political stability. Specifically, authoritarian regimes have exemplified a mixture of miracles and disasters, while democracies have historically been more stable and sustainable on average. Although democracies have experienced fewer instances of 'economic miracles', they have in turn proved to be less susceptible to the major disasters that swept across autocracies on the periphery – until the Great Recession undermined both Western industrialized states and the whole global economy. Democracies can better allocate the available resources to productive uses. In short, the book makes a strong argument in favour of democracies by showing that there is no trade-off between growth and openness; also, it casts significant doubt on the proposition that authoritarian regimes are in a more advantageous position to extract countries out of the poverty trap. Although the book disproves the endogenous theory of democratization – the inevitability of democratization as incomes rise to a certain level – it emphasizes the viability of successful economic growth under a more liberal and democratic political system.

Echoing the book's main arguments, especially on the absence of a correlation between GDP growth rates and political regimes, Ruchir Sharma (2011), head of Emerging Markets and Global Macro at Morgan Stanley Investment Management, analysed how 'at least over the short to medium term, what matters is not the type of political system a country has but rather the presence of leaders who understand and can implement the reforms required for growth'. The argument is based on his study of 124 emerging-market countries, which successfully managed an average 5 per cent GDP growth rate for a decade, with 48 per cent happening to be authoritarian and 52 per cent democracies.

The rentier state

Looking at modern Arab regimes, especially the non-petro-rich republics, we can clearly see how they have been unable to increase overall productivity and rein in strong population growth, and have had less major successes to show for their decades of top-to-bottom reform, large-scale projects and economic experimentations.

Nasr (2009) provides an interesting account of how the Arab regimes represent a well-intended project of modernization and development that went badly wrong. Discussing what he describes as 'the tragic failures of secularism', Nasr (ibid.: 85) described the 'perverse effects' of authoritarian imposition of Western-style modernity on the region's populations in the previous century. He identifies two fundamental problems with these regimes, which explain their poor economic performance and lack of democracy:

> An overreliance on top-down economic decision-making led to patronage states ... and a great deal of mismanagement and corruption. Those on top got wealthy but few economic benefits accrued to the teeming masses below. Another crucial problem was the failure of a true bourgeoisie to develop, a middle class of merchants and professionals with their own bases of economic power, independent from state sponsorship.

As Nasr (ibid.) correctly points out, the Arab regimes, especially in their first decades of rule in the post-colonial era, were interventionist and enclosed, both in their political and their developmental strategies. They not only blocked access to political institutions, and denied freedom to the larger population, but also prevented the rise of a vibrant middle class and a powerful, independent entrepreneurial sector. As a result, Arab regimes practically clogged varying extra-state channels through which the region could move forward. It was statism in its destructive form.

Ironically, the Arab regimes' strong presence in critical sectors of the economy, considerable hold on daily political and social affairs, as well as (direct and otherwise) access to strategic rent and hydrocarbon riches only encouraged institutional stagnation and political insularity. Instead of becoming engines of growth and prosperity, they became 'rentier states': regimes that derive a significant portion of their resources from external strategic aid and/or petro-dollars.

Given their relatively low reliance on taxation, almost negligible in the case of oil-exporting monarchies, these regimes exercise tremendous leverage over society, because (a) they can prop up elaborate systems of patronage to garner the loyalty of critical sectors, especially the bourgeoisie and the military, and (b) they have less incentive to cede power to civil and political society. Although a series of economic shocks and military debacles would place tremendous pressure on these regimes to introduce economic liberalization and democratic reform, practically none of these 'rentier' states evolved into liberal democratic regimes with vibrant economies. Instead, they adeptly avoided meaningful reforms, while soliciting support from outside and reconfiguring their patronage-based sources of support and self-perpetuation. By the 1980s, it was increasingly clear that 'Arab socialism' was in tatters. The 1979 Egypt–Israel peace treaty marked the end of pan-Arabist political and military adventures, while the introduction of economic reforms throughout the Arab world led to the collapse of the quasi-socialist state.

For analysts such as Geneva-based Middle East scholar Rolf Schwarz (2008: 599–616), the pattern of state formation among rentier states is distinct, with a considerable gulf between the regime and the greater populace. For Schwarz, the Arab region is by and large home to two types of rentier states: first, oil rentier states, comprising Algeria, Bahrain, Oman, the United Arab Emirates (UAE) and Kuwait, which levy negligible tax on their citizens; secondly, non-oil or semi-rentier states, which either rely more heavily on taxation (Tunisia, Morocco and Lebanon), or use indirect taxation and strategic rents to sustain their finances (Egypt, Jordan, Palestine, Syria and Yemen).

By indirect taxation, Schwarz (ibid.: 603–6) is referring to the use of tariffs, sales tax, licensing fees and taxes on state-owned companies (mainly the oil industry) to generate revenues. Overall, across the Arab world, he argues, taxes are mainly indirect, generally low and largely evaded, with states lacking legitimacy and a strong tax-collection capacity in the absence of the voluntary compliance of citizens. Despite some differences in the extent to which varying Arab regimes rely on taxes to sustain themselves, Schwarz (ibid.: 604) argues that the rentier state is by and large a common phenomenon across the Arab world. Overall, he argues that Arab states have been strong in terms of security function, and in welfare provision during the oil boom period, but weak when it comes to political representation, coping with economic shocks and welfare crisis.

Lacking political legitimacy, and weak in terms of sustained welfare provision and economic growth, rentier states have relied on instruments of coercion, and also patronage. As German political scientist Oliver Schlumberger (2008: 626) argues, the notion of '*Wasta*' (intercession or intermediation in Arabic) captures the ways by which Arab autocrats have used an iterated game of favours to targeted groups in exchange for loyalty and support, in order to sustain themselves in power: 'In fact, neo-patrimonial socio-political systems, extremely personalized patterns of political rule, and socially dominant patronage networks as well as search for *Wasta* dominate the Arab world's socio-political systems without exception.' These informal networks of patronage, Schlumberger argues, apply to all aspects of even formal life, including 'political decision-making, elite formation and recruitment mechanisms, law endorsement and enforcement, and even agreements of a contractual nature between non-state actors'.

The path to disaster

The Arab Spring was aimed at dislodging this unsavoury political economy, giving birth to a combination of autocratic states with little developmental success to show for it. To be sure, many autocratic states, especially oil-rich monarchies, were able to build vast financial, travel and cultural hubs (e.g. Dubai, Doha and Abu Dhabi), while extreme poverty is relatively lower in the Arab world as compared to other developing regions (see the first AHDR report). But development isn't only about rising income, eye-catching skyscrapers and shiny infrastructure.

For decades, what we have seen in the Arab world is narrow improvements in certain dimensions of development, especially economic and to a certain degree in basic social indicators such as health and education, but, overall, crony capitalism and autocratic governance have been the defining themes of the Arab space. Yet it is too simplistic to understand the Arab state's development debacle in isolation, given the region's constant interaction with the broader global system. This necessitates an understanding of the evolution of the international economic system and its impact on the Arab regimes and societies, especially since the advent of economic globalization, which failed to remedy past failures, while precipitating the Arab Spring in response to three decades of an exclusionary political economy.

At this point, it is important to understand how a dialectic interaction between rentier Arab regimes and economic globalization led to the collapse of sultanistic regimes in the Middle East, while placing almost all monarchies on the defensive. The Arab Spring was an unlikely yet somehow inevitable outcome of this marriage. As Goldstone (2011) correctly puts it, revolutions are a rare commodity, necessitating a perfect convergence of discontent among the elites (civil and military), broader sections of the population across socio-economic classes and ethno-religious lines, and international powers. Otherwise, an uprising could end up in civil war, stalemate and slow-motion disintegration of the state (e.g. Syria). Therefore, we should proceed by analysing in greater detail the explosive dynamic of institutional decay and economic shocks which gave birth to the Arab Spring.

3 | THE ADVENT OF ECONOMIC GLOBALIZATION: A PRELUDE TO CRISIS

> The strictest law sometimes becomes the strictest Injustice. (Benjamin Franklin)

The mid-1970s marked the beginning of a major 'paradigm shift' in economics, amid what could be described as the emergence of a late stage of capitalism, as centre economies shifted into a post-industrial mode of production, and struggled to maintain the impressive economic performance (in the so-called 'golden age') of the post-Second World War era.

For decades, beginning with President Roosevelt's 'New Deal', Keynesian economics – emphasizing the central role of the state in ensuring social cohesion by targeting full employment and instituting counter-cyclical measures to battle economic downturn – was the order of the day. Both in the South and the North, the state was the ultimate economic arbiter, whereby wealth creation and development were the prerogative of its strategic trade and industrial policies. Such a state-centric economic paradigm was also reflected in the global economic architecture of the so-called Bretton Woods System (BWS), which provided, among other things, for considerable economic and trade policy autonomy for individual states, especially in the developing world. But, eventually, a series of acute fiscal crises, coupled with a systemic monetary conundrum, precipitated the unravelling of the Keynesian age (Skidelsky 2009; Kaletsky 2010).

By the 1970s the BWS was beginning to crumble. In the North, 'welfare states' witnessed rising inflation, coupled with declines in employment opportunities and economic growth. Centre economies were gradually entering a period of recession, while trade protectionism as well as currency manipulation soured international trade. When the 'fixed-exchange regime' – undermined by the USA's weakening finances, growing imbalances in the international system, and the rise of the phenomenon of 'stagflation' in centre economies –

collapsed in 1971, a new period of uncertainty kicked in. The result was an era of unprecedented capital mobility, ending decades of 'Fordist' economics.[1] And states began to compete for capital by dismantling regulatory regimes deemed to constrain the entry of external economic actors (Kiely 2007).

Enter the neoliberals, the proponents of libertarian market-driven economies, who characterized the so-called 'Keynesian [welfare] state' as 'excessively' intrusive, bloated and unsustainable. In their view, the problem lay in the state. Richard Posner (in Przeworski 1996) succinctly summarized the neoliberal critique when he stated, 'The economist recognizes that government can do some things better than the free market can do but he has no reason to believe that democratic processes will keep government from exceeding the limits of optimal intervention.' In short, the bureaucrats, neoliberals argued, simply took Keynesian ideas to their logical extreme: the state, in their view, became an arena for private-interest-jostling and regulatory capture, coupled with rigid labour markets, with labour unions powerful enough to constantly push for wage hikes – with no reference to productivity gains – while monopolistic industries, mainly in steel and car manufacturing, dictated market prices. There were, however, external factors at play too: the costs of the Vietnam War, compounding the welfare expenditures of the pre-Nixon administration, brought the national budget to its knees. The oil shocks of the 1970s worsened the situation by pushing up the prices of basic commodities, inducing upward inflationary pressure. The combination of domestic economic contradictions and external shocks resulted in stagflation in the North: a simultaneous increase in inflation and unemployment. It was during this time that the prominent Chicago University economist Milton Friedman came into the picture – the high priest of neoclassical economics (and the neoliberal paradigm). Friedman (in Skidelsky 2009: 105), a former Keynesian by some accounts,[2] argued that in the short run, 'changes in the rate of growth of the money stock are capable of exerting sizeable influence on the rate of growth of output as well'. His central claim was that to combat the stagflation, the government needs to adopt a 'stable policy regime', wherein money supply changes alongside long-term rates of output growth. In his view, growing rigidities in the labour market and increasing inflation rates – due to expansionary monetary policies – undermined the stability of Keynesian economic policies. In exchange, Friedman introduced the concept of 'natural rate' as the equilibrium level of unemployment – supplanting the more socially acceptable concept of 'full employment' – which, he argued, could be established under conditions of 'stable inflation' (ibid.: 106).

In 1976, British prime minister James Callaghan embraced Friedman's views by stating that governments could no longer spend their way out of recession without risking further inflation. This period, some would argue, marked the alliance between neoclassical economists and the political leadership (ibid.: 107). While massive unemployment made Keynesianism a palatable political project, high rates of inflation turned neoclassical economics into the dominant ideology. Friedman's solution to downturns was lighter taxes, minimal regulation and unfettered market economics.[3] At the heart of this new paradigm were four main microeconomic theories: (1) the 'efficient market theory', which contended that markets are self-correcting systems and are capable of making speedy and necessary adjustments to avoid the occurrence and/or deepening of a crisis; (2) the 'rational expectations hypothesis', which contends that the expectations of agents about relevant economic variables are largely predictable, and thus can be accounted by precise mathematical/statistical models; (3) the 'policy ineffectiveness proposition', which posits that inflation-inducing expansionary fiscal policies do not solve unemployment, since the 'money illusion' – created by higher liquidity – is countered by a 'wage–price hike spiral', whereby suppliers and workers continuously push for higher prices in order to cope with inflation, with 'stagflation' a possible outcome; and lastly, the 'Ricardian Equivalence', which posits that government's spending policies do not have any major impact on consumer spending, since people will internalize government's 'budget constraints' (Kaletsky 2010: 168–78). On top of these microeconomic assumptions, the classical theory of comparative advantage, posited by David Ricardo, became the bedrock of subsequent hypotheses, which defined the contours of international trade regimes. The theory assumed complete markets, perfect information, perfect competition, non-mobility of capital, full employment, and perfect mobility of factors of production. With these assumptions, the theory posited that all parties are to gain from trade if each specializes in the production of what it is most efficient at or has comparative advantage in. The Hecksher-Ohlin theorem, built on the Ricardian theory, argued that countries could maximize their utility by specializing in the production of commodities which require their comparatively abundant factors of production (e.g. capital or labour). The Stopler-Samuelson theorem extended neoclassical analysis on two levels: first, an increase in the price of a commodity would lead to an increase in the return on the utilized abundant factor of production, and conversely, a decrease in the return on the less abundant factor of production; and secondly, trade liberalization is opposed by sectors which employ the less abundant/inefficient factor endowments. The neoclassical paradigm was also found in the 'trickle-down' effect proposition, wherein it is presumed that the increase in the national economic pie, on a macro level, would eventually translate into poverty alleviation, hunger reduction and development throughout society. Therefore, following such a proposition, there is no need for the state to disrupt economic operations and engage in distributionary policies, because the 'market' most efficiently allocates resources automatically (Kiely 2007; Skidelsky 2009; Kaletsky 2010).

Neoliberalism was elevated to a global ideology when, by the early 1980s, major states and international organizations began to internalize its basic assumptions into their policy paradigm. On the national level, President Ronald Reagan and Prime Minister Margaret Thatcher gradually dismantled the 'welfare state' system, embedding neoclassical economics in the fabric of the world's leading economies. The United Kingdom and the United States became the main beachhead for the neoliberal experiment, which, over succeeding years, gradually permeated the rest of the capitalist world – eventually sweeping across (and further intensifying in) eastern Europe, the Middle East, Central Asia and Russia by the 1990s. On the global level, the neoclassical economic assumptions formed the foundation of an economic paradigm that has traversed the world under the auspices of the IFIs, notably the 'triad' of the World Trade Organization (WTO), the International Monetary Fund (IMF) and the World Bank (WB). Soon, the global trade regimes began to emphasize the need for state economic disengagement in favour of a market-led economics. Thus began economic globalization (Kiely 2007; Goddard 2003).

Transforming the global South

By the 1980s, profligate capital expenditures and gross mismanagement of the economy – compounded by rising interest rates on capital – resulted in double-digit inflation rates and staggering amounts of debt among developing countries. From the Philippines in Asia to Mexico and Brazil in Latin America, developing economies called upon the IFIs for aid (Bello et al. 1982). And this was a period of tremendous influence for the IMF and the WB. In the new era of capital mobility, the IMF was bequeathed the role of ensuring the overall stability of a global flexible exchange regime run by fiat money. As a result of the expansion in its scope and functions, the IMF also became a central player in the determination of the overall macroeconomic direction of developing economies (Goddard 2003). The World Bank, similarly, was tasked with ensuring economic stability, and post-crisis recovery, among developing states (Kiely 2007). Together, they pushed for a package of structural adjustment programmes aimed at dismantling ISI policies, state subsidy regimes and state-held industries in favour of export-oriented industrialization, foreign capital and the domestic private sector. So, the state was defanged and subsidies were abolished, while a tiny private sector was forced to step in and fill up the investment and production vacuum. The broader aim was to integrate developing economies into an emerging international economic order, underpinned by capital mobility and new divisions of labour between South and North. And this was the era of economic globalization (Bello 2003).

The General Agreement on Tariffs and Trade (GATT) would be replaced by the WTO, which, in turn, pushed for more aggressive liberalization of markets and the dismantling of state-centred development in the South. Unlike the GATT, the WTO emphasized three main principles: first, a strict compliance with the rules of the organization lest 'penalties' be imposed; secondly, not only merchandise trade, but also investment policies, the service sector, agriculture and intellectual property rights to be subject to negotiations (and subsequent rules to emanate from agreement among members); and lastly, developing countries – with the exception of a few very poor small economies – expected to 'graduate' from 'special and differential treatment' provisions as soon as possible. The WTO facilitated the implementation of a much more aggressive liberal international order, featuring an expansion in FDIs, intercontinental trade and economic liberalization (Bello 2000; Cohen 2003; Mirza 2008).

The false economic paradigm In the aftermath of the 'oil shocks' of the 1980s, most Arab countries, facing the double evil of a deteriorating trade balance and a contracting fiscal space, initiated decisive periods of economic reforms. After decades of state-led, welfare-oriented economics, within the ambit of 'Arab socialism', the region – notwithstanding the divergence among individual states, especially between petro-states and resource-poor countries – gradually moved towards market-oriented, export-led economics, whereby international trade, FDIs, tourism and services became the engines of economic life. This trend was part of a broader global push towards a post-Keynesian international order.

In more specific terms, economic globalization in the Arab world contained the following elements: a reduction in both conventional (tariff) and unconventional (non-tariff) barriers to trade, followed by a gradual move towards capital account liberalization, primarily to encourage FDI and foreign portfolio investments; restructuring of the domestic economy in the direction of export-oriented industrialization and export-market-dependent growth; gradual withdrawal of the state from the national economy in exchange for growing private sector participation in all key aspects of the economy; securing macroeconomic stability, through fiscal discipline (i.e. budget deficit reduction) and monetary 'restraint' (i.e. inflation- and interest-rates-targeting); reorientation of industrial policy, through the abolition of interventionist macro-industrial management, and specialization of production under a comparative-advantage framework; and most fundamentally, the transformation of the state from a maximalist 'social state' into a minimalist 'regulatory state', designed to ensure the proper functioning of (real and financial) markets and protection of private property rights, while relegating 'welfare' responsibilities to the private sector, but retaining token safety nets to maintain social cohesion as well as ameliorate the impact of reforms and at times crises (Beinin 2009; Richter 2007; Pioppi 2007).

However, the reforms – aimed at integrating regional economies into global chains of production and unleashing private sector dynamism to remedy state-led economic ossification – had a profoundly counterproductive effect: they actually increased the Arab economies' exposure to the embedded volatility in international markets without a parallel effort to improve their resilience and coping mechanisms. Under the guidance of the IFIs, retaining low inflation and a balanced budget (low fiscal deficit) was prioritized over employment generation and inclusive growth. While privatization was encouraged, there were few prescriptions and programmes focused on public sector development (Stiglitz 1999). In contrast, more successful developing countries, notably the newly industrialized countries (NICs) and tiger economies in East Asia, already had a strong industrial and institutional foundation in place once economic globalization kicked in. In short, they were, unlike their Arab counterparts, in a particularly solid position to reap the benefits of trade liberalization and – especially in the case of less capital-intensive economies such as China and Thailand – attract investments from abroad (Gallagher 2005). In many ways, one could trace the origins of the 2010/11 Arab uprisings to this imbalanced and premature foray into international markets by Arab states, which largely came under external pressure.

Crony capitalism par excellence Unlike their visionary predecessors, Ben Ali in Tunisia and Anwar Sadat and Hosni Mubarak in Egypt progressively abandoned the more egalitarian and welfare-oriented policies of Arab socialism in favour of economic opening and deregulation. It was not so much their penchant for laissez-faire economics as their desperate attempt to win external aid from the West and the IFIs, balance the books and relieve their bloated regimes by dispensing with unsustainable levels of welfare, as the overall economy ground to a halt.

Egypt's market reforms began in the 1970s, after the Yom Kippur War, when the state confronted a severe economic crisis: a huge budget deficit, high foreign debt, double-digit inflation rates, and a creeping balance of payment crisis. Under the guidance of the IMF, the Egyptian state aggressively privatized state enterprises. By the early 1990s, a looming economic crisis had forced the government to reconsider a new round of economic reforms. As a result, subsidies were further reduced, social services – from healthcare and transportation to education and housing – were slashed, while long-time government guarantees of state employment for university graduates were suspended – this worsened the unemployment problem among restive and frustrated graduates in coming years. Across the region, the 1980s marked the beginning of the market-reform saga, with resource-poor Arab countries experiencing an across-the-board welfare crunch, while sparsely populated petro-states in the Persian Gulf were also forced to exercise a measure of fiscal prudence. It was crunch time across the region, but less endowed Arab republics, and to a certain degree also monarchies such as Jordan and Morocco, faced a particularly difficult period of belt-tightening and cutbacks. The regimes managed to survive the onslaught of downsizing and welfare reduction at the expense of the ordinary people, while the top brass of the security services and pro-regime business classes benefited from large-scale privatization schemes and new opportunities emerging in real estate, tourism, financial markets and import-export ventures. There was resistance to genuine economic reform across the board, since autocrats feared the political consequences of a full-scale rollback of subsidies and the impact of 'good governance' – namely, transparency-boosting and anti-corruption measures – reforms on varying systems of patronage. Nonetheless, the Arab regimes adeptly managed the period of reform. While avoiding any sort of policy adjustment or reform deemed to be regime-threatening, the autocrats were able to appease patrons without and clients within, at least to a certain point. They targeted the kinds of economic reforms which would allow them to secure loans from IFIs, and project a veneer of change, while stealthily tinkering with these policies later in order to enrich allies in the military and business community – and of course members of their own family, with both Ben Ali's and Mubarak's family and entourage amassing tens of billions of dollars in wealth to the chagrin of the masses (Kim 2011; Mariani 2013). This was accomplished through a predatory process of privatization: in the absence of a truly competitive market and rule of law, the autocrats manipulated bidding procedures during major privatization schemes of major state industries, banks and corporations (Richter 2007; Pioppi 2007; Schlumberger 2008).

In places such as Egypt, the military expanded its reach into the civilian economy, eventually controlling between 25 and 30 per cent of the economy by some estimates (Pravda 2011), while regime cronies, both military and civilian, benefited from cheap and easy credit, which was largely used to prop up newly privatized state assets and interests. The security sector, across many Arab countries, was particularly aggressive, using its impeccable organizational capacity as well as its strategic importance (to autocrats) to reach into and dominate critical sectors of the economy (Droz-Vincent 2007). In effect, the economic reforms were adulterated: they simply led to a recycling of state resources into the hands of top figures within the regime and their civilian and military allies. Soon, it became clear that not only was the regime able to maintain the loyalty of crucial allies and clients, but it was also able to deepen and expand its channels of patronage vis-à-vis critical elite circles. The result was a neo-patrimonial state, overseeing crony capitalism in its crudest form (Richter 2007; Pioppi 2007; Schlumberger 2008).

Indeed, some signs of trouble emerged early on. In 1997/98, Egypt experienced a liquidity crunch, resulting from a toxic mixture of external downturn and an internal money glut, which, earlier, fuelled large-scale speculative real estate investments, and an unsustainable surge in imports (Hussain and Nos'hy n.d.: 6). The regime cronies – by borrowing cheap, recycling funds from the banks to their own businesses, and prompting high rates of non-performing loans – constantly placed the financial system on the brink. But the party went on. Whenever the oligarchs fell into trouble, ranging from banking crises to trade disruptions, and the Great Recession of 2008, the regime would utilize resources at its disposal to bail out allies, stimulate flailing sectors, and provide alternative ventures for profit-making. After all, any stimulus programme or counter-cyclical measure would be directed at major sectors of the economy, which were unsurprisingly controlled by regime cronies. In this sense, the autocrats were not only adulterating economic reforms by artificially rewarding favoured economic agents; they also discouraged prudence and economic productivity. Since political calculations predominated in economic decision-making, the greatest beneficiaries of economic reforms were not exactly the most meritocratic actors. There was hardly any 'benchmark of performance' (or the so-called reciprocal mechanism) imposed on regime clients in exchange for economic carrots and special privileges. Thus, the regime manipulated reforms to favour incompetent allies and/or discouraged prudent investment and economic decision-making by engendering a deep systemic 'moral hazard': the implied guarantee of state support in the event of crisis. Given such an opaque and corrupt political system, there was, quite understandably, little interest from abroad in substantial 'greenfield' investments in countries such as Egypt, even after a period of supposed reform (Richter 2007; Pioppi 2007; Schlumberger 2008). Yet, even as Arab leaders astutely co-opted the process of economic reforms, the so-called Economic Reforms and Structural Adjustment Programmes, to sustain their regime and appease critical allies, the IMF and World Bank began to tout Egypt and Tunisia as regional cases of globalization's success. As late as 2010, top indices, measuring market openness and economic liberalization, painted a largely positive picture of the two North African countries. In the 2009/10 Economic Competitiveness Index (World Economic Forum 2010), Tunisia was ranked 32nd, outshining leading emerging markets such as Brazil and Turkey, while Egypt, ranked 70th, stood above European countries like Greece. More impressively, the 2010 KOF Globalization Index ranked Egypt and Tunisia 12th and 35th respectively in terms of the diffusion of government policies.[5]

The fundamental problem with the IFIs' strategy of reform in the Arab world was that it failed to appreciate and foresee the savvy machinations of autocratic regimes, hinged on a shrewd sense of survival, to co-opt reforms. More importantly, the IFIs overlooked the harmful mixture of shallow – if not counterproductive – economic reforms with weak, enclosed political institutions. In short, the reforms were off balance and one-sided, strengthening the autocrats, at least in the short to medium run, at the expense of genuine economic development. So, IFI-pushed economic liberalization did not lead to advanced market economies, but instead enabled Tunisian and Egyptian autocrats to institute a mafia-like system that allowed favoured cliques to dominate the tourism, real estate and banking sectors. In both Tunisia and Egypt, the minimalist regulatory doctrine imposed by IFIs prevented the state from becoming a central player in implementing industrial-trade policies to foster sustained industrialization and economic growth. As a result, despite decades of impressive economic growth, a significant portion of the population is impoverished, and the unemployment rates are sky high. The absence of globally competitive industries meant that these countries were hugely dependent on sectors fraught with speculative practices, fraud and uncertainty: real estate, banking and tourism. Economic liberalization and regulatory capture (in which special-interest groups influence and co-opt the very state agencies designed to regulate them) meant that the state had less budgetary and fiscal leverage to deal with sudden price rises in basic commodities. Owing to rampant deregulation and openness, commodity prices in Tunisia and Egypt were increasingly determined by variables beyond national boundaries. Therefore, Arab states reduced social safety nets – acting as shock absorbers – just when they opened up their economies to the vagaries of international trade. This proved a lethal combination.

Jordan – increasingly in the throes of revolutionary upheaval as protesters have begun to call for the king to step down, the main opposition groups have boycotted the last parliamentary elections, while a looming economic collapse coupled with an energy crisis has prompted an emergency IMF bailout proposal – is another Arab country which has engaged in aggressive market reforms in recent decades. It also enjoys comparatively high rankings in different competitiveness and economic openness indices. However, a few sectors, from construction to telecommunications, have been the main economic engines. Jobs in the manufacturing sector are limited to a few export zones, where the wages are generally low – many employees are actually non-Jordanian (Saif 2008a). This jobless growth – hovering around an annual rate of 6 per cent – also failed to reduce income inequality in the country, since the GINI coefficient hardly changed between 1997 and 2006 (ibid.).

Socialism with capitalist characteristics In the last decade, Libya and Syria have also instituted a series of economic reforms in order to revitalize their lethargic economies. Both countries have greatly relied on oil exports for revenue generation. The Gaddafi and Assad clans ruled their respective countries for more than four decades, allowing the leadership to establish an entrenched network of patronage. Although the income differential between the two countries is huge, they both share the same characteristics, albeit in different degrees: (1) there has been no significant trickle-down of hydrocarbon revenues to the wider population, since the leaders prioritized their own tribes and henchmen to ensure loyalty and continued support; (2) privatization schemes have either been minimal or a complete sham, since favoured clients were handed monopolies over new economic spaces, supposedly for the private sector; (3) a significant proportion of revenues was allocated to the maintenance of the coercive organs of the state, from the security forces to the intelligence and interior ministry; and lastly, while Syria devoted a huge amount of funds and attention to propping up its military and supporting proxies in Palestine and Lebanon, Libya's ambition, under Mu'ammer Gaddafi, of becoming a continental leader was accompanied by a significant reallocation of state revenues to different regional bureaucratic organs (e.g. the African Union) and economies (from Kenya to Niger, Gambia, Chad and Nigeria) (Reuters 2011a).

For a long time, Gaddafi's Libya touted itself as a socialist, pan-Arabist state, setting itself apart from its pro-Western, market-oriented peers, both republican and monarchic. The Libyan regime was among the most intransigent and audacious sponsors/supporters of anti-establishment organizations and revolutionary movements – from the Irish Republican Army (IRA) and the mujahedin groups in Afghanistan to revolutionary Iran – across the world. Gaddafi was a proud patron of sabotage, conspiracy, assassination plots and a whole host of activities, which eventually prompted America to conduct military operations, beginning in the 1980s, against Tripoli. Over succeeding years, the ominous Libyan regime further worried the Western countries by harbouring plans to build a nuclear capability. However, the last decade has witnessed a dramatic change in the country's posturing (see Fisk 2005), which precipitated an economic opening. The ease with which the coalition forces toppled Saddam Husain engendered a deep sense of vulnerability in the Libyan leadership, empowering so-called reformists such as Saif al-Islam, who used his growing influence to encourage rapprochement with the West for both economic and security reasons. The Libyan regime also faced growing challenges from Islamist movements in North Africa, which vehemently opposed Gaddafi's brand of secular autocracy. These factors facilitated a gradual and steady process of reconciliation and growing intimacy with the West, especially European countries, which became a top energy customer and source of investments for Libya. The normalization of ties with the West was followed by the influx of foreign investors, who were bent on exploiting the country's large, high-quality hydrocarbon reserves. Within a few years, major multinational energy companies, from ExxonMobil to BP and ENI, began to establish strongholds across Libya's hydrocarbon-rich landscape, among the biggest in the world. The regime was intent on improving its balance sheet, boosting its fiscal resources, and improving the country's overall economic conditions. It was a mutually beneficial arrangement. Intent on winning greater praise from the international community, amid smoothening and expanding linkages with the world's business and political elite, Saif al-Islam sought political reforms in order to improve the country's image. Ultimately, he wanted to position himself as the upcoming reform-minded leader of the country. Interestingly, among his constituencies was Libya's army of educated youth, who would eventually turn against him and the entire Libyan regime (Gumuchian 2011).

Nonetheless, despite Saif's supposed efforts in the direction of political and economic liberalization, the Libyan leadership had little respect for human rights, political freedom and civil liberties. Revolutionary committees and Gaddafi's tribal brethren ruled the country. There were no democratic elections, and the circle of power was practically confined to Gaddafi's nuclear family. His sons controlled all major organs of the state. The Libyan regime was anchored in a state of fear instilled by the leadership's carefully woven, complex web of 'sleeper cells', spies, security forces and tribe-based armies. It was an essentially personalistic police state built around a paranoid, brutal and repressive leader. What was more frustrating for many Libyans was that despite the country's wealth and high per capita income, among the highest in the developing world, a combination of staggering cronyism, corruption and misallocation of funds allowed a small circle of clients to amass immense wealth. Major infrastructural projects went unfinished, because the contractors siphoned off the funds or exhausted allocated revenues, thanks to a weak or non-existent independent auditing regime. Kickbacks, and other types of predatory corruption, ravaged the country's economic potential. On the other hand, instead of investing the country's whopping oil revenues in the domestic economy, the regime chose to invest a significant proportion of the country's cash reserves in pan-African projects and/or directly in Gaddafi and his associates' overseas accounts. The most disturbing fact for many ordinary Libyans in economic terms was that the country suffered from double-digit rates of youth unemployment, while average incomes were in actuality comparable to poorer neighbouring countries[6] (Joffe 2011; Gumuchian 2011).

In Syria, a decade of lopsided economic liberalization, beginning with the ascent of Bashar Al-Assad, led to the concentration of wealth in the hands of a small number of pro-regime oligarchs, on one hand, and a gradual decline in state services and the real income of the majority of people on the other. Moreover, the relaxation of trade restrictions also led to the influx of cheap imported products, which undermined small and medium-sized enterprises (SMEs) across the country. As a result, the middle class was severely hit by the economic reforms. Although the regime's roots were in its rural, peasant-led revolutionary past, gross neglect of rural areas – from weak administration to negligible infrastructural development – led to poverty, corruption, massive abuse by authorities, instability and tremendous disenchantment among the country's large rural population. Weak industrial policy and over-reliance on services and raw materials exports – mainly oil – turned Syria into one of the poorest Arab countries with one of the highest rates of youth unemployment. While manufacturing allows for the creation of large-scale quality employment opportunities, service-oriented economics tends to concentrate economic activity within a narrow circle of skilled and connected population. Also, there was hardly any proper trickle-down of the country's modest oil revenues, since the bulk of the fiscal resources were injected into the country's vast internal security apparatus, major arms-procurement deals, and pockets of major regime clients. Despite promises of political liberalization, the young Assad continued a strategy of reliance on coercive security measures. As such, the Syrian regime was practically a 'police state', composed of a vast and complex array of security and intelligence divisions, keeping opponents at bay and instilling a profound atmosphere of fear in the country. Alongside coercion, there was a weakening and marginalization of the national army – in an attempt to prevent a coup – that stripped the country of a neutral, coherent and professional national force, which could have prevented Syria from falling into a state of total chaos in the event of a major political earthquake, such as the Arab Spring[7] (International Crisis Group 2012a).

The demographic conundrum

Looking at the roots of the Arab Spring, there is another perennial problem, which has further compounded the Arab world's myriad economic challenges (and continues to do so). And this was by no means addressed by economic globalization, whereby the widespread availability of cheap surplus labour is always a welcome phenomenon for global suppliers and investors intent on cost-cutting and achieving competitive prices. The region is experiencing one of the most dramatic cases of youth bulge in modern history: an excessive and disproportionate number of young and unemployed educated people. The Arab world has the highest level of unemployment in the world, and youth unemployment rates are astronomical – averaging over 23 per cent in the region. The global average stands at 14 per cent (Shehata 2011: 26–32). Worse, 60 per cent of the Arab world is under the age of thirty. In addition, the average population growth rate in the Arab world is 1.9 per cent, which is much higher than the global average of 1.2 per cent (Akhtar 2011). So demographics are bound to be a long-term challenge for the Arab world.

Looking at the composition and anatomy of the Arab uprisings, the youth has obviously played a crucial role in organizing events, mobilizing the public, and circumventing state regulations. In this sense, the Arab uprisings should remind us of events in 1968, when the 'baby boomer generation' launched protests across the world, from Berlin and Berkeley to Paris and Prague. The 68ers represented a similar demographic reality, which had profound political and sociocultural implications for many countries in the West as well as the communist bloc. British historian Niall Ferguson captured the nexus between the post-war youth bulge and the widespread social movements and protests that rocked the West and even major capitals in the East:

> Nineteen-sixty-eight was a year of revolution in all kinds of ways, from Paris to Prague, from Berlin to Berkeley, and even in Beijing. But the common factor in all these disruptions to the Cold War duopoly of power was youth. Rarely in modern times have people aged between fifteen and twenty-four accounted for so large a share of the population as in the decade after 1968. Having dropped as low as 11 percent of the US population in the mid-1950s, the youth share reached a peak of 17 percent in the mid-1970s. By 1968 university students made up more than 3 percent of the entire American population, compared with less than 1 percent in 1928. (Ferguson 2011)

Looking at the Arab Spring, especially the largely non-violent protests in Tunisia and Egypt, through the lens of the 68ers' protests, renowned Yale sociologist Immanuel Wallerstein considered two fundamental 'currents' equally present in the 1968 'world-revolutions' and 2011 Arab uprisings: 'First, the revolutionaries of 1968 were protesting against the inherently undemocratic behaviour of those in authority ... in favour of horizontal decision-making – participatory and therefore popular ... [Secondly] the world-revolution of 1968 included in a very major way a revolution of the "forgotten peoples"' (Wallerstein 2011).

The 1970s represented a decade of mega-changes in the demographic make-up of many countries. A greater share of the population was under the age of thirty, while the number of university graduates increased exponentially. It was a decade that witnessed increasingly violent and widespread protests in streets and universities, forcing certain regimes to consider major social and political reform. In Czechoslovakia, it took a Soviet intervention to reverse concessions and reforms instituted and promised by Dubcek's government.

Nevertheless, the 68ers successfully pushed for the 'Prague spring', gender equality, counter-cultural trends, and reforms in the realm of civil rights and political freedom (Ferguson 2011: 315). Interestingly, the youth of the Arab Spring is pushing for similar reforms, mostly along liberal democratic lines. Their demands focus on equal economic opportunities, freedom of assembly and expression, individual civil liberties, and political rights (Anderson 2011).

The Arab youth bulge is as dramatic (if not more so) as its 1968 counterpart. Since 1990, the youth population, aged between fifteen and twenty-nine years old, has grown by 65 per cent in Egypt, 50 per cent in Libya and Tunisia, and 125 per cent in Yemen (Goldstone 2011: 8–16). This would overwhelm most labour markets' annual absorption capacity, unless there were a high level of employment-generating annual GDP growth. To the credit of Arab autocrats, modernization programmes resulted in tremendous improvement in basic healthcare and education. This is evident in the fact that many Arab countries, in recent decades, have registered noticeable improvements on the Human Development Index (see the 2002 AHDR). However, improvements proved to be a double-edged sword for autocrats. In recent decades, college enrolment increased fourfold in Egypt, while tripling in Tunisia and increasing tenfold in Libya (Shehata 2011: 26–32). This dramatic growth in college education was not accompanied by significant improvements in the labour market (owing predominantly to mismanaged economic policies).

Astonishingly, the highest levels of unemployment are among high school and university graduates, adding to the frustration of an increasingly rebellious and idealistic youth. This explains their growing audacity in confronting the state. In Egypt, 95 per cent of young individuals with secondary or higher education are unemployed (ibid.). Egypt's youth unemployment rate increased from 23.1 per cent in 1998 to 34.1 per cent in 2005 (see United Nations Statistics Division n.d.). Faced with the prospect of unemployment or low-paying jobs, many postpone their plans for marriage. Almost half of Egyptians between the ages of twenty-five and twenty-nine are unmarried (ibid.: 26–32). Unable to find a job and form a meaningful relationship, Arab youth finds a distinct resonance in revolutionary agitations.

The combination of the demographic problem in the Arab world, largely emanating from the lack of a proactive population management policy (see Chapter 8), and the co-optation of economic reforms, benefiting the elites at the expense of the people, provided the underpinnings of state failure and autocratic ossification. Overall, what one observes is that far from transforming Arab economies into new hubs of economic dynamism and social mobility, the advent of economic globalization brought about further structural vulnerabilities – which, in turn, provided the underpinnings of a political upheaval once a combination of commodity-based and financial-economic crises hit the Arab states and their main economic partners in the West. The Arab world was a powder keg awaiting an economic shock and a political fire.

4 | THE GREAT RECESSION: THE COLLAPSE OF ARAB CRONY CAPITALISM

> It is better to be roughly right than precisely wrong.
> (John Maynard Keynes)[1]

While the markets – thanks to increasing deregulation – played a crucial role in transforming the structure of the global economy, the 2008 global financial crisis exposed the paucity of a system in which a number of prominent financial institutions, such as Lehman Brothers, brought the world to the brink of collapse. In an interdependent world, a crisis essentially rooted in 'Wall Street' instantly transformed into a global contagion, causing a worldwide economic downturn amid persistent uncertainly in financial markets. As a result, many developing countries experienced a dramatic collapse in their commodity exports, exacerbated by declines in equity markets, with the major emerging economies of Brazil, Russia, South Africa and to a certain degree even China experiencing an economic downturn after a decade of rapid expansion, while in Europe the so-called PIGS (Portugal, Italy, Ireland, Greece and Spain) economies fell into disarray, precipitating a profound sovereign debt crisis, which sent ripples across the global financial system, while threatening to compromise the viability of the Eurozone – and the greater EU project, for that matter. No Arab economy was immune to the so-called Great Recession of 2008, the second-most severe economic crisis since the Great Depression.

More or less, there is a consensus on the genesis of the recent economic crisis: essentially, the crisis began with the bursting of the housing bubble in the over-leveraged and overvalued housing sector, thanks to the sub-prime crisis, with the subsequent collapse of Lehman Brothers in 2008 compromising gigantic, complex financial chains, which for decades served as the foundation of the global financial markets. The result was the overnight evaporation of trillions of dollars in financial assets, a recessionary credit crunch, a decline in overall consumption, a steep fall in production, and unprecedented emergency bailouts by jittery states desperate to rescue the economy from a free fall akin to the Great Depression (Kaletsky 2010: 128–81; Skidelsky 2009: 3–29; El-Erian 2008: 39–63).

Although different scholars focused on varying specific factors behind the crisis, the Great Recession was a by-product of a number of interacting factors: (1) the emergence of 'unsustainable' levels of imbalances in the global trading system, mainly between the 'locomotive' economies (e.g. Japan, China and Germany), on one hand, and 'consumerist' economies (e.g. the USA, the UK and southern European nations), on the other; (2) the absence of 'decoupling' between emerging economies, on one hand, and developed economies, on the other, facilitating the spread of the contagion from US markets to the rest of the world; (3) the dominance of market fundamentalists' influence in all levels of governance, leading to elimination of much-needed (effective and proactive) regulation to stave off the emergence as well as the spread of the contagion; and (4) the excessive confidence in often fundamentally flawed financial models, which supposedly provided precise and reliable formulas to guide stable expansion in financial activities, but instead created an illusion of stability in a casino-like finance-driven economics. In an ideal neoclassical world, trade imbalances – absent protectionism and imponderable disturbances in factors of trade – are supposed to be self-correcting: currency appreciation is tied to trade balance; thus, in the long run, trade surpluses are cleared as a result of currency appreciation. However, in the 'real' world, trade patterns follow a very different logic: on the part of export-oriented economies such as China and Japan, patterns of spending – owing to the culture as well as the socio-economic structure of these countries – have been extremely conservative; therefore a subsequent 'saving glut' has prevented other economies such as the USA commensurately tapping into market opportunities in these countries. The horrors of the 1997 Asian financial crisis also inspired many of the Asian economies to amass huge sums in foreign currency reserves as a cushion lest another currency crisis devastate their economy. Moreover, these countries have had a very strong mercantilist mentality in terms of their trading policies. Bent on deepening inroads into lucrative

Western markets, they have created a so-called 'manipulative cycle' in recent decades. Flushed with billions of dollars in trade surpluses, countries such as China and Germany have been 'recycling' their export earnings by granting credit to their consumers in the USA and southern Europe. This prevented the appreciation of their currencies. The result has been a 'money glut', whereby easy availability of credit has allowed many consumerist economies to sustain their already 'excessive' levels of imports and consumer spending – thanks to treasury bills bought by Asian and Arab central banks, or credit lending by German financial institutions. This lethal combination has given rise to a high level of imbalance in global trade, and excessive rates of credit availability, risk-taking and borrowing among indebted nations (Terzulli and Ascari 2009; Skidelsky 2009: 3–29; Kaletsky 2010: 209–67; El-Erian 2008: 19–39).

Emerging economies have also been highly tied to developed countries. Despite the appeal of the idea of 'decoupling', emerging economies have been highly dependent on investments from the North – as reflected in the composition of their equity markets and their trade balances. In addition, many emerging economies have been increasingly investing in the North, exposing themselves to the perils of financial instability in centre economies. In this context, the credit crunch in the USA easily spread throughout the emerging economies, shattering equity markets and compromising investments in financial sectors of the North. With many of emerging economies dependent on exports to the North, the credit crunch severely disrupted import and consumption patterns (United Nations 2009; Terzulli and Ascari 2009).

Beyond global trade and capital flow imbalances, the crisis was also a product of a chronic regulatory deficit. Regulation is indispensable to the life of any organization and activity. However, in the post-Keynesian climate of economic globalization, any sort of regulation was seen as an adulteration of the sanctity of rational, self-correcting and 'enlightened' markets. Neoclassical economics not only encouraged the withdrawal of the state, but also justified the growing centrality of financial markets as engines of wealth creation. As a result, 'stock markets', once again, became the nucleus of economic activity. The 'consumer boom' and the 'stock market bubbles' were the natural result of this development. With most regulators themselves being trained in top American universities, with a heavy dose of neoclassical curriculum, any sort of stringent government regulation was seen as a form of sinister intervention. From their viewpoint, to see regulation as a bedrock of economic stability would create some sort of psychological dissonance in an era of market-centred economics. So there was also 'thought contagion' of market fundamentalism. Crucially, regulators, however, simply overlooked a number of variables, which always threatened the foundations of the economy: (1) the 'too big to fail' syndrome empowered many large financial corporations to take huge amounts of risk, precisely because they knew that there was always an 'implicit' guarantee – on the part of the state – in the event of disaster; (2) embedded financial regulators – from credit agencies to other risk-evaluating institutions – were highly interlinked with the very institutions which they were supposed to regulate (e.g. banks and investment institutions); (3) large information asymmetries led to a situation where markets failed to adequately and properly reflect prices and risks, especially in booming sectors such as real estate (Terzulli and Ascari 2009; El-Erian 2008; Skidelsky 2009; Kaletsky 2010).

In an era of relatively stable rates of inflation and real interest there emerged an overall impression that the sands of time had transformed markets into even more predictable variables. The Rational Expectations Hypothesis (REH) allowed many economists and finance experts to introduce increasingly sophisticated, complex sets of algorithms and statistical models in an effort to analyse and predict patterns of economic behaviour. The introduction of securitization, risk-management models and derivatives allowed for an unprecedented expansion in economic speculation and financial transactions – separating borrowers/consumers from lenders/producers by the injection of a myriad of 'middlemen' mediating financial transactions and housing loans, while, on the macroeconomic level, the real economy was, in actuality, relegated to the background. With growing confidence in the utility as well as the value of financial models, regulation was increasingly 'internalized' by the financial sector itself: the introduction of mark-to-market accounting and risk-weighted capital requirements allowed for the 'transfer' of regulation from the state to the financial institutions. There were other structural factors in play. As a result of decades of stable macroeconomic conditions, illiquid assets (i.e. housing) became increasingly valuable. The introduction of mortgage-backed loans not only allowed for more borrowing based on house ownership, but also pushed real estate prices to new historic levels. With credit being easily available, and new financial instruments allowing for more risky lending, the stage was set for a precarious expansion in the housing sector. The combustible combination of regulation deficit, on one hand, and an increasing reliance on fundamentally flawed financial models, on the other, created the necessary conditions for an all-out economic meltdown (Kaletsky 2010: 85–181; Skidelsky 2009: 29–55; El-Erian 2008: 19–99).

On the global level, under the aegis of the international financial institutions, regulation in energy markets and financial activities was also increasingly liberalized – paving the way for the expansion of future markets and pervasive speculative activities, which precipitated precarious bubbles in commodity markets (think of oil and food, which almost choked off fragile economies and pushed tens of millions of people below the poverty line). It was this global economic mayhem, originating in Wall Street, which set the stage for a sustained phase of popular uprisings in the world's last regional autocratic stronghold (Terzulli and Ascari 2009).

The impact on the Arab world

The Great Recession – peaking in around 2007/08, but stubbornly sending shock waves over succeeding years – accentuated the failure of economic liberalization to (a) adequately spread the region's wealth and (b) improve the capacity of states to cope with global economic shocks. Significant declines in the tourism industry and the inflow of remittances as well as disruptions in the financial and real estate sectors due to the financial crisis crippled the few well-functioning economic engines in non-oil-based economies.

Macroeconomic disruption Although crony capitalism is a common feature among many Arab economies, especially among resource-poor states that underwent successive rounds of economic reform, the Great Recession had a differential impact across nations. Overall, though, a combination of massive currency reserves (especially among petro-states), low market capitalization (as in Lebanon and Jordan) and relative financial isolation (as in Yemen and Syria, but to a certain degree also states such as Egypt) led many analysts, at least initially, to project a relatively limited macroeconomic downturn among Arab economies in the aftermath of the global financial crisis. After all, the Arab economies were relatively insulated from global financial channels, and less integrated in the global chains of production as compared to, for example, export-oriented, rapidly developing East Asian economies. Meanwhile, the Arab petro-states – although suffering a significant blow to their investments abroad as well as oil-based export earnings – were able to reach into their deep currency reserves, thanks to the pre-crisis boom (2003–08) in global oil prices, to withstand the storm. A long period of liberalization also encouraged significant reforms in the banking and financial sectors, with many Arab governments tirelessly implementing appropriate measures to avoid a financial meltdown (Mashal 2012: 100–2). The advent of 'Islamic financing' also encouraged prudent investments – especially away from exotic financial instruments and derivatives – among many regional financial actors (Nasr 2009: 1–27). Also, as analysts pointed out, the dramatic collapse in oil prices should have been a blessing to oil-importing Arab economies. And yet the Arab world would be rocked by successive rounds of massive protests and political upheavals in the few years following the global financial crisis (Behrendt and Kamel 2009; Habibi 2009: 6–9; Orozco and Lesaca 2009).

What earlier (somehow superficial) assessments missed, however, was the fact that the global financial crisis of 2007/08 was followed by a stubborn downturn in global output, which fanned the flames of pre-existing structural maladies in the Arab world, ranging from massive unemployment rates, and growing inequality, to persistent borderline poverty among vulnerable sections, which heavily depended on state subsidies, a steady stream of generous foreign tourists, remittances from overseas workers in petro-states, and low inflation rates to avoid falling into extreme poverty and a state of food insecurity (Behrendt and Kamel 2009; Habibi 2009: 6–9; Orozco and

Lesaca 2009). At the time of the crisis, Egypt was host to 3 million individuals employed in the tourism sector, while the figure stood at 420,000 in Jordan, and 450,000 in Tunisia (Drine 2009). In short, the global financial crisis was extremely burdensome to most vulnerable sectors, which would later – after staging repeated protests against food price spikes – join the ranks of middle-class democratic forces that steered the course of the Arab revolutions.

In addition, in the absence of an actual 'trickle-down' resulting from the growing national economic pie, and attempts to rein in explosive demographics, many Arab economies had no choice but to retain relatively high rates of economic growth (in the neighbourhood of 6 per cent annual GDP growth and above) to genuinely improve per capita living standards and avoid large-scale economic dislocations – precisely what the Great Recession (coupled with global food crises) undermined in an increasingly vicious manner. Meanwhile, some Arab economies had to resort to relatively large fiscal expansionary policies to counter the downturn in critical sectors such as real estate and tourism, placing extra pressure on already fragile finances in less-endowed Arab economies outside the Persian Gulf. Egypt, for instance, introduced three series of stimulus programmes in the 2008/09 period, collectively amounting to as much as 15 billion Egyptian pounds (EGP) (Reuters 2009). So, ironically, economic globalization – after years of sustained pressure to streamline social expenditures and state finances – spurred massive state-sponsored counter-cyclical as well as palliative expenditures to rein in the destabilizing impact of a crisis born out of excessive deregulation and consumption in the North.

With their large-scale investments in the USA and Europe taking a massive hit during the global financial crisis, and places such as Dubai suffering a liquidity crisis amid a real estate collapse, many Gulf Cooperation Council (GCC) states began to reduce their investments in other Arab states. Moreover, Arab overseas workers had to contend with not only fewer jobs in the GCC as the monarchies wound down mega-projects, but also considerable reversals in the private sector coupled with new employment policies (in response to domestic pressure) that favoured GCC citizens (Behrendt and Kamel 2009: 11–21). For oil-importing countries, notably Jordan, Egypt and

TABLE 4.1 Average GDP growth in MENA (2000–11)

	2000–05 average	2006	2007	2008	2009	2010	2011 proj.
MENA	5.2	5.9	6.1	4.7	2.1	3.9	3.9
Oil exporters	5.6	5.7	6.2	4.7	0.7	3.5	4.9
Algeria	4.5	2.0	3.0	2.4	2.4	3.3	3.6
Bahrain	6.0	6.7	8.4	6.3	3.1	4.1	3.1
Iran IR	5.5	5.8	7.8	1.0	0.1	1.0	−0.0
Iraq	–	6.2	1.5	9.5	4.2	0.8	9.6
Kuwait	7.1	5.3	4.5	5.0	−5.2	2.0	5.3
Libya	4.3	6.7	7.5	2.3	−2.3	4.2	–
Oman	3.3	5.5	6.7	12.9	1.1	4.2	4.4
Qatar	8.7	18.6	26.8	25.4	8.6	16.3	20.0
Saudi Arabia	4.0	3.2	2.0	4.2	0.6	3.7	7.5
UAE	8.1	8.8	6.5	5.3	−3.2	3.2	3.3
Yemen	4.5	3.2	3.3	3.6	3.9	8.0	3.4
Oil importers	4.4	6.3	6.1	4.8	4.7	4.7	2.3
Afghanistan	–	5.6	13.7	3.6	20.9	8.2	8.0
Djibouti	2.4	4.8	5.1	5.8	5.0	4.5	4.8
Egypt	4.0	6.8	7.1	7.2	4.7	5.1	1.0
Jordan	6.0	7.9	8.5	7.6	2.3	3.1	3.3
Lebanon	3.4	0.6	7.5	9.3	8.5	7.5	2.5
Mauritania	3.7	11.4	1.0	3.5	−1.2	4.7	5.2
Morocco	4.4	7.8	2.7	5.6	4.9	3.2	3.9
Pakistan	4.9	6.1	5.6	1.6	3.4	4.8	2.8
Syrian AR	3.8	5.0	5.7	4.5	6.0	3.2	3.0
Tunisia	4.4	5.7	6.3	4.5	3.1	3.7	1.3

Source: IMF (2012)

Tunisia, the Great Recession had a relatively high macroeconomic impact, as exhibited in their precipitous decline in annual GDP growth after the Great Recession of 2008 (see Table 4.1). One must also note the 'psychological dimension' of the deleterious impact of the global economic downturn, which punctuated almost half a decade of relentless expansion and growth in many Arab economies, buoyed by growing intra-regional investments, trade and tourism. The massive downturn in Europe – exacerbated by the sovereign

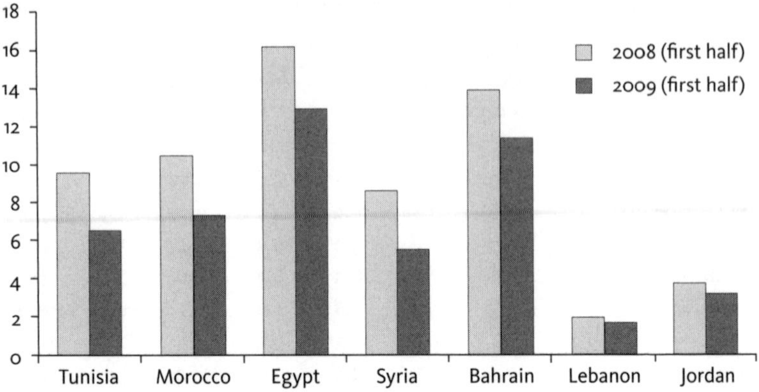

4.1 Merchandise exports of selected MENA countries (2008/09, US$ millions) (*source*: Direction of Trade Statistics, IMF)

debt crisis among several Eurozone economies – also slashed the non-oil exports of many Arab economies, which heavily depended on merchandise trade with their neighbours across the Mediterranean (see Figure 4.1). The overall impact on the current account balance of many oil-importing countries was substantial, with Oman, Egypt and Yemen slipping into negative territory, while Jordan, Morocco, Lebanon and Tunisia continued to struggle with a current account deficit (see Figure 4.2).

Accustomed to favourable economic fortunes, many Arab citizens suddenly faced the abyss of long-term unemployment, a cut in remittances, and overall austerity, while many Arab states – already squeezed by privatization of government assets, rationalization of tax revenues, and increasingly strict fiscal and monetary benchmarks – struggled to respond to the breadth of the incoming storm in a timely and sufficient manner (Heydarian 2011). After an initial expansionary fiscal response, growing volatilities in the global markets made belt-tightening among Arab economies an inevitability, which not only hurt the working classes and vulnerable sectors, but also the aspirational Arab middle class – a growing political force, which has opposed Arab autocracies with increasing dynamism and indignation in the run-up to the revolutions (see Chapters 1 and 2).

As prominent Marxist philosopher Slavoj Žižek (2012: 9–10) points

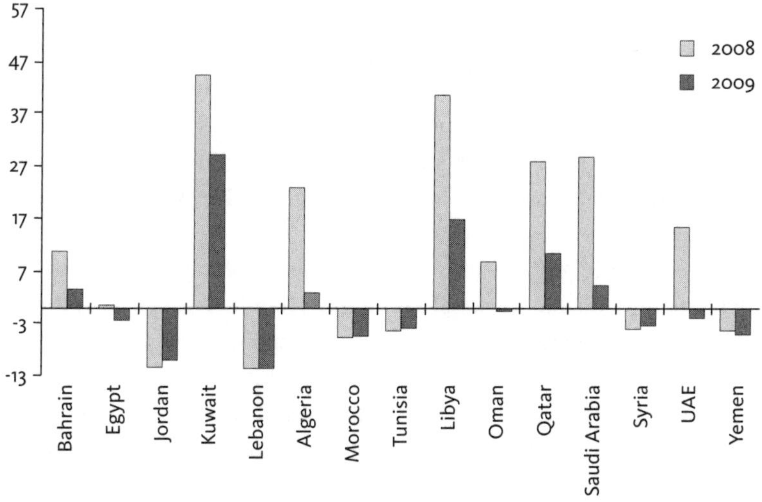

4.2 Current account balance as percentage of GDP (2008/09) (*source*: IMF, World Economic Outlook Database, October 2009, www.imf.org); 2009 values are IMF projections

out, the middle class, or what he calls the members of the lower-level 'salaried bourgeoisie', played a pivotal role in galvanizing the Arab populace against the embattled regimes, largely in reaction to a growing fear of an irreversible erosion in their own personal fortunes as the economic downturn dragged on:

> In times of crisis, the obvious candidates for 'belt-tightening' are the lower levels of the salaried bourgeoisie: political protest is their only recourse if they are to avoid joining the proletariat … This also accounts for the wave of student protests: their main motivation is arguably the fear that higher education will no longer guarantee them a surplus wage in later life …

In short, as Arab autocrats (predictably) jumped to the rescue of their crisis-hit cronies by implementing fiscal expansionary policies to counter the downturn in sectors such as real estate, the Great Recession begun to severely undermine the fortunes of both the working classes and the 'salaried bourgeoisie' – the two forces that eventually coalesced against Arab autocracies, especially during the initial waves of Arab revolutions.

Food insecurity and protests

A macroeconomic downturn was not all that Arab economies had to contend with. The global financial crisis was accompanied by successive rounds of commodity price spikes, which transformed the supposedly passive Arab street into a potent source of opposition against Arab autocracies – and their neoliberal economic policies by extension.

As economic globalization gained pace – notably the increasing deregulation in international commodity markets – across the developing and emerging world in the early 2000s, there was a steady upward fluctuation in the price of basic commodities, notably food and oil. This trend, a by-product of a complex interplay of several variables, would reverse decades of relentless post-Second World War progress in global food production (Bello 2009).

From 1950 to 1990, three factors contributed to an impressive rise in land productivity and an increase in global food production: first, the tripling of world irrigated agricultural lands; secondly, almost a tenfold increase in the total use of fertilizers to enhance crop yield; and lastly, the spread of high-yield GMO seed varieties such as hybrid corns in the USA and dwarf wheat and rice in Asia.[2]

Under the auspices of the BWS and the General Agreement on Tariffs and Trade, developing countries were granted necessary policy space in order to augment their agricultural sectors and subsidize poor farmers, who could not afford the gifts of modern science. The result was a steady and impressive expansion in agricultural output in many countries, from sub-Saharan Africa to East Asia and Latin America. Concurrently, many poor countries became surplus producers of agricultural goods, therefore becoming major exporters of food to developed countries. Although the terms of trade between agricultural producers, on one hand, and the industrial food importers, on the other, continuously deteriorated over decades, what was ensured in many poor countries was an encouraging pattern of increased food production, almost guaranteeing minimum food security for millions of poor living within a subsistence economy. The advent of economic globalization, however, marked a disconcerting decline in the agricultural landscape of many developing countries, including the Arab world. Under the watchful supervision of the

IFIs, more than ninety developing countries were forced to withdraw their direct support (e.g. agricultural subsidies and soft loans) from agriculture, as part of a broader effort to disengage the state from the national economy (ibid.). In October 2008, an independent report from the World Bank acknowledged the disastrous effects of the policies of the 1980s. According to the report, '[World] Bank policies in the 1980s and 1990s that pushed African governments to cut or eliminate fertilizer subsidies, decontrol prices and privatize might have improved fiscal discipline but did not accomplish much for food production ...'[3] Meanwhile, the West continued to support its agricultural sector aggressively, pouring in as much as $388 billion in state subsidies in 2004, the same year the World Trade Organization came into effect. As a result, tens of millions of farmers in the developing world, lacking any substantial state support and basic financing infrastructure, found themselves at the mercy of cheap, subsidized imported food flooding increasingly liberalized national economies in the South. This new disequilibrium in production led to extreme food dependency among the many developing countries, which used to have solid agricultural foundations (ibid.).

While economic globalization – with China joining the WTO and becoming a global factory on the back of its cheap and heavily regulated labour – allowed for a dramatic drop in the prices of certain commodities to the benefit of many consumers, basic commodities such as food and oil would become increasingly unaffordable products for hundreds of millions of people struggling with poverty across the South. Analysts have looked at several factors to explain this phenomenon. Some looked at the introduction of large-scale agro-fuel industry, which used agricultural commodities, derived from sugar cane, corn or palm oil, to produce fuel for transportation. On 3 July 2008, based on a leaked 'secret report' by the World Bank, the *Guardian* (ibid.) came up with an exposé, which claimed that the agro-fuel policies of Western countries were responsible for three-quarters of the shocking 140 per cent increase in food prices between 2002 and 2008.[4] However, looking at the bigger picture, the push for agro-fuel production was probably more of an 'aggravating' factor, but nevertheless in the last decade there has been a gigantic push for bio-fuel production across the West and in agricultural superpowers such as Brazil – thanks to the rising market value of such products (ibid.).

Others looked at the impact of rising demand from China and other major developing countries. They emphasized China's seemingly insatiable appetite for raw materials to feed its gigantic industries, coupled with the increasingly meat-based diet of its rising middle classes, as a major factor behind an upward trend in global commodities prices. But there is a more structural explanation for the rising volatility in commodity markets. In recent decades, especially since the 1990s, zealous pro-market technocrats in the West have allowed for relentless deregulation in previously off-limits, sensitive markets such as the international trade in basic commodities. Soon, hedge funds and other financial institutions – the harbingers of finance-driven economics in the North, which eventually led to the Great Recession – would benefit from betting in newly established futures markets, with university endowments and pension funds being invested in speculative market practices. Now not only current global demand, but also projections of future demands, have pushed a growing pool of investments into buying future shares in commodity markets such as oil – an attempt to hedge their bets against an eventual oil peak or other forms of supply shocks. As a result, influential financial institutions have increasingly determined the movement of commodity prices on the global stage. With food prices tied to energy prices – largely because of a global shift to large-scale fuel-intensive agricultural production, accentuated by the introduction of agro-fuels more recently – the result has been greater volatility in energy and food markets and the emergence of speculation-driven bubbles (ibid.; Terzulli and Ascari 2009; Sharma 2011; El-Erian 2008).

From 2006 to 2008, three bubbles were to emerge: a real estate bubble in the US housing market, and food-energy bubbles in the global market (Terzulli and Ascari 2009). Given the interconnected nature of financial markets, founded on investor sentiments and overall confidence in the soundness of the underlying economic regimes, there was almost a simultaneous bursting of all three bubbles as the financial crisis exposed large-scale market failures: the inability of the markets to truly reflect the prices of goods, thus leading to overvaluation of many assets and investments (ibid.). But that was not all, since more commodity price spikes were to follow. Three years on, the 2011 *Global Risk Report* argued that food was one of the three biggest threats to global security (World Economic Forum 2011), while prominent economists such as Robert Schiller (2011) warned about how an excessive speculative drive into food and energy markets – given the meltdown and continuing uncertainty in traditional areas of financial investment – was a recipe for even larger commodity bubbles in coming years.

The Arab world, especially the non-oil agricultural states, was a major victim of this broader trend. Increasing integration into global markets and privatization of state enterprises meant that many agricultural countries, such as Egypt, would increasingly depend on food imports. For arid and semi-arid Arab countries, a combination of a rapidly growing population, elimination of tariffs on agricultural imports, and lack of available water and fertile land has transformed the region into the world's biggest food-importing region. For instance, owing largely to aggressive trade liberalization, Egypt and Morocco were transformed from agricultural net-exporting into net-importing countries (Saif 2008b). Arab countries import around 58 per cent of their cereal and 75 per cent of their sugar consumption – constituting 61 per cent of per capita caloric consumption (Akhtar 2011). This highlights the Arab world's distinct vulnerability to movements in international commodity markets. The greatest vulnerability is among non-oil-exporting economies, which have had fragile current account balances with which to cope with ballooning food imports prices. In the last four decades, these countries have experienced violent protests in response to food price hikes (due either to subsidy cuts or supply–demand dynamics), starting in Egypt (1977), Morocco (1981), Tunisia (1984) and Jordan (1996) – before all-out pan-Arab food-related protests in 2008 (Rosenberg 2011).

Among the biggest shortcomings of Arab regimes in recent decades has been a relative neglect of agriculture. Scholars such as David Rosenberg (ibid.) have looked at the parlous state of agriculture in the region, identifying poor public policy as one of the key manifestations of a broader regional agricultural decline, which has made the Arab world, on both individual and national levels, food insecure. As Rosenberg correctly points out, a deteriorating regional agricultural landscape not only has direct food security implications, but given that about 45 per cent of the general population is in one way or another involved in agriculture, there are larger socio-political ramifications:

> A large part of the [Arab] population is highly sensitive to changes in farm prices and conditions. Moreover, in the most critical countries of the region, farming accounts for a larger proportion of GDP ... The critical role of agriculture as a source of employment also applies to many of MENA's most important oil-exporting countries.

While in Egypt and Syria agriculture employs up to 32 per cent and 17 per cent of the labour force respectively, for the oil-exporting countries of Iraq and Algeria the figure stands at 21.6 per cent and 14 per cent respectively (ibid.).

From 2006 to 2008, a combination of food and energy price hikes led to massive hunger and poverty across the world.[5] From 2008 to 2011, succeeding rounds of unprecedented price increases placed a huge economic burden on food-importing Arab countries with weak fiscal positions. As a result, protests erupted across the Arab world, from Morocco to Egypt and Yemen; corresponding state efforts to cope with rising commodity prices – from instituting new subsidy programmes to double-digit increases in wages – led to budget deficit and inflation (Bello 2009).

Although successive waves of global commodity fluctuations led to a tremendous rise in hunger, food riots and palliative measures such as emergency food aid across the developing world, what must be noted is that the effects of food price hikes were uniquely devastating in the Arab world. Prices of the two principal food commodities, cereal and sugar, increased by 40 per cent and 77 per cent respectively (Akhtar 2011). In Egypt, bread prices experienced a fivefold increase (Saif 2008b). According to the United Nations Food and Agricultural Organization (in Kovalyova 2011), 'food prices [are] up for the seventh month in a row, [and] the closely watched FAO Food Price Index touched its highest since records began in 1990, in nominal terms, and topped the high of 224.1 in June 2008, during the food crisis of 2007/08. The index, which measures monthly changes for a food basket composed of cereals, oilseeds, dairy, meat and sugar, averaged 230.7 points in January, up from 223.1 points in December' (ibid.). The situation was further aggravated by 2011. Based on the UN FAO report, January 2011 saw record high increases in global food prices, surpassing even the 2008 levels (Akhtar 2011).

Because the region's governments have little fiscal power – thanks to privatization, FDI-friendly tax incentives, regulatory capture, and bureaucratic streamlining – and have increasingly shied away from providing economic subsidies to benefit the populace, the food crisis over the last decade has pushed millions of people in food-importing Arab nations into abject poverty and hunger (World Bank et al. 2009). Worsening matters, foreign aid from the richer countries diminished by around 28 per cent as a result of the economic crisis (Diouf 2009). With prices of basic goods dramatically increasing, a significant proportion of society was affected; not to mention the secondary effects of food price hikes on non-food inflation (IMF 2010: 35). Another issue is that although Arab countries have registered some improvements in reducing extreme poverty, a large proportion of the population lives close to the poverty line (living on less than $2/day), with most of their income allocated to the procurement of food and basic needs. After all, the poor spend around 65 per cent of their income on food alone; thus very small changes in global commodity prices push millions of people below the poverty line (Akhtar 2011).

Bearing in mind the momentous impact of the food crisis on Arab countries, some analysts have gone so far as to suggest a monocausal hypothesis, whereby the Arab Spring is more or less seen as the culmination of food-related protests. For instance, according to Marco Lagi, Karla Bertrand and Yaneer Bar-Yam of the New England Complex Systems Institute, 'Despite the many possible contributing factors, the timing of violent protests in North Africa and the Middle East in 2011 as well as earlier riots in 2008 coincides with large peaks in global food prices'; therefore, 'These observations suggest that protests may reflect not only long-standing political failings of governments, but also the sudden desperate straits of vulnerable populations. If food prices remain high, there is likely to be persistent and increasing global social disruption' (Lagi et al. 2011: 1). The three scientists, accordingly, have identified a specific 'food price threshold' above which the likelihood of protests is almost certain. Emphasizing the central role of bio-fuels and speculative investments in commodity markets, the authors have looked at how 2004 marked the beginning of a steady increase in food prices, with riots breaking out beyond the threshold of the FAO Price Index of 2010.

Yet it is important to keep in mind that the food-related protests in the Arab world were a reflection of the larger phenomenon of economic globalization, which at once weakened individual states' ability to ensure food security and cope with shocks. Also, economic globalization unleashed a destructive storm of speculative practices in the global commodity markets. For instance, in July 2008, only four swap dealers controlled about 30 per cent of all NYMEX oil contracts, and estimated that prices would increase, according to a *Washington Post* investigative report (Cho 2008). This cycle of speculation has made oil markets (which have a direct bearing on food production and prices) increasingly more reflective of investor sentiments, rather than actual supply-and-demand dynamics.

The Arab world has been grappling with a whole new commodities dynamic on the global level, which Ruchir Sharma, the author of the best-selling book *Breakout Nations*, has termed 'commodity.com'. The rapid growth in China's and other major developing economies' demand for basic commodities, from food to raw materials for production, and oil has created an illusion of a 'commodity super cycle' – a relentless upward movement in the prices of basic commodities. This phenomenon, Sharma (2011) argues, is akin to the mania that surrounded the internet bubble, which gripped global investors in the late 1990s, deceptively raising the hopes for a 'Goldilocks' economy of high growth and low inflation in the twenty-first century. When the technology bubble burst, shortly after peaking at around 30 per cent of all stocks, there was a wholesale foray into the commodity markets, with speculators starting to trade oil far beyond actual consumption patterns, while other commodities such as copper piled up in bond warehouses until prices could be jacked up for huge profits. By 2011, commodity stocks reached the 30 per cent mark. For Sharma, the commodity.com bubble is far more dangerous than the preceding dotcom bubble in 2001:

> No bubble is a good bubble ... but the commodity.com era has had a larger and more negative impact on the global economy than tech boom did. The hype has created a new industry that turns commodities into financial products that can be traded like stocks ... as speculative investments ... while rising prices for stocks – techs one included – generally boost the economy, high prices for staples like oil impose unavoidable costs on businesses and consumers and act as a profound drag on the economy ... Excitement about rising commodity prices exists only among the investors, financiers, and speculators who can gain from it. (Ibid.: 224–5)

With ten out of eleven post-war recessions following a sharp increase in oil prices, Sharma rightly underscores the macroeconomic and humanitarian costs of the commodity mania, which has, in his words, invented a 'new paradigm' to justify 'irrationally high oil prices' just as in all previous manias.

So what's next?

The absence of democratic institutions in the Arab world prevented people from constructively airing their basic economic grievances. Faced with growing state brutality and deepening economic insecurity, more and more people joined the ranks of the anti-government protesters, who eventually toppled Ben Ali and Mubarak. In Tunisia and Egypt, labour unions bridged the gap between the Facebook-friendly middle class and the broader disenfranchised masses. Economic desperation served as the rallying cry around which all sectors and classes coalesced. Similar grievances are continuing to fuel protests across the Arab world.

The Arab Spring was successful in dislodging a number of autocrats across the region, portending a gradual transition to a more pluralistic and democratic political system, but practically all post-revolutionary regimes continue to face structural as well as short-term economic challenges. With secular autocrats in Egypt, Tunisia, Libya, Yemen and elsewhere relegated to the dustbin of history, the world is closely watching a new generation of power brokers across the region, notably the Egyptian Muslim Brotherhood and its many

Islamist offshoots across the region, which have either taken over the government (as in Egypt under the Justice and Freedom Party of President Mohammad Morsi, Tunisia under Ennahda, and Morocco under the Justice and Development Party), or have been influential players behind the scenes and on the streets (as in Libya), or in a strong position to overturn a flailing regime (as in Syria and Jordan).

Political Islam is on the rise, so the next question is whether these new powerful forces are intent on tackling the region's profound economic and political challenges, and in a position to do so. The new power brokers face the double challenge of ensuring economic stability and democratic opening in the short run, while paving the way for actual democratic consolidation and an optimal development paradigm in the long run. Otherwise, they will face similar waves of protests and public discontent to those faced by their predecessors – precisely what has been happening across the region.

In order to understand and properly assess the Islamists' potential role in revamping the regional landscape and introducing a new development paradigm, we must first look at their origins as socio-religious organizations, their subsequent evolution as political parties, and their current behaviour (whether as ruling parties or an essential element of the opposition), ruling within a new structure of political opportunity as the region moves into a new season – an Arab summer in the eyes of many, but a winter in the eyes of sceptics.

The eventual downfall of the Morsi government in Egypt, accomplished through the July 2013 coup, was a sobering reminder of the fragility of post-revolutionary governments, no matter how deep their socio-religious and political roots. The ensuing crackdown on the Muslim Brotherhood, and similar outbreaks of violence and protests against leading Islamist parties across the region, was largely a product of their inefficacy in addressing short-term demands for economic stability, their perceived betrayal of the liberal tenets of the revolution, and ultimately the absence of a clear vision for dislodging crony capitalism and autocracy in favour of a more democratic and egalitarian political economy.

5 | THE NEW POWER BROKERS: POLITICAL ISLAM AND THE ARAB SUMMER

> Economics has more to do with determining the pecking order in the Middle East than the region's miasmic tumults of feuds, wars, and saber rattlings would lead one to believe. (Nasr 2009: 5)

It was perhaps inevitable. After almost a century of increasingly active and overt participation in modern politics, widening influence within the larger sociocultural sphere, and unflinching struggle against secular autocracies (and monarchies), moderate (mass-based) Islamist political parties have emerged as one of the largest winners of the Arab Spring – ushering in a new era of political Islam amid a contentious process of democratization.

At the onset of the Arab spring, liberal-secular opposition forces, especially in places such as Tunisia and Egypt, played a pivotal role in galvanizing mass protests against sultanistic regimes. They successfully turbo-charged the uprisings through a savvy optimization of new media, while consciously framing the protests as a non-violent movement for democracy. Also, they were careful to reassure the West that the revolutions were not against them, but instead represented a new wave of democratization – portending a friendly, liberal-democratic enclave in the Near East. These democratic forces were keen on proving one fundamental argument: that the majority was fed up with autocracies and extremism. The age-old 'silent majority' was no longer silent, as evidenced by the sound and fury of their audacious stand-off with brutal reactionary regimes. They screamed the 'death of fear', which, by then, was even louder than the sound of the gun. The democratic trailblazers in the run-up to the Arab Spring were a vast but loose coalition of trade unions, middle-class seculars and liberal opposition figures and youth protesters. This was, at least initially, what the global media saw and continuously covered until the reality kicked in.

Soon after the downfall of Mubarak and Ben Ali, and the attendant euphoria, it became increasingly clear that the Islamists were the most organizationally consolidated and well-established contenders for power in the new emerging order. More radical Salafi elements would join the fray later (see Chapter 7). The mass-based moderate Islamist parties were, as an organization per se, largely inconspicuous in the earlier stages of the Arab Spring, despite the attendance of many young members in the secular-bannered protests. And sooner rather than later they came to relish how electoral democracy – the selection of top political leaders through majoritarian vote – was clearly in their favour. After all, they had a deep cache of electoral experience to bank on. Occasionally accommodated by autocratic regimes in recent decades, despite facing constitutional bans in certain cases, Islamists gradually honed their electoral campaigning skills, developing a formidable array of organizational capabilities to increasingly outmanoeuvre, outnumber and outwit their secular rivals, who were then beset by internal dispute, unending ideological bickering and brutal state crackdown.

Eric Trager (2011), a specialist on the Muslim Brotherhood (MB) at the conservative think thank the Institute for Near East Policy, put forward a persuasive case for how the powerful Egyptian Islamist organizations stand out as the most potent political force in the post-Arab Spring transitional phase. He argues, 'whereas Egypt's liberal and leftist political parties are nearly as easy to join as parties in the West', the Muslim Brotherhood has an established five-to-eight-year process during which it can closely watch and ensure the loyalty of members to the cause. Trager (ibid.) describes a rigid and multi-faceted system, which progressively ensures the full indoctrination of members and their full political compliance in crucial political periods such as the aftermath of the Arab Spring:

> This intricate system for recruitment and internal promotion produces members who are strongly committed to the organization's purpose, enabling its leaders to mobilize its followers as they see fit ... virtually [guaranteeing] that only those who are deeply committed to its cause become full members ... its pyramid-shaped hierarchy ensures that these members dutifully execute the aims of its national leadership at the local level.

Arab autocrats were no fans of the Islamists, but the gradual decline of the socialist welfare system in the aftermath of economic globalization – precipitating a steady erosion of the legitimacy of the autocratic state – made the 'conditional' and 'semi-managed' accommodation of Islamist parties a fait accompli, or a matter of political necessity for autocrats. Given the latter's growing influence within the Arab social landscape, impeccable organizational coherence and strong record on social services, Arab regimes had no choice but to accommodate the Islamists' rise, but only to a certain degree. Once it became clear that the Islamists could dominate even elections heavily rigged by the regime, there was a knee-jerk crackdown by the autocrats (Al Jazeera 2012; Sivan 2003). Nonetheless, the Islamists preserved their internal strength as well as their external appeal among the people – two key factors which would prepare them for the aftermath of the Arab Spring and facilitate their eventual rise to power.

For decades, major Islamist organizations were able not only to attract a huge pool of professionals and influential intellectuals to build their organizational competency and credibility, but also to make significant inroads into society by offering generous and reliable welfare, especially when the state institutions repeatedly failed on a massive scale. From one (man-made or natural) disaster to the other, Islamists were always there to help out and make up for whatever the governments lacked in resources and political will. This was the case with major Islamist movements across the Muslim world. From the 1992 earthquake in Cairo to those that followed in Istanbul in 1999 and on Pakistan's frontiers in Kashmir in 2005, the Islamists were constantly and visibly there on the ground, providing food, shelter, medical relief and all sorts of services one normally expects from the state (Nasr 2009: 171).

Moreover, despite their occasional engagements – or, as some would call them, back-door deals – with the autocrats, and their ability to draw in a huge pool of aid and charity from across the region and beyond, the Islamist parties tirelessly preserved a venerable image unblemished by corruption and all the maladies pervading not only the autocrats, but also liberal opposition forces. It was an image of pious, caring men reconciling the heavenly duties of

Islam with earthly services to address ordinary people's most basic necessities. And this explains why they were able to expand their social capital within their respective countries, while continuously drawing in support, new recruits and charity. In Egypt, by the late 1980s, Islamist movements were able to account for almost half of all welfare-related organizations, with about four thousand *Zakat* committees – bodies which draw their resources from religiously based taxes and donations – serving up to 15 million people by the first decade of the twenty-first century (ibid.). In this way, mainstream Islamist parties were able to tap into anti-establishment discontent among rural and urban poor, while projecting a clean, uncompromised image to the general public.

This successful strategy was predicated on a fundamental tactical realization among the top leadership of many Islamic political parties, ranging from the Muslim Brotherhood in Egypt, to Ennahda in Tunisia, the Justice and Development Party (PJD) of Morocco, and most visibly in the case of the highly successful AKP (and its progenitors) in Turkey: directly confronting the state would only invite brutal crackdown by Arab autocrats, with, of course, the tacit support of their external patrons. After all, in Libya, Syria and Algeria, Islamists bore the brunt of heavy security-military countermeasures, while in Egypt and Tunisia top leaders were exiled, killed and/or imprisoned. In Egypt, the Muslim Brotherhood was officially banned after an assassination attempt against Nasser in 1954, followed by some accommodation during Anwar Sadat's presidency, which ended with his assassination in 1981. Mubarak, despite occasional accommodations, even considered fiddling with the constitutional provisions to ban any religious-based political party (Al Jazeera 2012; Sivan 2003).

As a result, the Muslim Brotherhood members were not able to join elections as a party per se, only as an amalgamation of varying members running in different districts, albeit with similar platforms (Al Jazeera 2012). One after the other, Islamic revolts, namely in Egypt (1981), Syria (1982), Algeria (1991) and Saudi Arabia (1979 and the post-9/11 era), were crushed by the state. Creating Islamic states through direct confrontation was no longer a viable option (Nasr 2009: 145–74).

After all, this was perhaps the only area where the autocratic Arab regimes were strong: namely, in garnering (a) enough domestic and international support, especially from the armed forces, cronies and Western allies, and (b) resources, both in financial and coercive terms, to crush any domestic rebellion, be it from the secular (e.g. communist forces in the past) or Islamist elements (Sivan 2003).

It was this profound realization which explains the increasing trend, especially in the 2000s, of Islamic political parties transcending the usual slogan of 'Islam is the Solution' (*al-Islam huwa al-hall*) to instead incorporate a more down-to-earth but highly appealing slogan that combined an emphasis on good governance initiatives, provision of social services and denunciation of extremist violence. This tactical 'pragmatic turn' by major Islamist political parties, or at least in the leadership's more politically oriented circles, explains the 'splits' within the Islamist organization, strengthening the ranks of more radical Salafi and Wahhabi elements, which not only continued to pursue a path of confrontation against autocracies (and their Western patrons), but also went so far as to dismiss mainstream Islamist organizations as sell-outs which had abandoned the principles of the original Islamist struggle (Nasr 2009: 145–202).

Overall, the strategy of working from within the system proved quite effective for the mainstream Islamist organization, despite some setbacks here and there. The Egyptian Muslim Brotherhood was even able to win as much as 22 per cent of parliamentary seats in 2005, while its offshoot in Palestine, Hamas, won the largely democratic elections in 2006, thanks to its uncompromising rhetoric vis-à-vis Israeli occupation, but also, perhaps more importantly, its uncorrupted and welfare-oriented pedigree. Their overwhelming electoral success drew the ire of autocrats and Western powers. Predictably, a few years of crackdown and isolation followed, but the Arab Spring had in store the best reward for the Islamists' pragmatic recalculations.

Today, years into the Arab uprisings, the Egyptian Muslim Brotherhood, formally established in 1928, and its many offshoots across the region are either in a position of power (as in Egypt and Tunisia), ruling based on a modus vivendi with the *ancien régime* (as in Morocco), an undeniable force behind the scenes (as in Libya), or a major element within the opposition-led protests across the Arab world, notably in Syria and Jordan. After a century of struggle and resistance, they have finally got the chance to reshape the regional landscape according to their ideology and political platforms, which have, in turn, evolved and been shaped by divergent geopolitical and economic circumstances across the Arab world (Hamid 2011a).

Yet Arab Islamists have not operated in a vacuum. They have been encouraged by more recent developments in the Islamic world. While the experience of Iran has shown them that it is possible to topple secular autocrats, outmanoeuvre secular-liberal rivals in the post-revolution vacuum, and overturn the regime to establish an Islamic republic, the Turkish example, in turn, especially under the AKP, has shown them that it is possible to simultaneously retain a certain Islamist agenda, improve the economy tremendously, preserve critical commercial and strategic ties with the West, expand influence internationally, and, perhaps most importantly, consistently win elections at home. Looking farther east into South-East Asia, Arab Islamists also see increasingly successful Muslim-majority countries such as Malaysia (a hybrid regime) and Indonesia (an electoral democracy), where Islamist parties have enjoyed considerable influence in recent decades amid economic prosperity and political opening.

Against this backdrop, a renewed sense of destiny among Arab Islamist parties is fuelling a drive for change in Arab politics, where Islam and democracy are the key themes of sociocultural struggle and political contestation. Yet, for the Islamists, the road to achieving and sustaining power as well as overcoming endemic socio-economic challenges is bumpy, to say the least. Facing divergent structures of political opportunity in their respective countries, Islamist political parties have developed (and will continue to have to develop) a distinct set of strategies to promote their specific agenda. The question is whether they have the necessary political will and capacity to do so. More fundamentally, it is also unclear what their specific agenda is: is it establishing an Islamic state à la Iran, going the AKP way, or perhaps a third way? This is where the Islamists' stance on and behaviour towards drafting post-revolutionary constitutions is of paramount analytic interest – and so are their policy and pronouncements on the basic rights of minority groups and the civil liberties of ordinary citizens.

However, what is clear is that for the Islamists to attain and sustain power in the Arab Summer, avoid fatal internal splits, and retain considerable legitimacy and popular mandate, they will have to make a decisive break with the discredited paradigms of the past. In short, they will have to not only work within the parameters of electoral democracy, but also introduce necessary structural economic reforms and effective developmental strategies in order to reverse decades of stagnation, and steer the Arab world into the twenty-first century. Otherwise, they will lose influence and popularity, forcing them to either step down from power, and operate on the political sidelines, or resort to despotic measures and risk a violent backlash, both internally and externally.

There is also the powerful resource endowment factor. Since none of the Arab Islamists has taken over a petro-state, undermining investment and commercial relations with the outside world is a non-starter. Overall, while some may argue that the Islamists are the 'only game in town', at least in some post-revolutionary Arab countries, undoubtedly 'political pragmatism' (realpolitik) is the name of the game – a fact that has radically reshaped and determined the overall ideological vortex in the Arab world (ibid.).

The evolution of political Islam

In order to understand the rise of Islamic political parties within the context of the democratic struggles in the aftermath of the Arab Spring, it is first necessary to analyse the dialectical relationship between democratic principles/struggles and Islamic thought(s) throughout the Muslim world in modern history. Thus, we should look at the dynamics of democratic struggles and popular revolts in the Islamic world and map the evolution of the 'Islam and democracy debate' therein.

The moderate, mass-based Islamist political parties are not only contending with a political environment that begets pragmatism and calculated manoeuvring, but they are also dealing with an evolving ideational dynamics, whereby democratic principles and Islam are increasingly reconciled as mutually favourable ideals, especially when both notions are seen in response to decades of disillusionment with secular autocracies and the fundamentalist nemesis they have inspired. Perhaps, just as conservative parties evolved in various

Asian and European democracies, notably the Christian Democrats in western Europe, the moderate Islamist political parties could follow a similar trajectory, whereby the exigencies of power would force them to not only adopt but even internalize political pragmatism and electoral contestation as the overarching strategy to win power.

Today, Islam is one of the world's biggest (and fastest-growing) religions, while democracy is considered a universal goal, which every nation should aspire to. However, there are lingering questions and increasingly intense discussions on the inherent and actual interrelationship between Islam and democracy. (To be sure, there are after all many forms of democracy, social, libertarian, minimalist and liberal, while there are many strands within the two major traditions of Sunni and Shia Islam. Nonetheless, the debate nowadays is predominantly generic, rather than concerning how certain forms of Islam fit into certain typologies of democracy.) Historically, the decline of the Islamic civilization was concomitant with the rise of European imperial powers, thus beginning a period of intense confrontation and accommodation between forces of modernization and conservatism. While Middle Eastern modernists argued for the adoption of European concepts of representative democracy and civil liberties, the conservatives, on the other hand, resisted such notions by calling instead for a return to traditions of the precolonial era. For more fundamentalist elements, the decline of the Middle Eastern empires was largely a product of the withdrawal of faith from the operations of the state. They argued that when Arab rulers, beginning with the Ummayad Dynasty (632–661 CE), followed by the Ottoman Empire (and to a certain degree the Safavid Empire in Iran), prioritized *raison d'état* over the principles of Islam, piety and simplicity, the so-called 'golden age' of Islam – when the first four caliphates successfully expanded the Islamic empire across three continents – came to an end, paving the way for European powers to dominate the Islamic societies over time (Nasr 2009: 153). In short, they argued, the only way to restore the glory and dignity of the Arab world was to build an Islamic state that reflected the features of the early days of the Islamic empire (ibid.: 145–75).

Such a divergence of ideological bents among Arab intellectuals and social movements precipitated frequent clashes, but also intellectual cross-fertilization and fierce debates among varying factions, which would predominantly morph into the following intellectual traditions: socialism, secular-liberalism, Islamism, and later Third Wordism.[1] But clearly over time some movements and intellectuals would come to combine varying intellectual and ideological currents to gain relevance and political capital amid the winds of change.

A common struggle against autocracy The twentieth century witnessed the rise of post-colonial states with increasingly modern and democratic socio-political features. However, much of the Islamic world continued to be plagued by autocratic regimes, which marginalized opposition forces while pitting the democrats and Islamists against one another. While some East Asian leaders invoked the notion of 'Asian Values/Democracy' in order to justify their illiberal, semi-autocratic manner of rule, many in the Middle East, including more radical Islamists as well as secular autocrats, dismissed principles of representative democracy as a mere 'Western construct', which should not trample upon the unique traditions of Islamic societies. The 1950s and 1960s saw a string of Arab coups against sitting monarchs and governments. In Egypt, an alliance of secular socialists and the Muslim Brotherhood toppled the pro-Western monarchy, which had earlier introduced some liberal reforms to win popular support. Overall, the first decades of the post-colonial era in the Middle East were dominated by 'the ideology of Third Worldism', whereby nationalist leaders (e.g. Mossadeq in Iran) and military officers (e.g. coups in Egypt, Syria, Iraq and Libya) built a new front against what they perceived as neocolonialism and unremitting Western hegemony in the region.

Initially, though, the Islamists had a working relationship with the secular-nationalist camp, since they both shared the same nemesis in the pliable monarchies. However, once new republics were established, there was a fierce showdown between the two former collaborators, most notably in the case of Egypt, where an assassination attempt on Nasser in 1954 provoked a heavy-handed state response. The ensuing clashes between secular autocrats, on one hand, and radical Islamist forces, on the other, resulted in further radicalization of the latter and greater brutality on the part of the state. Meanwhile, the democratic-liberal opposition was simply pushed to the margins. Neither the state nor the Islamists were for the establishment of (Western-patterned) democratic institutions. After all, liberal democracy upholds the sovereignty of a rational citizenry (akin to French philosopher Jean-Jacques Rousseau's concept of 'general will') as a foundation of the nation-state. This is something that many Islamist organizations at the time, which believed in the ultimate authority of religious principles, and secular autocrats, who held an unshakeable belief in the righteousness of their personal rule and their quasi-socialist-nationalist projects, vehemently opposed (Sivan 2003).[2]

But after two decades of constant oppression by secular autocrats came the upheavals of the 1970s. The secular-socialist projects of the autocrats fell into disarray, while the liberal opposition was largely pacified. The communists were a powerful and well-organized force across the region, but they were hamstrung on two fronts: first, they faced a battle against autocratic regimes backed by Western allies intent on rolling back Soviet influence in the region; and secondly, their ideology (mixing a convoluted notion of historical-materialist dialectics and atheism) failed to gain significant traction among a largely pious populace, even in the ultra-secularist states such as Turkey and Pahlavi Iran. Moreover, the communists, in the eyes of many people, were guilty by association, especially given the invasion of Afghanistan by the Soviet Union – the supposed embodiment of the communist motherland – which sparked a holy jihad across the Islamic world. The communists played a crucial role in mobilizing opposition and even insurgencies against powerful Middle Eastern powers, including Turkey and Iran, but they were heavily suppressed and constantly under attack. Meanwhile, the mosques remained largely outside the control of the autocratic states, providing ample opportunities for Islamists to build their organizational capacity, mobilize opposition, and expand their reach across the society (Nasr 2009).

Notwithstanding the inherent strengths of the Islamist organizations, Slavoj Žižek, beginning with a reflection on the experience of Afghanistan and Iran in the 1970s and ending with the Arab Spring, correctly identified the roots of the Arab Islamists' ability to outmanoeuvre secular-leftist rivals. For him, a large part of the Islamists' success had something to do with how the left was severely suppressed by the secular autocrats: 'The inevitable conclusion to be drawn is that the rise of radical Islamism was always the other side of the disappearance of the secular left in Muslim countries' (Žižek 2011).

No wonder, amid the gradual erosion of secular autocrats, that it was political Islam which seemed to be on the rise. The late 1970s saw the emergence of Islamists, after decades of failure by secular autocrats, as a potent force. In Iran, the 1979 revolution allowed Islamic republicans to take over a regional fulcrum, displacing the once-powerful Pahlavi dynasty. The Afghan 'jihad' against Soviet occupation also attracted scores of Arab Islamists, who would benefit from heavy financial-logistical support from Pakistan, the USA and Arab monarchies; this served as a crucial 'formative period', when radical Islamist groups were able to make inroads into South and Central Asia, gain operational experience in guerrilla warfare and sabotage activities, and develop transnational links, which underpinned the formation of groups such as Al-Qaeda and its many offshoots. It was a period that marked the rise of radical Islam, years after the death of Muslim Brotherhood radical thinker Sayyid Qutb, who, in his final years in prison, called for direct confrontation with both secular autocrats and their Western patrons. Iran's Khomeini, confidently riding on the support of millions of enthusiastic revolutionaries, called for a pan-Islamic revolution against *mustakberin* (oppressors) across the region and beyond. Soon, Tehran would emerge as a major supporter of resistance movements across the greater Middle East, placing itself at the centre of a new 'axis of resistance' against Western hegemony. The 1979 'hostage crisis' marked the beginning of an explicit international conflict between an Islamic powerhouse and an international great power. Meanwhile, in South Asia, the powerful Pakistani state, under General Zia, would also become increasingly Islamized, as the military regime began indoctrinating its officers with political Islam, while various Islamic movements gained growing influence within the ideological apparatus of the state (Nasr 2009). By 1981, radical Islamist groups, linked to the Muslim Brotherhood, went so far as to assassinate Egyptian president Anwar Sadat – almost also killing his successor, Hosni Mubarak, who was in the same area – for his supposed complicity with Israel after the 1979 peace agreement brokered by the Carter administration. In Turkey, the itary formed a tactical alliance with the Islamist forces to battle leftist and secular opposition groups, especially the Marxist Kurdish separatist elements. Over the succeeding decades, the Islamists in Sudan (1989) and the Taliban forces in Afghanistan (1996) would establish new Islamic republics on the edges of the Middle East. In 1991, Algeria's Islamic Salvation Front would win the first multiparty elections in the country's history, while the Saudi-born Osama Bin Laden would declare war on the West (and Saudi Arabian royalty), largely triggered by the Persian Gulf monarchies' consent to the coalition forces' intervention in the first Gulf War (Sivan 2003; Rubin 2003; Fisk 2005; Nasr 2009). After winning a majority of the vote in the 1989 elections, the Jordanian Muslim Brotherhood would form a power-sharing coalition, albeit briefly, with the Jordanian monarchy, wresting the control of the ministries of social development, education, justice, health and religious affairs (Hamid 2011a). In 1997, the Islamist Welfare Party would take over executive power in Turkey – arguably, the region's staunchest secularist state. By 2001, the extremists would manage to hit right into the heart of the Western world, targeting the World Trade Center and the Pentagon, and by 2006 Hamas (after the elections) and Hezbollah (after a decisive battle against the Israeli Defence Forces) would emerge as major players in Palestine and Lebanon. Yet this picture of constant empowerment and radicalization of Islamist movements, and/or their penetration into the political and sociocultural spaces, tends to overlook the larger landscape of dynamic changes, splits and debates within the Islamist movements, and how the brutal countermeasures by secular autocracies (with the support of Western powers) forced many Islamic movements, especially the Egyptian Muslim Brotherhood, to reconsider their strategy of confrontation against the system in favour of 'working from within' the system.

After all, no major Arab state was subject to a domino effect of Islamic revolutions. Even the Iranian regime began to enter a stage of 'Thermidor' after eight years of brutal warfare with Iraq and growing international isolation, whereby post-war reconstruction, normalization of ties with external powers and Arab neighbours, and internal political stabilization supplanted the revolutionary zeal of the early 1980s (Sick 2001; Nasr 2009; Ansari 2006; Takeyh 2006). In

Turkey, the military – fearing an Islamist counter-revolution within the laic system – issued a communiqué calling for the Welfare Party to step down, which was followed by the party's dissolution by the Turkish Constitutional Court. Hamas's electoral success was met by international isolation, suspension of loans, a total siege of Gaza, and repeated Israeli military incursions into the Hamas-held areas under Operation Cast Lead (2008) and Operation Pillar of Defence (2012), which led to a dramatic escalation of violence and the protracted humanitarian tragedy in the Gaza Strip.

Despite gaining popular support across the world, Al-Qaeda (AQ) would be at the receiving end of a tide of military backlash, under the banner of the Global War on Terror, spanning the greater Middle East, Central Asia and South-East Asia, while suffering estrangement from the Arab populace after repeated and indiscriminate bombings against innocent civilians, on top of untold destruction visited upon the Arab world after the 9/11 attacks. The first decade of the twenty-first century witnessed a wholesale global war against extremist elements, providing a pretext to crack down even on more moderate Islamist parties. Amid this black-and-white picture of confrontation and retribution, moderate mass-based Islamic movements maintained a pragmatic outlook in order not only to avoid imprisonment, death and exile, as they had suffered in the past, but also tap into new opportunities to wield influence and even occupy political office.

In *Living in the End Times*, Slavoj Žižek looked at modern capitalism, and, aptly citing the French psychoanalyst Jacques Lacan's notion of 'false binary opposition', he analysed how 'official antagonism' between capitalism (think of economic globalization under the rubric of Arab autocrats backed by Western power) and fundamentalism (as in extremism) conceals the 'true antagonism, [which] is not between liberal multiculturalism and fundamentalism, but between the field of their opposition and the excluded Third (radical emancipatory politics)' (Žižek 2010: 152). In this regard, one could argue that the Arab Spring was (and has been) precisely about creating this 'third way' of emancipatory politics, one that is free from both the dictates of autocrats and discredited market-driven reforms under economic globalization. One could argue that the more progressive – or, alternatively, the less reactionary – elements within the mainstream Islamist parties were also perhaps eyeing this more consequential battle for the soul of the Arab world, whereby neither neoliberalism nor autocratic rule could serve as a tenable basis of legitimacy and power. Whether they have done so – or are moving in that direction at least – in the aftermath of the Arab Spring is another question (see Chapter 7). Nonetheless, one thing is clear: the moderate Islamists realized that a direct confrontation with forces of economic globalization would only invite both symbolic and actual violence.

Shadi Hamid (2011a), a leading expert on Islamist political movements and a fellow at the Saban Center for Middle East Policy at the Brookings Institution, has provided us with one of the most compelling analyses of how pragmatism has been internalized by mass-based Islamic movements, which started with individual parties calling for a sharia-based state:

> At their core, however, mainstream Islamist organizations ... have strong pragmatic tendencies. When their survival has required it, they have proven willing to compromise their ideology and make difficult choices ... Beginning in the 1990s, however ... they increasingly focused on democratic reform, publicly committing themselves to the alternation of power, popular sovereignty, and judicial independence.

The art of peace and pragmatism The advent of economic globalization, coming on the heels of repeated military defeats, brought about massive social dislocation and an ideological vacuum in Arab society. While radical elements, often led by a highly educated cadre from a privileged background, were able to recruit scores of disenfranchised individuals from across the Muslim world to fill their ranks, large, moderate Islamic organizations – astutely identifying the strengths and weaknesses of the Arab states – saw an opening to rise within the system – and perhaps upend it from within. They knew that the Arab regimes were strong in terms of their ability to crack down on and gather intelligence on opposition elements, but at the same time increasingly weak in terms of welfare provision and electoral legitimacy. As great students of Sun Tzu's *Art of War*, the moderate Islamists understood both their enemies and themselves, specifically in terms of vulnerabilities and strengths. After all, for

Sun Tzu: 'If you know the enemy and know yourself, you need not fear the result of a hundred battles. If you know yourself but not the enemy, for every victory gained you will also suffer a defeat. If you know neither the enemy nor yourself, you will succumb in every battle' (Sun Tzu 2007: 57).

As Hamid (2011a) puts it, the Islamists have even risked alienating more conservative members as well as fundamentalist elements by constantly pushing the boundaries of their internal ideological reconfigurations, culminating in the 2006 so-called Reintroducing the Brotherhood to the West initiative. They have displayed considerable flexibility on crucial issues: instead of calling for the implementation of sharia as a basis of law, the Egyptian MB, in recent years, has instead called for a 'civil, democratic state with an Islamic reference', while expressing commitment to the separation of mosque and state. On Israel, geographical proximity has defined the intensity of the rhetoric, with the Jordanian MB featuring among the most hardline opponents, as opposed to the more measured approach of relatively distant Islamists in Morocco and Tunisia (ibid.). Yet even Hamas – despite its explicit opposition to the State of Israel in its 1998 Charter – has repeatedly signalled its willingness to negotiate along the lines of the 1967 borders for a two-state solution, following the stipulations of numerous international pronouncements, notably United Nations Resolution 242, calling for Israeli withdrawal from territories forcibly annexed after the 'Six-Day War' (Levy 2011).

But of course, it is natural to expect 'cyclical' escalation in not only Islamist but what is an almost universal antipathy in the region, including from the AKP, towards Israel whenever a new offensive is launched against the Occupied Territories. Yet it is by no means accurate to claim that the Islamists, by and large, categorically oppose the formation of the Israeli state, and actively seek to undermine its existence. Wary of the consequences of a direct confrontation with Israel, and the huge repercussions on Arab–American relations, major Islamic organizations have creatively sought to reconcile their attempts to tap into popular opposition to Israel's strategic impunity, on one hand, and the necessity to avoid confrontation with Israel and its Western allies, on the other.

Yet it is also unfair to say that this pragmatic turn is simply a tactical shift, which can be reversed once new circumstances emerge, notwithstanding the muscular policies of ruling Islamists in Egypt and elsewhere. The Islamist political parties had also to contend with broader ideational developments, which have reshaped the context of their strategic manoeuvrings, and the mindset of their own members, both young and old, especially those with a slightly liberal bent, as well as the broader population. Democracy and the preservation of stable relations with neighbouring states and international powers have seemingly been internalized by many moderate Islamist organizations, now vying to reshape the trajectory of the Arab Summer.

Islam and democracy From a Hegelian point of view, one could argue that material changes in the Middle East are a by-product of ideational dialectics, which have perforated the Islamic world's public space. The democratic discourse has been primarily a critique of the 'secular authoritarian' systems, which have ravaged Muslim countries for decades. To be sure, there are divergent opinions on whether the Islamic world should adopt liberal democratic values or rather develop its own version of democracy, but this is a secondary issue. The main threat to democracy has come from secular autocrats – from monarchies to republics – rather than European liberalism. The failure of democracy in the Middle East is largely explained by the tragic experiences of top-down secular autocracies (see Chapter 2).

Interestingly, the fiercest and most powerful arguments on the compatibility of Islamic values and democracy came from revolutionaries behind the 1979 Islamic revolution. Ali Shariati is widely recognized as one of the key – if not the primary – ideologues behind the so-called 'Islamic revival', yet what many analysts tend to overlook is how he had continuously emphasized the compatibility of Islamic values with an accountable, democratic and egalitarian government. The liberal democrats (think of prime minister Mehdi Bazargan, president Abdulhassan Banisadr and foreign minister Ebrahim Yazdi) who presided over the immediate post-revolutionary Iranian regime were actually the first officials in the region who vigorously sought to inject democratic principles into the fabric of a nascent regime and its constitution. Although, eventually, the more conservative elements from the Islamist factions, namely the Islamic Republican Party (IRP), dominated the new regime, ideas and legacies of these democratic visionaries, over decades, inspired reformists and liberals within Iran to widen the broader political discourse. The reverberations of their ideas were mostly confined to universities, but they gradually suffused national debates and penetrated halls of power. In 1997, the so-called 'reformist movement' propelled the liberal president Mohammad Khatami to power, despite vigorous attempts by conservatives to prevent this (Ansari 2006; Takeyh 2006; Abrahamian 2011). The conservatives, or the so-called 'old guards', managed to frustrate reformists' attempts to push for normalized ties with the West and more politico-social liberalization, but the movement was able to re-emerge under the leadership of Mehdi Karoubi and Mir Hossein Mousavi during the contentious 2009 elections, which precipitated the largest protests against the regime in its three-decade history. (A heavy crackdown followed, with both Karoubi and Mousavi under house arrest, but the reformists continued to preserve a semblance of relevance amid the ensuing battle among the conservatives over the succeeding years, especially ahead of the 2013 presidential elections.) However, while Iranians were battling for their own version of democracy, Arabs, Turks, Malays, Indonesians and South Asians also witnessed their own debates on Islam and democracy – and some managed to even experience the sweet melody of democratic change.

Before the 2011 Arab uprisings, two major Muslim countries went through a period of democratization. Today, by many estimates, both Indonesia and Turkey are considered 'electoral' democracies, with competitive and largely transparent elections for top political leaders. Meanwhile, their economic dynamism is adding fuel to the broader momentum towards greater political pluralism and liberalization, notwithstanding growing concerns over corruption and ethnic violence in Indonesia, while a large section of the Turkish society has expressed its growing dissatisfaction with Prime Minister Erdogan's authoritarian tendencies, as manifest in his crackdown on critics and journalists, allegedly tied to the 'deep state', and heavy-handed response to those who opposed the demolition of Istanbul's iconic Gezi Park. Growing popular discontent in these countries is a reflection of a deep yearning to move beyond majoritarian rule in favour of a more participatory democracy. Intellectuals, including leading

Islamist thinkers, in these countries have also been active in arguing that there are no inherent incompatibilities between Islam and democracy. After all, they argue, Islam has always emphasized the 'rule of law', protection of the weak and dispossessed, human dignity, social justice, charity, and accountability of rulers. The post-9/11 era also provided the impetus for moderates across the Islamic world to emphasize the virtues and wisdom of tolerance, pluralism, accountability and representation. While neoconservatives and extremists clashed with one another, the liberal-moderate Muslims gradually permeated the broader social discourse, laying down the foundations of the so-called Arab Spring. The successful experiments in certain major Islamic countries, Turkey and Indonesia, provided an actual model upon which the debate could be anchored, operationalized and further explored. The Arab Spring, by and large, was precisely about building a democratic and pluralistic society in place of Arab autocracies and extremism.

Even in the Arab world, many Islamist thinkers (based either in the region or in the West) have been riding the tide of pro-democracy discourse by emphasizing the significance of democratic elections and a welfare-oriented state. Meanwhile, they have also toned down their disapproval of proposed reforms on issues such as freedom of expression, women's emancipation, cultural pluralism and protection of minority rights. Islamic scholars such as Tariq Ramadan (in Constable 2007), the grandson of the Muslim Brotherhood founder Hassan Al-Banna, have been among the most prominent voices arguing in favour of and envisioning a perfect harmony between democratic principles and Islamic traditions. For him, 'There is no contradiction between Islamic teachings and democratic principles. The problem is not the concept; it's the terminology.' He buttresses this point by stating that there are five 'indisputable' principles in Islam that are fundamental to democracy: the rule of law, equal rights for all citizens, universal suffrage, accountability of government, and separation of powers. To better understand the context of the Islam and democracy discourse, one must note that, historically, religious scholars have, on many occasions, actually served as guardians of common social and religious values by exercising 'oversight' of the tyrannical predilections of rulers such as the Ottoman sultans[3] (Feldman in Fukuyama 2009).

The Middle East had a qualitatively different historical record. Yes, the religious scholars did exercise immense influence over many policies of the monarchs; however, the sultans (or kings) were still the absolute arbiters of power. On the other hand, the religious community, the so-called *Ulema*, was never monolithic. Once in a while, more progressive religious scholars emerged in different corners of the Islamic world, for instance supporting constitutional reforms in the Ottoman Empire (think of Tanzimat) and Qajar Iran (think of the 1905 Constitutional Revolution). Some used their religious influence to temper tyrannical sultans and push for a constitutional monarchy, while others pushed back reforms, or envisioned a much more empowered *Ulema*, as with Ayatollah Khomeini's *Velayat-e-Faqih* (the guardianship of the cleric). Departing from the so-called quietist tradition within Shiism, as well as Dr Ali Shariati's socialist-Islamist ideology of 'red Shiism', Ayatollah Khomeini envisioned a theocratic political system emanating from a revolutionary overthrow of the *ancien régime*. Over time, though, more liberal religious thinking would emerge in countries such as Turkey, Syria, Indonesia, Tunisia, Lebanon and Iran, among others (Nasr 2009).

According to pre-eminent Islamic scholars John Esposito and John O. Voll (2001), the Muslim world represents '... a broad spectrum of perspectives ranging from the extremes of those who deny a connection between Islam and democracy to those who argue that Islam requires a democratic system'. In the middle, they say, are 'a number of countries where Muslims are a majority, [and] many Muslims believe that Islam is a support for democracy even though their particular political system is not explicitly defined as Islamic'.

Looking at the tenets of Islam, one can identify a number of principles which are conducive to democracy and good governance. After all, Islam emphasizes two fundamental values which are akin to democratic principles: (1) shura or mutual consultation, which emphasizes accountability and democratic rule; and (2) caliphate embodies the broad responsibilities of men as stewards of God's creation. In this sense, Islam emphasizes how monarchs are not absolute rulers, but rather have responsibilities to the people (ibid.).

In *The Islamic Political System*, the influential Shia religious scholar Ayatollah Baqir al-Sadr (in ibid.) stated how people 'have a general right to dispose of their affairs on the basis of the principle of consultation'. In reference to Iran's constitutional system, based on principles set by Ayatollahs al-Sadr and Khomeini, President Khatami reaffirmed this principle by stating, 'people play a fundamental role in bringing a government to power, in supervising the government and possibly the replacement of the government without any tension and problems'.

For proponents of Islamic democracy, Islam can provide a solution to the 'spiritual vacuum' that plagues the contemporary world, while furnishing the institutional requisites of a democracy. In *On the Sociology of Islam*, Dr Ali Shariati (in ibid.), arguably Iran's main revolutionary ideologue, stated that the principle of Tauhid, 'in the sense of oneness of God is of course accepted by all monotheists. But Tauhid as a world view … means regarding the whole universe as a unity, instead of dividing it into this world and the hereafter … spirit and body.' In this sense, Islam provides a unified holistic paradigm, which fuses the material and the divine, the sublime and the earthly. Thus, human reason and popular sovereignty are not the all-encompassing essence of human life. The Islamic paradigm encourages an alignment between democratic and righteous politics on earth, on one hand, and faith in and compliance to the word of God as expressed in the Holy Qur'an, on the other.

In defence of his distinct 'Islamic democracy' thesis, President Khatami (in ibid.) stated, 'the existing democracies do not necessarily follow one formula or aspect. It is possible that a democracy may lead to a liberal system. It is possible that democracy may lead to a socialist system. Or it may be a democracy with the inclusion of religious norms in the government. We have accepted the third option.' For Abdolkarim Soroush (in Bosetti 2011), known as 'Islam's Luther', 'religious democracy' is about a 'moral' state, which ensures '… respect for the wishes of the majority and the rights of others, justice, compassion, and reciprocal trust'. For him, the state should provide a pluralistic social framework, featuring secularist and postmodern elements while guaranteeing the full freedom to criticize; it should provide a clear distinction between civil society and the state. In such a society, individuals should enjoy internal and external freedom. The former ensures individual spiritual emancipation, while the latter emphasizes the freedom of the citizen from tyranny and repression, allowing him/her to fully participate in the public sphere.

The discourse on and within Islam is a rich and diverse one. Scholars such as Dale Eickelman (2003) have identified various tropes within the Islamic discourse on sharia itself, namely silent, liberal and interpreted varieties, with each having a distinct interpretation of basic principles of the religion. In this light, other scholars such as Charles Kurzman (2003) have analysed 'liberal' strands within Islam, and their overlaps with principles of liberal democracy, especially on human, civil and political rights. Nasr (2009: 186) identified a number of prominent 'liberal' Muslim thinkers, namely Nurcholis Majid (Indonesia), Abdolkarim Soroush (Iran), Muhammad Shahrour (Syria), Khalid Abou El Fadl and Abdullahi an'Na'im (US-based Arabs) and Muhammad Arjoun (French-Algerian), who have sought to reconcile principles of modern democracies with a new interpretation of Islam.

Turkey, in particular, has emerged as a major source of experimentation on political democracy and Islam, especially in light of the country's cosmopolitan imperial past and pluralistic sociocultural context. The spiritual guides of the new Turkish (and global Muslim) middle classes – the supporters of the AKP and the backbone of the country's democratization and economic revival in recent decades – are men like Fethullah Gülen – the world's most influential intellectual in 2008, according to *Foreign Policy* – who boldly stress the centrality of Islamic values in the life and business of a citizen, while espousing pluralism and democratic values (Aras and Caha 2003; Narli 2003; Yavuz 2003; Nasr 2009). The Indonesian experience with Islam and democracy is quite similar to Turkey's. Owing to the deeply ingrained secular traditions of the country's constitution, anchored on the 'Five Moral Principles' of Pancasila, many pious intellectuals emphasized the compatibility between democratic values and Islamic religious beliefs. After the fall of Suharto, the transition to a more pluralistic and democratic system did not lead to inter-religious conflicts or the rise of fundamentalist forces – although recent years have witnessed growing incidents of sectarian violence and intercommunity tensions. Indonesia's successful transition indicates the broad-based acceptance of tolerance, secularism and moderation under the umbrella of a democratic system. In fact, the biggest issue in Indonesia is arguably corruption (Anwar 2010). Reflecting on the Arab Spring and Indonesia's thirteen years of democratic experience, Anies Basweden (in Spiegel 2011), Indonesia's most celebrated youthful intellectual, emphasized how democratization does not imply Islamization – establishment of an Islamic state. He has encouraged religious leaders to argue in favour of a secular state, which is inclusive, transparent and democratic. According to him, 'As long as there is openness, transparency and freedom of media, people will reject Islamic rule.'

Egyptian society has also experienced fierce debates on the Islam and democracy issue. For decades, feminists, elite secular democrats and highly influential intellectuals such as Naguib Mafouz argued against the rise of the Muslim Brotherhood and what they have perceived – and continue to perceive – as fundamentalist anti-development movements. But the cultural context is shifting as many women embrace their newly cherished Islamic piety; consider how 'Islamic fashion' has demonstrated the trendy aesthetics of the hijab. With the exponential increases in institutions for distributing Islamic charity, mosques are spreading across the country and Islamic lifestyle programmes are beginning to dominate the media space. The majority of Egyptians are not exactly embracing the specific interpretation of Islam provided by groups such as the Muslim Brotherhood, but nevertheless there is a growing appreciation of Islam and its broader societal message. Indeed, the cultural discourse in the country has become increasingly 'Islamized' and public opinion immensely critical of American influence on Egypt's foreign policy. 'Islamic' intellectuals have played a central role in shaping public opinion and paving the way for cultural shifts and subsequent political transitions. Recently, the Arab world's most influential Islamic scholars, such as the Doha-based Yusuf al-Qaradawi (in Al-Kuraysi n.d.), have repeatedly emphasized the importance of Islam in the lives of people. For al-Qaradawi, despite his controversial statements on suicide bombings and the targeting of Israeli civilians, democracy is the best antidote to tyranny. Major TV personalities such as Amir Khaled have called for 'Faith-based Development', in which religion plays a key role in the advancement of Muslim society. Aware of his immense charisma and inspirational impact on the youth, through his wide range of civic and social engagements, Khaled (in Dreyer 2010) said, 'I work to make the youth positive, and this is the first stage for democracy.' These world-renowned intellectuals have espoused ideas that are obviously contrary to secular authoritarianism, and, arguably, are in favour of a democratic society compatible with the conditions of the Islamic world. Democracy, after all, is not only about elections, but more importantly about engendering a deep sense of communitarian solidarity, increasing social capital, and espousing a civic culture of socio-political engagement.

On the relationship between Islam and democracy, Mohamed ElBaradei (in Thuman and von Randow 2010), leader of the liberal-secular opposition coalition the National Salvation Front (NSF), stated,

> Islam, like any religion, is what you make of it. In the past, it's true, fully developed civil societies have not emerged under Islam. There have been autocracies with absolute rulers. But that was once the case in Europe too, and it's changed in Europe. Why should Islam be different? In a Sura in the Koran it says: 'The ruler must rule through consultation.' We can start from there. After all, some Muslim countries have functioning democracies, like Turkey or Indonesia.

For ElBaradei, democratic principles such as 'freedom of opinion, religious freedom, freedom from fear and want' are universal and devoid of geo-cultural relativism (ibid.). It is precisely this generation of thinkers, reflecting on and analysing the literature on Islam and democracy, which is guiding the process of democratization in the Middle East. And it is upon these ideational foundations that the mainstream and moderate Islamist organizations are cruising to the Arab Summer.

As Olivier Roy (2012), author of *The Islamists are Coming*, succinctly puts it:

> The longstanding debate over whether Islam and democracy can coexist has reached a stunning turning point. Since the Arab uprisings began in late 2010, political Islam and democracy have become increasingly interdependent. The debate over whether they are compatible is now virtually obsolete. Neither can now survive without the other ...

From the peripheries to the core

As the revolutionary dust over the Arab uprisings settled, and countries such as Egypt, Tunisia, Yemen and Libya moved towards a post-authoritarian system, the public's focus increasingly centred on more fundamental issues of economic stability. Now, as the ruling parties, many Islamist organizations discovered a complex, growing package of problems on their hands.

On the political front, the primary issues were (and continue to be) security sector reform, public safety, protection of (cultural, tribal, sexual) minorities, and legal accountability on the part of authorities. It is a political picture that is fraught with uncertainties and deepening challenges. As in past revolutionary upheavals, from France to Russia and Iran, inter-factional jostling has dominated and determined the configuration of the new political economy, as well as the trajectory of the revolution. But political recovery and revolutionary consolidation demand stabilization in the economic sphere lest the country witness either a downward spiral of 'permanent revolution' or, worse, a counter-revolutionary takeover. The police forces, a backbone of previous regimes, have also been heavily marginalized, further undermining public safety and strengthening the hand of gangs and organized crime. In Egypt, the new Islamist leadership had to contend with protests even by police forces. Within a year of the Arab Spring, many large-scale private enterprises, belonging to (alleged and actual) cronies of the former regime, came under attack, as the new governments aimed to dismantle crony capitalism and reverse past economic injustices. On top of this, the revolutionary zeal inspired continuous mobilization and (sometimes random) strikes by workers, demanding better working conditions and higher wages, affecting production and further eroding business confidence. The bureaucracy also suffered from a constant state of paralysis and indecision, with policy-makers shunning major decisions on infrastructure and development projects lest they get embroiled in damaging corruption cases. The economic challenges were tremendous in both scope and depth. Post-revolutionary Arab states faced – and continue to face – both cyclical and structural economic problems (Economist 2012a).

In cyclical terms, the economic costs of the revolution were immense. While oil-rich Libya suffered staggering losses in infrastructural damage and forgone oil revenues, Egypt and Tunisia experienced significant decline in tourism, commodity exports, industrial activity and overall economic productivity. From 2010 to 2011, Libya's GDP shrank by more than 50 per cent, as the country suffered as much as $15 billion in infrastructural damage. Meanwhile, Tunisia's GDP growth slowed from 3 to 0 per cent. Egypt saw its GDP growth reduced to 1 per cent, as compared to 5 per cent in the previous year. The investment climate also significantly deteriorated – a huge blow to the investment-reliant Arab economies of Egypt and Tunisia. The Egyptian government saw FDI declining from almost $12 billion in 2007 to merely $500 million in 2011. In Tunisia, the FDI almost halved, while Libya saw almost no new investments in 2011 (see Figure 5.1). In the same year, Libya struggled to access around $170 billion in frozen assets, formerly held by the Gaddafi regime (ibid.).

Although Libya's small population, at least theoretically, was poised to benefit from a rapid recovery in oil output, thanks to the influx of multinational energy companies and steadily high oil prices, Tunisia and Egypt continued to struggle with an overall deterioration in terms of unemployment, foreign exchange reserves, budget balance and GDP growth rates. Within a year, Egypt's currency reserves declined from $36 billion to $10 billion, with the unemployment rate jumping from 10 to 15 per cent. Tunisia was battling a staggering 19 per cent unemployment rate, while Libya faced an even worse unemployment picture. The debt levels were also on the rise, while

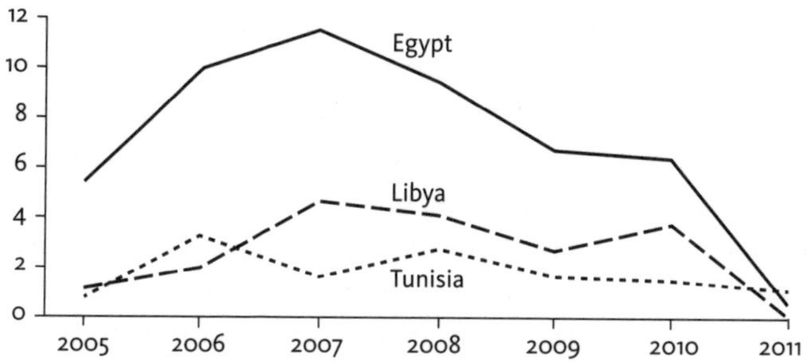

5.1 Declining foreign investment during the revolution (US$ billions)

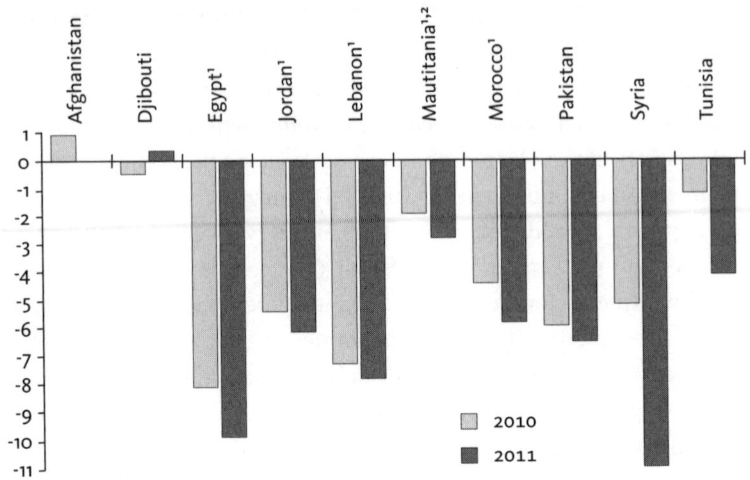

Notes: 1. Central government; 2. Includes oil revenue transferred to the oil fund

5.2 Rising budget deficits in post-revolution states (US$ billions) (*sources*: National authorities and IMF staff calculations)

budget deficits grew substantially. For instance, Egypt struggled with a budget deficit as great as 10 per cent in 2011 (see Figure 5.2).

In short, the ruling Islamist parties, in Egypt, Tunisia and Morocco, faced assaults on all fronts, with short-term economic shocks and a grim economic outlook. High levels of trade and budget deficit, coupled with growing debt, placed a downward pressure on the Arab transition countries' (ATCs) credit ratings, which, in turn, threatened rising borrowing costs just when governments were in a desperate scramble for cash to sustain commodity imports and get the state institutions running. For instance, even at yields close to 16 per cent, Egypt struggled to raise funds. Moreover, given Arab states' high dependence on food imports, falling currency reserves jeopardized food security, which has had serious socio-political implications for fragile post-revolutionary governments.

In the short and medium term, in order to reverse this cyclical trend, ATCs needed to simultaneously improve the political and economic picture, because the economic and political problems were mutually reinforcing. Arab states needed to tackle fundamental political questions to ensure that there was enough stability

TABLE 5.1 Egypt: selected economic indicators (2010–13)

	2009/10	2010/11	2011/12 estimated	2012/13 projected
GDP growth (%)	5.1	1.8	2.0	3.0
CPI inflation (%)	10.7	11.8	7.3	12.3
General government balance, excluding grants (% of GDP)	−8.2	−10.1	−11.8	−10.3
Current account, excl. grants (% of GDP)	−1.7	−2.3	−3.0	−3.0
Fiscal financing needs, excluding grants (US$ billions)[1]	18.5	25.1	31.6	31.7
External financing needs, excluding grants (US$ billions)[2]	7.1	11.5	11.7	12.7
Public debt (% of GDP)	73.2	76.4	79.7	81.1
External debt (% of GDP)	12.4	11.8	10.1	14.5
Reserves to short-term debt (%)[3]	306	297	326	327
Reserves in months of imports of goods and services[3]	6.9	4.7	2.7	3.0

Notes: 1. Budget deficit, excluding official grants, plus public external amortization. Assumes full domestic rollover; 2. Current account deficit, excluding official grants, plus amortization; 3. Official reserves including central bank foreign currency deposits held at banks

Sources: Egyptian authorities and IMF staff estimates

TABLE 5.2 Morocco: selected economic indicators (2010–13)

	2010	2011	Proj. 2012	Proj. 2013
GDP growth (%)	3.7	4.9	2.9	5.5
CPI inflation (%)[1]	1.0	0.9	2.2	2.5
Fiscal balance (% of GDP)[2]	−4.6	−7.1	−6.7	−6.5
Current account (% of GDP)[3]	−4.6	−8.4	−8.6	−6.8
Fiscal financing needs (US$ billions)[4]	4.9	7.9	7.4	7.5
External financing needs (US$ billions)[5]	5.4	9.8	9.9	8.5
Public debt (% of GDP)	51.3	54.3	58.1	58.9
External debt (% of GDP)[6]	24.7	23.6	25.4	24.9
Short-term debt, % of international reserves	0.02	0.02	0.02	0.02

Notes: 1. Period average; 2. Excluding grants; 3. Excluding official transfers; 4. Budget deficit excluding grants plus public external amortization. Assumes full domestic rollover; 5. Current account deficit excluding transfers plus external amortization; 6. Includes external publicly guaranteed debt

Source: IMF (2012)

TABLE 5.3 Tunisia: selected economic indicators (2010–13)

	2010	2011	Proj. 2012	Proj. 2013
Real GDP growth (%)[1]	3.0	0.0	2.7	3.3
CPI inflation (%)	4.4	3.5	5.0	4.0
Fiscal balance (% of GDP)[1]	−1.1	−3.5	−7.1	−5.6
Current account (% of GDP)	−4.8	−7.3	−7.9	−7.7
Fiscal financing needs (US$ billions)[2]	1.6	2.7	3.5	3.3
External financing needs (US$ billions)[3]	4.1	5.6	5.4	5.3
Public debt (% of GDP)	40.4	44.4	46.3	51.5
External debt (% of GDP)	48.8	50.2	54.6	56.7
Short-term debt, % of international reserves	52.3	68.5	64.1	67.5

Notes: 1. Overall fiscal deficit of the central government, excluding grants and privatization; 2. Overall budget deficit, excluding grants, plus public external amortization. Assumes full domestic rollover; 3. Current account deficit, excluding grants, plus amortization on external debt

Source: IMF (2012)

and confidence to rescue their anaemic economies. On the other hand, a weak economy meant further agitations, discontent and populist mobilizations across society, making it very difficult for the new governments to focus on realizing the political objectives of the revolution. Any move should have symbiotically tackled both economic and political hurdles.

Any solution in store?

Islamic political parties may have welcomed democratic elections as a tactical victory, but their strategic ends as ruling parties are yet to be deciphered. The ruling Islamic parties, from the PJD to the FJP and Ennahda, in varying forms and degrees signalled a similar model of governance: they all evoked Turkey's AKP as a source of inspiration, notwithstanding the Muslim Brotherhood's occasional criticism of the AKP's supposed compromise with Kemalist ultra-secularism, albeit not a primary model of governance. Just as the AKP supplanted an autocratic secular regime, laid down by Kemal Atatürk in the early twentieth century, Arab Islamic parties claimed to represent a moderate and democratic alternative to discredited secular Arab autocracies (see the final chapter). They claimed to represent social movements and political parties, which combine a moderate interpretation of Islamic values with a belief in basic tenets of free market economics and parliamentary democracy. In this sense, similar to the AKP, the Arab Islamists even resembled to some extent the political economy of Christian Democrats in western Europe (Nasr 2009; Hamid 2011a). Of course, these political parties fall along a spectrum, with the AKP and the FJP leaning more towards conservatism, while Ennahda has proved to be more secular and parliamentarian in its outlook – in light of its emphasis on the separation of religion and state and agreement to concentrate more state power in parliament – perhaps largely in response to the strong influence of labour unions, leftist groups and liberal parties in the country.

Looking at the – so far rudimentary – policy pronouncements of ruling (moderate) Islamic parties, one could identify a number of common but seemingly contradictory themes. On the one hand, they all emphasize macroeconomic stability by welcoming FDI, unrestrained tourism, a balanced budget, stable inflation, higher GDP growth and full employment. There is also a growing appreciation of regional economic integration, pan-Arabist solidarity and closer socio-economic ties with Europe, especially in the case of Tunisia and Morocco.

Simultaneously, there is a discourse on deepening the role of the state in spurring industrialization, raising domestic food production and minimum wages, and instituting strategic trade barriers to strengthen the domestic economy. Their key strength is in the realm of social welfare and charity, since Islam espouses social justice and economic equity. They also have a more critical view of modern capitalist finance. For instance, they condemn financial speculation and high-interest lending. Instead, they encourage banking-sector diversification by expanding Islamic finance, which shuns speculative capital and high lending yield, and tighter regulation of financial markets, from bonds to commodity trade. Then again, depending on the composition of the parliament, the internal balance of forces and the realities on the ground, the ruling Islamist parties have either leaned towards market-oriented economics or state-led development.

So far, what is clear is that they have all made contradictory statements, with no clear economic strategy to redress the immense structural imbalances common to all ATCs. What is unclear is how they will manage to balance growing economic integration and macroeconomic stability, on one hand, with social welfare, cautious protectionism, higher wages and subsidies, and tighter regulation, on the other. While Egypt initially rebuffed the IMF, the Islamists in Egypt and Tunisia have engaged in detailed negotiations over multibillion loans to refuel and restructure flailing economies.

Short-term political calculation and economic necessities seem to have overwhelmed their strategic calculus. Thus, the ruling Islamic parties are yet to flesh out a detailed programmatic approach on critical issues such as good governance, privatization, subsidy reforms, and streamlining of the bloated bureaucracy. So far, what we have are broad brushstrokes that say more about the broader political vision rather than concrete, technical policy proposals.

What is clear is that there are two systemic factors which have encouraged political moderation and ideological tolerance among dominant Islamic political parties: first, democratic elections are having a moderating effect on mainstream Islamic political parties by raising the stakes in terms of preserving and improving the status quo; and secondly, dependence on foreign trade, tourism and cordial ties with the West discourages radicalism and encourages political flexibility and economic openness. Thus, if these parties seek to retain and deepen their influence in the post-revolutionary landscape, then political moderation, based on compromise and flexibility, is the only game in town. The new power brokers simply have too much to lose now, significantly reducing the odds of radical resurgence.

These experiences only show that having an electoral majority is by no means a guarantee of smooth control of the transition process. Delicate compromise and a modicum of respect for the rule of law – and the influence of other centres of power – are necessary to translate electoral power into a measure of actual control. Otherwise, there will be a breakdown in the internal political order and a large-scale, unified backlash from secular and liberal forces. As Eric Trager (2013) has eloquently put it, the Brotherhood is powerful, but not in control.

Yet the Arab Spring was by no means confined to North African countries. And the newly empowered Islamist political parties have also been far from isolated from the developments across the Red Sea, where a group of rich, powerful and influential monarchies in the Persian Gulf have coordinated their efforts to not only withstand the onslaught of the popular uprisings, but also shape and steer their course. Saudi Arabia and Qatar, the two pillars of the GCC, have served as powerful forces directing and redirecting the momentum of the Arab Spring. Qatar has been a powerful backer of the Muslim Brotherhood and its many offshoots, providing much-needed finance and media exposure to its new allies in the post-Arab Spring states. It also played a critical role in directly helping armed Islamist rebels in Libya to topple Gaddafi. Most of all, Qatar's influential Al Jazeera channel, a backbone of the tiny kingdom's soft power, also played a critical role in galvanizing the Arab street and the international community (think of the NATO intervention in Libya) against now-fallen autocrats in North Africa. But once the Arab Spring hit Bahrain – and later other monarchies like Oman, Kuwait and Jordan – it became clear that the GCC powers were not ready for democratic change at home, and a subsequent entente between Saudi Arabia and Qatar facilitated the formation of a powerful counter-revolutionary bloc, which has reshaped the course of the Arab Spring.

6 | GULF EXCEPTIONALISM: HOW THE MONARCHIES HAVE RESHAPED THE ARAB SPRING

> The cost of liberty is less than the price of repression.
> (W. E. B. Du Bois)[1]

When the Arab Spring struck North Africa, there were mixed reactions among the Arab monarchies, and sheikhdoms in the Persian Gulf. In Riyadh, there was palpable concern over the downfall of Arab allies, especially in Egypt, and the region-wide reverberations of a democratic, people-driven regime change. As a result, the Saudi monarchy decided to shelter Ben Ali, after the Tunisian strongman was forced to renounce power in December 2010 in the face of unprecedented popular protests. When Hosni Mubarak, a key element in the regional cold war against Iran, was caught off guard amid a nationwide revolution, bringing the whole country to a standstill, Arab monarchies – led by Saudi Arabia – spared no efforts in pressurizing the West, especially Washington, dissuading the latter against siding with the popular uprisings. When the Obama administration eventually decided to withdraw its support from Mubarak, a development that was largely facilitated by the decision of the Egyptian military to form a so-called transitional Supreme Council of the Armed Forces (SCAF), the Saudis were furious, accusing the USA of throwing an old ally under the bus – thus sending a wrong message to other regional allies facing domestic upheaval.

There was also a lingering fear among Arab monarchies that the collapse of long-time allies would give birth to a new era dominated by more independent-minded and populist forces, including the Muslim Brotherhood and its many offshoots, which have had a tricky (and often conflictual) relationship with the Arab monarchies, ranging from Jordan to Saudi Arabia and the UAE.

In Doha, it was a totally different story. The monarchy in Qatar, in clear contrast to fellow Arab monarchies, was among the most vehement supporters of the Arab Spring (in its initial stages), using its deep pockets and 'soft power' to galvanize the Arab street against sultanistic regimes. Based in Doha and generously funded by the Qatari royalty, Al Jazeera – arguably the region's most powerful media outlet, and increasingly a global force to reckon with – played an indispensable role in not only reporting the ebbs and flows of the popular uprisings, but, more importantly, also providing a specific kind of coverage, anchored by a calculated political messaging, which energized the protesters, garnered global attention and sympathy for the Arab Spring, and continuously delegitimized the autocrats across Arab republics (Miles 2011; Al-Qassemi 2012a).

Qatar – along with Al Jazeera – also emerged as a major sponsor of varying Islamist groups across the region, notably the Muslim Brotherhood. The group's most influential cleric, Yussuf al-Qaradawi, has hosted a regular show on Al Jazeera, while the Brotherhood's top leaders, such as Deputy Supreme Guide, Khairet El Shater, and General Guide Mohammed Badie, have been, especially during the Egyptian revolution, regular guests on the network. When Mohammad Morsi, who earlier also appeared on Al Jazeera programmes along with other Brotherhood leaders, won the Egyptian presidency, the network's (Arabic-language) Cairo bureau chief Abdel Fattah Fayed went so far as to liken the then obscure Morsi to the charismatic pan-Arabist Egyptian leader Gamal Abdel Nasser, proclaiming: 'Mohammed Morsi reminds [the] Egyptians of President Gamal Abdul Nasser' (Al-Qassemi 2012b).

In many ways, Qatar's proactive role in the run-up to and during the Arab Spring had something to do with its leadership's (pragmatic) ambitions. The Qatari emir, Sheikh Hamad bin Khalifa, who took power through a coup against his own father, Sheikh Khalifa, in 1995, was intent on building a legacy for himself by elevating his tiny kingdom – enriched by booming hydrocarbon revenues – to the top of regional and international affairs. He also followed in his father's footsteps, albeit after an initial hiatus, by maintaining strong ties with the Islamists, especially the Brotherhood. In many ways, lacking military prowess and sheer economic size, he relied on Al Jazeera to espouse his visions for Qatar and the broader region, which, as many analysts would argue, made the network, especially in recent years, somehow an extension of Qatar's public diplomacy and foreign policy agenda (Al-Qassemi 2012a; Hashem 2012).

In *New Media and the New Middle East*, communication experts Shawn Powers and Eytan Gilboa looked into the 'public diplomacy' role of Al Jazeera, and how the news channel emerged as an important actor on the international stage, operating to a two-dimensional political agenda: 'The internal agenda promotes debates on values, customs, and norms in the Arab society and politics. The external agenda offers critical coverage and opinion on international events such as military interventions and wars in Afghanistan and Iraq' (Powers and Gilboa 2007: 75).

Al Jazeera provided an unprecedented and powerful platform for the Arab street to challenge mainstream, state-dominated media, which for decades monopolized sources of information and served as propaganda outlets for autocratic regimes. By breaking such an information monopoly, and injecting a quasi-progressive agenda into the regional discourse, Al Jazeera became the most trusted source of information and opinion-making in the region, while provoking the ire of Arab autocrats as well as hawkish elements in the West, notably the neoconservatives under the Bush administration. Upon his visit to the network's headquarters in Qatar in 2001, Mubarak, unable to conceal his long-time annoyance with Al Jazeera's critical coverage of his regime, reportedly quipped: 'All that noise from this little matchbox?' (Miles 2011).

A 2002 Gallup poll highlighted Al Jazeera's strength, from the perspective of Arab societies, especially in terms of providing daring, objective and comprehensive news coverage, with citizens in Kuwait, Saudi Arabia and Jordan registering remarkably high approval ratings (as compared to state-run channels and mainstream Western media) in this regard (Gallup 2002).

Emerging from the ashes of a failed BBC Arab news channel initiative, with Saudi funding, the influential and well-funded Al Jazeera was launched by Qatar in 1996, hiring staff and journalists from the earlier failed BBC project, which was allegedly closed after it aired a series of controversial documentaries on the Saudi royal family. 'This time they were assured that nothing would stop the new station, mainly because there were no limits, no red lines, and an unlimited budget,' stated a former Al Jazeera war correspondent, Ali Hashem (2012), in the *Guardian*. 'The new channel introduced counter-fire talk shows and documentaries from hotspots with an emphasis on controversial issues ... [Al Jazeera] emerged as the most credible news source in the region ...'

Although Al Jazeera claimed to be an independent, self-sustaining news outlet, it reportedly relied on the largesse of Qatar's emir to sustain its ambitious and wide-ranging operations. Following an initial $137 million grant for its first five years of operation, the Qatari emir had to extend consecutive loans over the succeeding years, highlighting the intimate bonds between the Qatari leadership and the powerful media network (ibid.). The growth of Al Jazeera, anchored in one of the world's richest kingdoms, and the rising profile of Qatar as a regional power broker went hand in hand, with the tiny Arab state playing a pivotal role in mediating various conflicts across the region, ranging from Syria and Sudan to Lebanon and even Iran, specifically over its nuclear programme and off-again, on-again tensions with Arab neighbours. (After all, Iran and Qatar share the world's largest deposit of natural gas in the Persian Gulf, the so-called South Pars/North Field complex, necessitating a pragmatic bilateral understanding.) It was, in many ways, a synergistic relationship between Al Jazeera and the state of Qatar, sending shock waves across the region and beyond. Within less than two decades, Qatar emerged as a global leader in the export of liquefied natural gas (LNG) and a patron and host of cutting-edge research in varying scientific fields, while Al Jazeera came to rival – if not surpass – global networks such as the BBC and CNN, especially on covering developments in the global South and the Middle East. *The Economist* (2011) aptly likened Qatar's astonishing rise to 'a pygmy with the punch of a giant', underscoring the new-found self-importance of the tiny sheikhdom.

> While cheerleading the Arab spring, Qatar has interposed itself, with mixed diplomatic success, in conflicts as far away as Lebanon, Palestine, Sudan, Syria and Yemen. Its sheikhs sit on an array of big European boards and own choice chunks of London. Their spreading portfolios embrace Chinese refineries, French fashion houses and Spanish football teams.

Aside from $70 billion in cash reserves, *The Economist* (ibid.) argued, a slim chain of command, dominated by the emir, his cousin, Sheikh Hamad bin Jassim al-Thani, and son, Crown Prince Tamim, allowed Qatar to efficiently put its assets into action, while other regional actors, including the USA, faced bouts of fiscal uncertainties and struggled to optimize a heavily bogged-down bureaucracy.

For many analysts, Qatar's shining moment truly arrived when the Arab Spring struck Egypt. After witnessing the smooth and swift downfall of Ben Ali, Al Jazeera, demonstrating its prescience, positioned itself for a potential meltdown in Egypt, sending its best journalists and staff to provide comprehensive and instantaneous coverage of a gathering popular storm against the Mubarak regime. The shock-and-awe of the Jasmine Revolution lay in its ability to undermine the myth of invincibility among the Arab autocrats, signalling the possibility of revolutionary change in the Arab heartland of Egypt (Miles 2011).

Cognizant of Al Jazeera's critical coverage of various Arab states, the Egyptian regime resorted to a combination of coercion, propaganda and satellite jamming to hamstring Al Jazeera's coverage of the widening protests, especially in Tahrir Square. The Egyptian Information Ministry ordered the offices of various Al Jazeera bureaus to be shut down, revoking the accreditation of all the network's journalists in addition to accusing them of inciting people against the state, while the government-run satellite transmission company, Nilesat, violated its contractual agreement with Al Jazeera Arabic by blocking its transmission at the height of the protests – forcing Al Jazeera to rely on private media outlets to reach the Egyptian people (ibid.).

'Al Jazeera's powerful images of angry crowds and bloody morgues undercut the Egyptian regime's self-serving arguments and stood in sharp contrast to the state-run TV channels, which promoted such a dishonest version of events that some of their journalists resigned in disgust,' explained Hugh Miles (ibid.), an Egypt-based journalist and author, who has written extensively on the Qatari network's influence across the region. 'Given Al Jazeera's enormous influence on the Arab street and its electrifying message that Arab dictatorships are, in fact, mortal, it is no wonder dictators and despots across the region have been left feeling rather rattled.' No wonder, in light of the network's indispensable role during the Egyptian revolution, protests in Tahrir Square and beyond chanted 'Long Live Al Jazeera', alongside similar praise and expressions of gratitude for social networking sites such as Facebook and Twitter, which also played a critical role in bypassing state-owned media propaganda (ibid.).

As a testament to Al Jazeera's influential role in the run-up to the Egyptian revolution, *Time* (2011) magazine nominated the news outlet for the 100 most influential actors in 2011, arguing, 'During the events of the so-called Arab Spring, no station covered itself in greater glory than the English- and Arabic-language channels of Al Jazeera,' while emphasizing that its 'subversive zeal and superior resources in the Middle East saw millions of people around the world flocking to its coverage of the uprisings in Tunisia, Egypt and elsewhere in the region'. Eventually, Ayman Mohyedlin, the lead Al Jazeera English reporter during the Egyptian revolution, was selected as a member of *Time*'s 100 most influential people in 2011 – unprecedented recognition for a reporter from a non-Western news channel, or for any journalist for that matter.

Yet one thing unified Qatar and Riyadh: the self-serving belief that the Arab Spring was not really against monarchies, but instead bankrupt, discredited and corrupt leaders of Arab republics. This is precisely why they came to the rescue of Jordan and Morocco, extending an invitation to the two relatively poor and distant Arab monarchies, which had repeatedly flirted with popular upheaval in recent decades, to join the GCC just months into the Arab Spring. If they were about democracy and politico-economic freedom per se, then a strange aspect of the popular uprisings – and Al Jazeera's expressed support for them – was that they emerged in Tunisia (arguably, the Arab world's most liberal society and diversified economy) and took off in Egypt (the Arab world's sociocultural heart, buoyed by a vibrant civil society), while the more autocratic rulers and single-dimensional economies were in the Persian Gulf.

What made this tactical, timely alliance more interesting is that for years Saudi Arabia and Qatar squabbled over a whole host of issues, including Al Jazeera's 'critical' coverage of politics in the Persian Gulf, especially in Saudi Arabia, the tiny kingdom's 'cordial ties' with Iran, disagreements over regional hydrocarbon projects (as in the \$3.5 billion UAE–Qatar gas deal), and disputes over a sixty-kilometre-long maritime–land border, precipitating a border clash in 1992 that reportedly led to the death of two Qatari soldiers. Qatar even arrested a number of Saudi citizens for allegedly participating in a foiled 1996 coup attempt to restore the old king, Sheikh Khalifa (Al-Qassemi 2011). From 2007 onwards, Qatar initiated several attempts to mend frayed ties, including a modus vivendi of some sort with Saudi Arabia, as reported by the *New York Times* in 2008, whereby Al Jazeera would stop hosting Saudi dissidents and tone down any critical coverage against Riyadh. Then, in 2010, the Emir of Qatar also pardoned Saudis implicated in the 1996 coup attempt. Nonetheless, Saudi Arabia continued to deride Qatar's foray into Lebanese politics, supposedly a Saudi turf. Disagreements further intensified during the Arab Spring, when Qatar repeatedly called for the downfall of Arab leaders, especially Mubarak, and even committed troops (first among Arab states) to NATO operations against Gaddafi, despite Saudi objections. But when the Arab Spring hit the Kingdom of Bahrain (and Oman), the GCC – the force behind a loose politico-economic integration of semi-like-minded oil-rich Arab kingdoms – suddenly began to act in unison, largely toeing the Saudi line. Immediately, there was a rapprochement between Riyadh and Doha, with the two wealthy kingdoms not only resolving their border issues, but also, perhaps most crucially, combining their resources and influence to keep democratic uprisings at bay – and mould their trajectory thereafter. When the Arab Spring gained momentum in Syria, Qatar and Saudi Arabia began to find another common ground: while Saudi Arabia was largely concerned with the Damascus–Tehran axis, and how a new regime could break that alliance, Doha responded to Qaradawi's support for the uprising, which was, in turn, dominated by the Syrian Muslim Brotherhood (Al-Qassemi 2011, 2013).

Once the Saudi–Qatari gloves were off, Al Jazeera's reputation – as supposedly an independent institution – was undermined, raising concerns over the influence of the Al-Thani Khalifa on the network's coverage and agenda, especially after Ahmed bin Jassim Al Thani replaced Wadah Khanfar as Al Jazeera's director-general in September 2011. The chairman of Al Jazeera is another royal family member,

Hamad bin Thamer Al Thani, placing the network, as some analysts would argue, quite firmly under the command of the ruling family. The growing grip of the Qatari leadership over Al Jazeera, as many commentators would assert, reached its apogee when the Syrian revolution evolved into an all-out regional proxy struggle, pitting Sunni powers like Qatar and Saudi Arabia, backed by the West, against Iran, Iraq, Russia and to a certain degree China (Al-Qassemi 2012a) (see Chapter 7).

'Al Jazeera had noticeably ramped up its coverage of the Syrian protest movement, privileging YouTube clips and eyewitness accounts over government claims that the protests were a foreign-backed Islamist conspiracy,' argued Al-Qassemi (ibid.), describing how a Qatar–Saudi rapprochement could spell the early end of the Arab Spring in terms of its peaceful, democratic and internally generated character.

For journalists such as Ali Hashem (2012), the Qatari leadership's increasingly overt interference in Al Jazeera's coverage, starting with the Bahraini revolution and peaking during the Syrian uprisings, prompted his resignation from the network. 'I was one of those who experienced it when Al Jazeera, the channel I used to work for, refused to air footage of gunmen fighting the Syrian regime on the borders between Lebanon and Syria.' Ali Hashem (ibid.) described how GCC-financed networks prioritized strategic considerations over anything else in their coverage. 'It was clear to me, though, that these instructions were not coming from Al Jazeera itself: that the decision was a political one taken by people outside the TV centre – the same people who asked the channel to cover up the situation in Bahrain.'

Multiple diplomatic cables, released thanks to Wikileaks, also revealed that there were extensive discussions between Al Jazeera management, led by then managing director Khanfar, and Washington officials, notably from the Defense and State departments. While an outright conspiracy is far from established, Omar Chatriwala (2011), another former Al Jazeera employee, makes a persuasive case that the cables suggest instead 'an organization struggling to maintain professional standards'.

Unlike their resource-poor counterparts, the Persian Gulf monarchies, under the aegis of Qatar and Saudi Arabia, were able to adeptly 'manage' – at least in the short run – protests and calls for democratic reform by devising a powerful counter-revolutionary strategy based on an astute combination of four factors: cash, leveraging petro-politics and the 'Iran card', coercion, and revolutionary redirection/diversion. This four-point strategy explains the ability of Arab monarchies to, so far, avoid the onslaught of the uprisings.

The counter-revolution

Facing a common threat, the GCC launched an ambitious project of counter-revolution, strategizing ways to stave off short-term systemic threats, especially with respect to more vulnerable monarchies such as Bahrain and Oman, and taking the reins of the new popular uprisings in the medium to long run.

Simply looking at higher income levels in the GCC is by no means a sufficient and appropriate way to consider the trajectory of the Arab Spring, since protest-hit states such as Bahrain are considerably wealthier (think of per capita income) than many other Arab countries, which have, so far, prevented protests from mushrooming into an all-out uprising (e.g. Algeria, Sudan and Morocco). The Arab populace shares many common grievances (see Chapter 2), ranging from the lack of political freedom to staggering unemployment rates and perennial structural economic problems, but revolutions are rarely about the sheer ferocity of protesters; they are also, perhaps in equal measure, a reflection of the ability of the state and the ruling regime to adopt new tactics, and employ more effective counter-strategies to prevent its downfall.

While describing sultanistic regimes as 'paper tigers', Professor Goldstone (2011: 13) has looked into why monarchies are comparatively in a better position to manage popular discontent, underscoring their flexible political structure, whereby they 'can retain considerable executive power while ceding legislative power to elected parliaments'. So, his argument goes, in times of upheaval protesters tend to call rather for 'legislative change than for abandonment of the monarchy', giving monarchs considerable flexibility to placate opposition forces.

Moreover, as Goldstone (ibid.: 13–14) notes, monarchies such as Morocco were able to project an image of change upon succession of power, especially when it involved an older monarch passing his throne on to a younger, seemingly reform-minded heir. Thus monarchies, he argued, could avoid a violent downfall if they considered sharing their power with elected officials or handing the reins to a younger family member who heralds significant reforms. While it is arguable whether Morocco's king, Mohammed VI, initiated genuine steps towards a constitutional monarchy since his accession to power in 1999, it is clear that the monarchs have that extra 'wiggle room' to use their 'traditional authority', in Weberian parlance, to cope with modern-day challenges of governance, specifically by 'outsourcing' some state obligations, and executive powers, to an elected leadership in the legislature, as with the PJD in Morocco in recent years. This, quite shrewdly, also allows monarchs to enjoy a measure of 'plausible deniability' by shifting the blame to the elected parliament whenever problems arise: conveniently distancing themselves from controversial issues feeding popular discontent. Sultanistic regimes, in contrast, lacked traditional authority, so they largely depended on 'charismatic leadership' (think of Egypt's Nasser) or some form of rational-legal authority (think of Tunisia's Bourguiba).

Throwing money at the problem Unlike (now-fallen or soon-to-fall) Arab republics, GCC states by and large have enjoyed substantial fiscal clout because of favourable oil prices in the last decade. Despite incurring significant losses during the Great Recession of 2008, after large-scale investments in and integration with Western financial institutions, the GCC continued to carry significant cash in its coffers, having in its possession among the world's biggest sovereign wealth funds (SWFs). From 1998 to 2009, the GCC's real GDP grew by an average of 5.2 per cent annually, a cumulative total of 65 per cent (Economist Intelligence Unit 2009). Despite taking a huge hit during the Great Recession, the GCC by and large maintained a strong economic record (see Table 6.1).

Eager to tap into America's safe financial havens, especially in the form of treasury bills, build a powerful reserve for external investments and, to a lesser degree, avoid the vagaries of a so-called 'Dutch Disease',[2] the GCC has been at the forefront of building an impeccable SWF, amounting to as much as $1.861 trillion in 2012. The UAE leads the pack, holding around $932 billion, followed by Saudi

TABLE 6.1 GCC key economic indicators (2007–20) (US$ billions)

	2007	2008	2009	2010	2015	2020
Trade balance	294.5	365.8	4.9	86.6	98.8	105.9
% of GDP	36.0	35.9	0.6	9.3	7.1	5.3
Exports	559.3	698.2	332.1	438.5	621.4	860.6
Oil and gas	410.9	549.8	183.3	283.7	391.3	522.5
% oil	73.5	78.7	55.2	64.7	63.0	60.7
Non-oil	148.3	148.4	148.8	154.8	230.1	338.1
Imports	−264.8	−332.4	−327.2	−351.9	−522.6	−754.7
Services	−79.5	−104.8	−104.7	−110.3	−172.9	−248.1
Income	18.8	9.1	13.3	17.2	60.3	138.3
Current transfers	−40.0	−42.4	−41.1	−44.5	−62.7	−91.0
Current account balance	193.7	227.7	−127.5	6.0	14.4	33.3
% of GDP	23.7	22.3	−16.4	0.6	1.0	1.7

Note: Estimates and forecasts were generated in early 2010
Source: Economist Intelligence Unit (2009)

Arabia ($533 billion), Kuwait ($296 billion) and Qatar ($100 billion) (El-Erian 2008; European Investment Bank 2012: 6). Such a liquidity glut allows petro-monarchies to shift large amounts of money to designated investment destinations, serving the double purpose of (a) aiding (internal and external) allies and (b) influencing foreign partners, including industrialized states. As a result, GCC states have emerged as major shareholders in a range of flashy and high-profile assets in the West, with Qatar's SWF owning 95 per cent of London's Shard, the tallest building in western Europe (GlobalPost 2013).

So, when the Arab Spring jolted the GCC, particularly hurting monarchies in Bahrain and Oman, member countries engaged in a massive dole-out programme, handing huge sums to allies, clients, consultancy firms, public relations (PR) experts and citizens in order to stave off growing protests and appease basic economic grievances. In addition, they stepped up their efforts to woo a fiscally challenged Washington by finalizing historically high arms purchases, notably Saudi Arabia's $60 billion arms deal, which was initially announced in 2010, but operationalized over succeeding years. By placing themselves firmly at the top of the list of Western defence industries and America's arms exports destinations, GCC states deepened their leverage over Western partners (Landler and Myers 2011).

The GCC also jumped to the aid of its more vulnerable members, Oman and Bahrain, in an attempt to cover their flank, offering their brethren $20 billion in development package loans (Murphy 2011). Then, in May 2011, the GCC also extended membership to monarchies in Jordan and Morocco, which are technically outside the Persian Gulf. (In contrast, states such Yemen, despite their geographical proximity to the GCC, have been denied membership, mainly because of their divergent political system.) While the official language suggested 'economic reasons' as the basis for such an unprecedented decision to expand the GCC, it was clear to many that containment of the Arab Spring was at the heart of the Saudi-led GCC calculus (Khalaf and Allam 2011).

Back in 1979 (after a violent crackdown, involving Western security forces, to end the occupation of the Grand Mosque by the Juhayman Islamist forces) and 1990 (after the entry of 500,000 US troops into the kingdom during the Gulf War), GCC states such as Saudi Arabia engaged in a massive dole-out programme to temper a popular backlash, featuring reduced government fees and increased subsidies, among other things. Yet they paled in comparison to the kingdom's $130 billion spending programme, announced in the wake of the Arab Spring in 2011 – roughly a 40 per cent hike in government spending. The new patronage writ large was a multi-phased measure that included, among other things, ambitious programmes such as the establishment of 500,000 houses, the creation of 60,000 new jobs in the Ministry of Interior, the establishment of a general unemployment assistance scheme, and the raising of the minimum wage to $800. To ensure the loyalty of bureaucrats and religious institutions, it also included supplementary budgets for religious institutions, large bonuses for civil servants, and budget increases for various public credit agencies (Hertog 2011).

Aided by their GCC big brothers, Bahrain and Oman stepped up to the plate. Bahrain announced 20,000 new jobs at its interior ministry, while Oman – aside from new subsidies for basic goods and expanded pension payments and welfare schemes – announced

35,000 new jobs in the public sector, as part of a larger pledge to create 50,000 new employment opportunities. Less-populated and well-endowed kingdoms in the UAE, Qatar and Kuwait, felt less pressure to engage in a new massive patronage scheme, but the UAE, more or less, pushed ahead with targeted measures, including subsidies for basic food, a 70 per cent increase in military pensions, and a $1.6 billion infrastructure project in poorer emirates in the north (ibid.). Kuwait's handouts were particularly large: amounting to $2,600 per family, surpassing Bahrain's $1,000 rate (Sharma 2011: 216). Whether these measures are sustainable is another question.

Flushed with booming hydrocarbon profits and home to a compact, ethnically homogeneous citizenry, the Qatari emirate, as Hugh Miles (2011) suggests, faces a different kind of problem: 'How to motivate a population of soon-to-be millionaires to keep showing up for work in the morning.' Whether the emir and the Qatari monarchy fall is another question, but rumours of repeated coup attempts continue to circulate in the regional media. In response, Qatar raised military personnel pensions by 70 per cent (Sharma 2011: 216). So it is far from clear whether the country will in fact hold democratic elections any time soon, in spite of earlier promises of parliamentary elections in 2013. To ensure a smooth transition in leadership, and amid rumours of increasing health issues, Qatar's Emir Hamad bin Khalifa Al Thani bequeathed power to his fourth son, Tamim bin Hamad Al Thani, trained at the British Royal Military Academy, Sandhurst, and known for his diligence and ambition (Henderson 2013).

'For the high-rent countries, the issue will remain largely academic for decades to come. But depending on oil price developments, it could become an existential worry for Bahrain, Oman and Saudi Arabia before the end of the decade,' argued London School of Economics lecturer and GCC expert Steffen Hertog (2011) in *Foreign Policy*, emphasizing how the new dole-out programmes considerably undermine the region's attempt to create more sustainable, diversified economies. 'The breakeven oil prices for GCC budgets have increased significantly in the past few months ... These should be sobering numbers for those who believe that the GCC can always buy its way out of trouble.' Bahrain and Saudi Arabia, he notes, will now probably need per-barrel prices of oil to hover above $100 and

$110 respectively. Aside from facing a higher threshold of oil prices to keep their fiscal house in order, countries such as Saudi Arabia and the UAE increased their oil dependency rates by 10 per cent and 2 per cent respectively in the 2001–10 period. Prior to the Arab Spring, as much as 45 per cent of Saudi Arabia's GDP was oil based, while the UAE figure stood at 31 per cent (Sharma 2011: 218). Another big problem with the GCC spending spree is that they have a minimal tax base, with Saudi Arabia abolishing income tax in 1975, while the UAE – home to investment hubs like Dubai – has one of the world's lowest corporate income tax rates (ibid.: 214).

Coercion and containment As far as the GCC is concerned, the Arab Spring is a short-term systemic threat, which needs an immediate response. By no means, based on various reports by human rights groups and international media, have the regional popular upheavals encouraged genuine democratic reform to appease the legitimate needs of the masses.

In a blatant expression of the counter-revolution, a so-called GCC Peninsula Shield Force, composed of around 1,200 Saudi troops and 500 Emirati police forces, came to the rescue of the Sunni Al-Khalafi royal family amid a popular uprising, largely comprising the majority Shia population of Bahrain, which has borne the brunt of decades-long repression, marginalization and employment discrimination.

'While some observers here have blamed Saudi Arabia and its neighbouring Sunni-led sheikhdoms as a major source of the icy winds that are blasting through the Gulf, the growing contradictions between the US and Western "values" and their interests are adding to the unseasonable weather,' argued Jim Lobe (2011), Washington Bureau Chief of the Inter Press Service, explaining how American acquiescence, based on strategic calculations, provided the GCC with carte blanche to silence the democratic uprisings. '[Such] failure to clearly and publicly denounce the Saudi-backed repression is only the most blatant example of this trend.' After all, Bahrain hosts the US Navy Fifth Fleet, while Qatar's Ul Udeid airbase is host to the forward headquarters of United States Central Command. The direct US military interests in the highly strategic region of the Persian Gulf couldn't be any less self-evident.

'After the Obama administration acquiesced to the Egyptian regime's collapse, Saudi Arabia, the most powerful Gulf state, began doubting the United States' commitment to regional stability. So it has taken matters into its own hands. In a time of unprecedented upheaval, the Saudis are digging in ... stepping well beyond [their] traditional sphere of influence,' Shadi Hamid (2011b) wrote in *The National*, explaining why the Saudi-led GCC, intent on 'stabilizing' the region, assumed an uncharacteristic level of assertiveness vis-à-vis Washington.

What followed was an emboldened group of monarchies determined to rein in dissent. The UAE silenced calls for an elected parliament with executive powers, responding to protests with ruthless efficiency. The authorities detained prominent intellectuals and pro-democracy figures such as Nasser bin Ghaith, Fahad Salem al-Shehhi and Ahmed Mansour (BBC 2011), suspended the board of directors of one of the most prominent civil society organizations, the Jurist Association, and revoked the citizenship of seven members of the Islamist Al-Islah group (Lobe 2011; Kerr 2011), while keeping a watchful eye on Islamist elements with links to the Egyptian Brotherhood, culminating in the arrest of eleven Egyptian citizens in 2013 for allegedly plotting the overthrow of the Emirati sheikhdom in favour of an Islamic state (Reuters 2013b).

The Omani ruler, Sultan Qabus bin Said Al Said, initially faced nationwide protests, from the port city of Salalah in the south, to the capital in Muscat and the industrial town of Sohar in the north, demanding political reforms and employment opportunities. Intent on avoiding a direct confrontation with the masses, he initiated symbolic but seemingly consequential reforms, notably a restructuring of the cabinet, firing the Inspector General of the Police and Customs Lieutenant General Malik bin Suleiman Al Maamary, and ceding some legislative and regulatory powers to the largely elected Council of Oman. These measures, coupled with development aid from the GCC, and reportedly the imprisonment and intimidation of many opposition activists and leaders, enabled him to head off an all-out revolution, at least for now, but in the absence of a clear heir, Oman faces a potentially catastrophic succession problem in the near future (Human Rights Watch 2013; Reuters 2012).

But more heterogeneous societies such as Bahrain, Saudi Arabia and to a certain degree Kuwait are simmering with domestic discontent. Bahrain remains the most volatile monarchy among GCC members. The opposition forces, led by the Al-Wefaq movement and guided by top Shia clerics, consistently presented the uprising as the continuation of decade-long legitimate demands for a constitutional monarchy, whereby the Shia majority could also enjoy equal rights of citizenship. A combination of Western acquiescence and tacit GCC security and financial support, however, consistently strengthened the hand of hardliners – the so-called triumvirate of Prime Minister Khalifa bin Salman, Royal Court Minister Khalid bin Ahmad bin Salman al-Khalifa and the commander of the Bahrain Defence Forces, Khalifa bin Ahmed al-Khalifa – calling for a heavy crackdown and open confrontation at the expense of so-called reformers such as Crown Prince Salman, and to a certain degree King Hamad himself. This was precisely why repeated attempts by the king to appease the protesters failed to bear fruit: promises of a national dialogue with the opposition forces, amending the constitution to empower the Shura Council and parliament, ensuring accountability for security forces responsible for the death, torture and injury of protesters, and instituting necessary political reforms, precipitously gave way to an uncompromising, maximalist position by the ruling establishment. What followed was a further brutal crackdown on not only protesters but also medical personnel who came their rescue, and total obliteration of the Pearl Roundabout, Bahrain's version of Tahrir Square (Wehrey 2012). In addition, in an attempt to discredit the uprising and justify further suppression, the authorities upped the ante by accusing the opposition of conniving with Iran, despite repeated protests by prominent opposition leaders such as Sheikh Ali Salem against Iranian interference. Later, the King Hamad-appointed Bahrain Independent Commission for Inquiry itself cleared the protesters of any involvement with Iran (Farhi 2012). Instead of pondering real dialogue and compromise after a string of bloody crackdowns, sparking unrelenting and ever-growing protests, the authorities reportedly revoked the citizenship of thirty-one activists, destroyed Shia mosques, with security forces said to have shot dead a teenager during the second anniversary of the Bahraini uprisings (Reuters

2013a), and imprisoned prominent opposition leaders such as Said Yousif Al-Muhafdha and Nabeel Rajab (Bahrain Centre for Human Rights 2013), while others such as Abdulhadi Al-Khawaja and his daughter Zainab al-Khawaja are on hunger strike (El-Dahshan 2013). In short, the GCC counter-revolution encouraged a maximalist position on the part of the ruling establishment, under the guidance of hardliners, which, in turn, has increasingly radicalized the opposition forces – all to the detriment of the country itself. With so much blood spilled, with hawks still in power, it is far from clear whether the new rounds of national dialogue, and the appointment of reformer Prince Salman to the position of deputy prime minister, will lead to a positive change (Abdo 2013).

Similar to Bahrain, Kuwait has also been among the more liberal monarchies within the GCC, known for its age-old civic activism and relatively open politics and sociocultural life. Just as in Bahrain, social movements advocating political reform and state accountability pre-dated the Arab Spring. Yet the country, increasingly since its liberation from Iraqi occupation in 1991, has splintered along social classes and generational lines. Aside from an intensifying struggle between the traditional (pre-oil-era) liberal-urban elite (*hadhar*) and the post-oil-boom Bedouin-conservative tribal population (*badu*) over parliamentary seats, a youthful generation of tech-savvy and cosmopolitan individuals, highly critical of gerrymandering and bureaucratic red tape, also gave birth to the so-called 'Orange Movement' in 2006. These changes gradually reconfigured the balance of power between the ruling family and the executive cabinet, on one hand, and the elected parliament, on the other. What followed, after decisive gains by opposition elements within the parliament, was heightened bickering between the two poles, which, in turn, produced political paralysis, indecisive elections, cabinet reshuffles and delays in developmental projects, while the rest of the GCC moved ahead with mind-boggling infrastructure projects at a numbing speed. The Arab Spring played into this explosive chemistry, inspiring the opposition to push the boundaries of politics and more openly challenge the *ancien régime*. In the February 2012 elections, the opposition managed to score a landslide victory, winning 34 out of 50 parliamentary seats. Soon, a refurbished conservative bloc within the parliament were advocating measures that threatened the generally liberal sociocultural state of affairs in the country, while the showdown between the ruling establishment and opposition representatives intensified. Then the Emir of Kuwait, Sheikh Sabah Al-Sabah, took the unprecedented step of activating Article 106 of the constitution in June, suspending the National Assembly for a month. This was followed by the Constitutional Court's more draconian decision to dissolve the parliament and reinstate the previous assembly. The country was plunged into all-out crisis, prompting massive protests met by teargas and rubber bullets, the forcible occupation of parliament by protesters, and the boycott of parliamentary elections by opposition forces composed of Islamists, liberals and Bedouins (bringing total turnout from 59 per cent in February down to 40 per cent in December), with the Orange Movement – carrying slogans bearing the caption 'national dignity' – at the centre of unprecedented rallies calling for a constitutional monarchy and a parliament-designated government (Ulrichsen 2012; Economist 2012b). The Shia bloc, in contrast, participated in the elections, winning 17 out of 50 parliamentary seats – their best-ever electoral performance. However, while the Shia groups managed to more accurately reflect the country's 30 per cent Shia population in the parliamentary balance of forces, they risked further estrangement vis-à-vis the opposition, especially the Islamist groups, which have not only stood by the Saudi-Bahraini leaderships' response to the Shia-led protests, but have also advocated measures (such as toughening the anti-blasphemy law) that could marginalize the Kuwaiti Shia population. In short, the country is stuck in a grinding deadlock, increasingly polarized along ideological, sectarian and even class-based lines (Economist 2012b).

While in Kuwait and Bahrain the pro-democracy movements have advocated pushing the boundaries of and actualizing the earlier reform initiatives, especially those in the last two decades, Saudi Arabia stands as a unique case of double suppression of the Shia minority and the liberal-democratic forces. Despite certain efforts by King Abdullah to introduce some reforms, notably the appointment of women to the Shura Council, the introduction of municipal council elections, establishment and expansion of so-called 'liberal enclaves' (especially in and around university campuses), the country is, even by regional standards, a highly conservative society, with an absolute monarchy, in tandem with puritan Wahhabi religious authorities, denying civil liberties and basic political rights enjoyed by citizens of Arab countries such as Lebanon and other neighbours such as Turkey and Iran (think of female employment, females being allowed to drive and election of parliamentarians). Aside from growing signs of civic activism in places such as Riyadh, with democratic opposition forces staging unprecedented protests in front of government offices, the situation of the Shia population, located in the oil-rich Eastern Province, has become particularly explosive. The Shia community is seen as a heretical population by the strict Wahhabi establishment. Often, they have also been accused of serving as Iran's 'fifth column'. The fact that the bulk of Saudi Arabia's oil facilities and reserves are located in Shia-populated regions hardly allays the ruling family's suspicions and anxieties. Facing tremendous suppression and economic marginalization, and inspired by the Arab Spring and the largely Shia uprising in neighbouring Bahrain, sporadic protests by Shia citizens have rocked the Eastern Province, with the governorate of Al-Qatif serving as a flashpoint of confrontations between protesters and security forces, often ending in deaths and injuries on both sides. In addition to the deaths of at least sixteen individuals due to a heavy-handed security crackdown on a gathering storm of protests since 2011, the calls by a Saudi prosecutor for 'death by crucifixion' of prominent Shia cleric Sheikh Nimr al-Nimr, whose arrest in July 2012 sparked massive protests, threatens further estrangement between the monarchy and the Shia community (PressTV 2013). In light of the festering security situation in the Eastern Province, King Abdullah went so far as to sack Prince Mohamad bin Fahad bin Abdulaziz in favour of Prince Saud bin Nayef bin Abdulaziz in January 2013. Given the ongoing jostling over succession with the death of Crown Prince Nayef bin Abdul Aziz Al Saud and uncertainties over the health of his successor, Deputy Prime Minister Prince Salman, the decision to replace the governorship of the restive province carried additional political significance. Amid a flurry of speculation about the ongoing deliberations over the issue of succession, King Abdullah's decision to appoint his adviser Muqrin bin Abdulaziz as the second deputy prime minister has prompted some analysts to suspect that the current king is actually positioning his own son Mutaib by elevating a supposedly pliable ally in Muqrin (Al-Akhbar 2013). What one increasingly sees in Saudi Arabia is a combination of growing protests in Shia-populated regions, audacious expressions of discontent by liberal intelligentsia and pro-democratic groups, and an unprecedented succession dilemma, which is consuming the royal court. Meanwhile, the harsh sentencing of Abdullah al-Hamed and Mohammed Fahad al-Qahtani, founding members of the now-banned Saudi Civil and Political Rights Association, in March 2013, underscored the resistance to any form of dissent (Al-Omran 2013). Given growing tensions with Iran over the nuclear issue, and to a certain degree Syria and Bahrain, and an increasingly unsustainable spending spree to appease allies at home and in the West, the kingdom could be more than at any time in its modern history ripe for upheaval. In short, neither compromise nor democratic reform is on the cards.

Petropolitics and the bogeyman The year 2011 marked a precarious resurgence in popular protests against autocratic states, but it also represented a period of intensified conflict between Iran and the West over the nuclear issue. When the Arab Spring hit Libya, forcing the North African state to halt its energy exports, the world's attention suddenly focused on Saudi Arabia's spare capacity – and its ability to fill the vacuum. With the introduction of unilateral, debilitating sanctions against Iran's hydrocarbon and financial sectors in late 2011, the West required not only the political support of GCC states, but also a coordinated effort to avoid a global energy crisis, especially amid a weak global economic recovery, as a result of shutting out the OPEC's second-largest exporter, Iran. Saudi Arabia tapped into its spare capacity, increasing its total output to compensate for the Iranian oil loss in global markets, while other GCC states such as Qatar and the UAE stepped up their energy deals and investments with top Asian customers such as Japan, South Korea, Turkey, India and China. This allowed GCC members to increase their market shares and more importantly isolate Iran even further. Such efforts – combined with an increase in North America's hydrocarbon output as well as global non-conventional oil production – prevented an all-out panic in global energy markets, facilitating large-scale hydrocarbon divestments against Iran and an almost 50 per cent collapse in its oil exports within a year or so (EIA 2013). So when Iran, in response to what it perceived as an 'act of economic warfare', threatened to close the Strait of Hormuz, through which almost a third of global seaborne oil passes daily, the USA lavished even more military assistance on GCC allies, while increasing its own footprint in the region: moving a squadron of F-22 fighters to the UAE, positioning the large floating base USS *Ponce*, deploying a second aircraft carrier and a Sea Fox undersea drone, and stepping up multinational minesweeping exercises, among other things – all supposedly to ensure 'security of supply' in the region (Jones 2012).

Looking at Iran's actual capabilities and military spending, the sheer degree of the US military presence and the GCC arms build-up borders on hysteria. Back in the 1970s as much as 80 per cent of total oil revenues went into arms purchases, military expenditure and conflicts. The oil crisis in the 1980s encouraged the GCC states, in the first decade of the twenty-first century, to invest up to 70 per cent of their revenues in debt payments and savings, shoring up their sovereign wealth fund (Sharma 2011: 217). By 2012, however, the GCC states were expected to spend as much as $123 billion on arms purchases over a five-year period (UPI 2013). In terms of percentage of GDP, the GCC is the world's most profligate military spender, with Saudi Arabia allocating as much as 10 per cent of its GDP to military expenditure, compared with a 2.4 per cent global average. In contrast, Iran's military – composed of largely Cold War-era technology and relics of pre-revolutionary hardware – has barely spent beyond $10 billion annually in recent years, hardly above 3 per cent of its GDP (SIPRI 2010; Greenwald 2012).

Yet despite Iran's brewing economic crisis, and indisputable conventional military inferiority, as a result of the sanctions, the West was also worried about the implications of the collapse of the Mubarak and Ben Ali regimes, which provided a historic opening for Iran to reach out to new post-revolutionary regimes. Overall, an almost obsessive pursuit of containment of Iran provided a perfect strategic pretext for the GCC to silence domestic opposition and target unsavoury Arab states, namely Libya and Syria. Arab monarchies continuously used the 'Iran card' – a systematic exaggeration of Iran's supposedly destabilizing/hegemonic plans in the Persian Gulf to justify external support – in order to discourage Western pressure, ensure unflinching support and tighten the screw against Iran. Domestically, the GCC states never stopped using Iran as a bogeyman to intimidate and discredit genuine democratic uprisings, especially in Bahrain and Saudi Arabia. Since the Arab Spring, Iran has been accused of staging unrest and coups by Bahrain and Saudi Arabia, with early 2013 witnessing the arrest of sixteen Saudis, as well as Iranian and Lebanese, on grounds of espionage. In response, Shia clerics in Saudi Arabia and the Al-Wefaq group in Bahrain have denounced such allegations as a pretext to discredit the opposition (Spyer 2013).

'Arab Gulf monarchs have summoned the specter of an Iranian threat ever since the 1979 Islamic Revolution. Today, however, anti-Iranian hysteria is at an all-time high, whipped up by Iran's perceived strategic benefit from the toppling of Saddam Hussein, the rise of Shia Islamist parties to power in post-Saddam Iraq, Iran's posture of "resistance" during Israel's wars on Lebanon and Gaza, and now the Arab revolts,' lamented Toby Jones (2012) of the Middle East Research and Information project, arguing that the USA's obsession with containing Iran encouraged the GCC to behave badly and step up violence against protesters. 'Here, the Gulf regimes appear to have calculated correctly, for to date Washington has paid far more attention to Iranian maneuvering, real and imagined, than to the excessive force used to grind down pro-democracy and human rights activists on the Arab side of the Gulf.'

In similar vein, Diamond (2010: 99), shortly before the Arab Spring, aptly identified the two key pillars of Arab authoritarianism: 'the patterns and institutions by which authoritarian regimes manage their politics and keep their hold on power, along with the external forces that help to sustain their rule. These authoritarian structures and practices are not unique to the Arab world, but Arab rulers have raised them to a high pitch of refinement, and wield them with unusual skill.'

The Arab Spring reprocessed Aside from suppression at home, aided by external support and internal finances, one of the GCC's – namely

Saudi Arabia and Qatar – most powerful weapons against the Arab Spring was (and continues to be) their decision and ability to re-direct the course of the uprisings – a phenomenon that gathered momentum in Libya, deepened in the case of Yemen, but reached its peak in Syria.

With the decline of Egypt into post-revolutionary mayhem, the GCC, especially Saudi Arabia, Qatar and to a certain degree the UAE, have become major voices within the Arab League, setting the regional agenda with unprecedented traction and ferocity, actualizing a NATO-led military intervention in Libya, while espousing an Arab–NATO military campaign in Syria.

Other post-revolutionary Arab states, namely Egypt and Tunisia, have also been in the cross hairs of the GCC, while Jordan and Morocco have moved ever closer to the GCC orbit. If there was one thing the GCC learned from Brazilian footballers it is this: the best defence is offence. They did not settle for just containing uprisings at home. Instead, they took the battle back to unfriendly sultanistic regimes – and also to the so-called axis of resistance, or the Shia crescent.

7 | PEERING INTO THE ABYSS: THE ARAB SPRING AT THE CROSSROADS

> We must accept finite disappointment, but never lose infinite hope. (Martin Luther King, Jr)[1]

After a few hopeful months of revolutionary idealism, the Arab Spring met not only a fierce countervailing force, namely in the form of a determined and well-endowed grouping of absolute monarchies, but also demons from within. Long oppressed under the shadow of cruel, unapologetic autocrats, the spontaneous convergence among a vast array of opposition parties, mass movements and ordinary protesters, however, primarily focused on one concrete objective: toppling the figure on top. This was a period of savvy youngsters – consumed by a common passion for change – circumventing outdated modes of state censorship and propaganda. Yet, as soon as the autocrats were gone, the opposition forces and protesters, hailing from divergent ideological and organizational backgrounds, began turning on each other, providing a perfect opportunity for reactionary forces to sabotage and hijack the revolution.

For Professor Sheri Berman of Columbia University, the post-revolutionary chaos is in many ways a product of how autocrats in the past, lacking popular legitimacy, manipulated and deepened 'communal cleavages in order to divide potential opponents and generate support among [the] favored groups'. Given the lack of prior experience, he argues, of 'regular, peaceful articulation and organization of popular demands', initial democratic transition is characterized by the explosion of 'pent-up distrust and animosity', where citizens 'express their grievances in a volatile and disorganized way, through a dizzying array of parties, extremist rhetoric and behavior, and street protests and even battles' (Berman 2013).

Worryingly, the initially non-violent protests turned into a vicious cycle of violence, tribal warfare, sectarian tensions and civil war, most notably in Syria. As a result, many observers' attention, approaching the second anniversary of the uprisings, focused on risks and uncertainties rather than the contours of a supposedly Arab summer of democratic consolidation and economic recovery. Securing the gains of the revolution became a challenge amid the ensuing chaos, inspiring renewed bouts of anxiety. The global consultancy firm Eurasia Group, specifically looking into the Syrian conflict and the vagaries of post-revolutionary politics in places such as Egypt, identified the Arab Spring as the third-largest source of risk in 2013, echoing concerns with messy transitions and politico-economic regressions across the region (Bremmer 2013).

In a twisted turn of events, Arab spring optimists, notably former UN diplomat Jean-Marie Guéhenno, were proved right about one thing: that the uprisings were not a caricature of Facebook/Twitter-powered revolutions, copycatting Western liberal democracies à la 1989 collapse of the European communist states. The uprisings, instead, took on a unique character and trajectory by reflecting age-old wounds and the internal contradictions of the Arab world.

'There are no recent examples of extended power-sharing or peaceful transitions to democracy in the Arab world. When dictatorships crack, budding democracies are more than likely to be greeted by violence and paralysis,' Vali Nasr stated, presciently identifying dangers lurking in the uprisings in late 2011, warning about a new wave of conflicts and challenges ahead. 'Sectarian divisions ... will then emerge, as competing groups settle old scores and vie for power' (Nasr 2011).

Social networking sites, which were initially hailed (rather naively) as the precursor/progenitor of the uprisings, began to evince their dark side, morphing into a 'devolutionary' force undermining the Arab Spring. A general predilection for hyperbole – primarily to capture attention amid an overflowing stream of data – severely undercut the credibility of many social networking sites, which played a pivotal role during the initial days of protests, while allowing the authorities to co-opt the technology, sabotage opposition sites, and easily identify the sources of dissent as well as detect planned protest activities. Also, an obsession with instantaneous protests, sensationalism and leaderless mobilization diverted much-needed attention from the more methodical, time-consuming and patient game of investing in organizational capacity, party-building and political strategizing. This provided a perfect opportunity for organized Islamist groups to dominate the post-revolutionary electoral contest, which, in turn, brewed cynicism among more liberal and secular forces. Regrettably, many social networking sites collapsed into a polarizing, partisan and parochial platform, instead of fostering dialogue and political consensus within and across Arab states. Incitement to violence and divisive, sectarian discourse took over many social networking platforms, which enabled a swift spread of hatred amid the chaos of democratic transition and/or political upheaval in places such as Syria. For these reasons, Marc Lynch (2013) aptly underscored how technology is inherently a double-edged sword. For him, in the case of the Arab Spring, Facebook/Twitter, notwithstanding their initial positive role, assumed an increasingly negative role over time: 'The net effects of the empowerment of diverse voices and the free flow of information strike me as positive. But if we believe in the transformative power of these changes, we really cannot avoid considering the negatives alongside the positives. And the current state of the Arab revolutions offers us far too many negatives from which to choose.'

Yet it would be a mistake to look into the trajectory of the Arab Spring without taking into consideration the role of GCC powers, which waged a unified campaign to shape, contain and co-opt the Arab Spring – a project that took off among monarchies such as Bahrain, Oman, Morocco and Jordan, but intensified in Yemen, Libya and, most importantly, Syria. Organized and flushed with cash, Qatar and Saudi Arabia took the reins of the Arab League, filling in the political vacuum as a result of Mubarak's downfall and Egypt's descent into chaos. Through their sponsorship for a whole host of Salafi Islamist groups as well as mainstream Islamist groups, the GCC was able to increase its footprint across the Arab world, at the expense of the liberal-democratic forces as well as moderate Islamic factions. A huge cache of sovereign wealth funds (SWFs) also portended growing GCC leverage over Arab secular elements and Western powers. Meanwhile, in an attempt to reshape the regional balance of power, the GCC powers sponsored the armed rebels and extremist groups against Gaddafi and Assad, which, in turn, led to a regional sectarian conflict and the creation of new havens of terror across Levant and North Africa. Triumphant in the aftermath of the Egyptian revolution, Al Jazeera was also transformed into a powerful source of what some would term propaganda against Gaddafi and Assad, compromising its image and reputation as a source of unbiased and comprehensive coverage. Thus, the GCC diverted the winds of change and reshaped the course of the Arab Spring, hoping to avoid an upheaval at home.

Back to Year Zero

Libya's violent revolution was a testament to how the Arab Spring spelled the death of fear for millions of emboldened Libyans, who felt that enough was enough.[2] The more force the regime used, the more determined were the protesters. When Libya reached the tipping point of revolution, no amount of violence could contain the raging torrent. Ironically, what spelled the Libyan regime's end was the very thing that sustained it for decades: indiscriminate use of brutal force, which galvanized the international community in the wake of an impending humanitarian crisis as Gaddafi's forces closed in on Benghazi in mid-2011, threatening to eliminate all traces of resistance and opposition. This was the beginning of the end for Gaddafi.

UN Security Council (UNSC) Resolution 1970, condemning the use of violence by Gaddafi forces, was a crucial precursor to an eventual humanitarian intervention in Libya. It directly held the leadership accountable, referring the case to the International Court of Justice (ICJ), while imposing sanctions – from an asset freeze to travel bans – against prominent leaders within the Libyan regime. It was the first critical step in mobilizing the international community against the Libyan leadership. Crucially, the resolution garnered unanimous support among neighbouring countries as well as global powers. The subsequent approval and implementation of UNSC Resolution 1973 marked a decisive shift on two critical levels: first, the resolution was a landmark event in the sense that it secured the acquiescence of Russia, China and many of the world's emerging powers; and secondly, more interestingly, it also enjoyed significant support from regional actors, especially the Arab League, now led by the trio of Qatar, Saudi Arabia and to a certain degree the UAE. With post-revolutionary Egypt and Turkey on board, the GCC played a crucial role in instigating, facilitating and implementing the imposition of a 'no-fly zone'.[3] In parallel, the Arab League's suspension of Libya and unequivocal condemnation of state-sponsored use of systemic violence and commitment of mass atrocities paved the way for a decisive and 'muscular' international response to the ongoing civil war in Libya.

There were several factors that encouraged such an uncharacteristic move by the Arab League. First of all, there was no love lost between Libya and the GCC states. Gaddafi's flamboyant disregard of and disrespect for other Arab leaders, and intermittent intransigence, especially against Arab monarchies, drove a wedge between the two sides[4] – a potential factor behind the Libyan strongman's greater interest in his role within the African Union rather than the Arab League. Also, with growing protests in other Arab countries, autocratic states were interested in focusing global attention on the Libyan revolution in an attempt to drive away 'international scrutiny' from the GCC intervention in Bahrain. Thirdly, the Arab countries were simply responding to the new mood created by the Arab Spring. On one hand, countries such as Qatar were interested in boosting their profile and appeal to the Arab street by aiding revolutionary brethren in Libya. Other Arab countries were also interested in showcasing their solidarity with the Libyan people in order to win more political points at home. Lastly, there were also pragmatic calculations at play. Although it would be utterly reductionist to see the Libyan intervention as motivated by a desire to lock up hydrocarbon resources, one could say that some Arab countries, such as Qatar, harboured long-term plans to establish strong business and political ties with the post-revolutionary order.

There were other immediate concerns too: the dangers of spillover. The Libyan revolution led to the growing displacement of people and a mass influx of refugees into neighbouring Egypt and Tunisia. Fragile in the wake of their revolutions, both countries were interested in avoiding a disastrous humanitarian crisis on their doorsteps. Chaos and an ongoing civil war in Libya could also mean a 'security vacuum', providing a safe haven for all sorts of agents saboteurs and extremist elements, who could threaten other Arab states. With all the international and regional powers, more or less, on board, the

NATO forces were able to decisively reverse the Libyan regime's military advance. As French warplanes and American warships pounded Libya's military installations, the downfall of the regime became once again a realistic prospect. After months of frustrating stalemates and intense military jostling, the rebels – under the supervision of the Benghazi-based National Transitional Council (NTC) – were able to eventually overrun the loyalists, and reclaim Tripoli. The imposition of the 'no-fly zone' not only prevented a possible massacre in Benghazi, but also spelled a critical shift in the military balance of opposing forces on the ground.

The 'no-fly zone', however, turned into an increasingly controversial undertaking, with critics pointing out that a predominantly Western military intervention was tarnishing a genuinely indigenous Libyan revolution, with imperial machinations and foreign interests looming large over Libya's precious hydrocarbon resources. The most damning criticism came from those who pointed out the intense escalation in casualties, infrastructural damage and overall destruction in the aftermath of the resolution's implementation. For them, the 'no-fly zone' simply worsened the vicious cycle of military confrontation between rebels and the regime.[5] Fundamentally, many individuals as well as nation-states, notably Russia, China and other emerging powers, vehemently censured the way NATO clearly went beyond its original mandate – supposedly confined to the imposition of a no-fly zone – by engaging in whole-scale military operations against the Libyan regime. NATO forces were not only protecting civilians, they argued, but also providing real-time intelligence, surveillance and logistical support to rebel forces, complemented by the presence of Western and Arab Special Forces and an extensive air and naval 'back-up' campaign by NATO. While Al Jazeera correspondents were embedded among rebel groups throughout the advances against Gaddafi forces, with the al-Thani family providing logistical, military and humanitarian support to rebel groups, the Qatari Special Forces were reportedly at the forefront of final advances against Gaddafi, giving the GCC powers their first taste of shaping the Arab Spring through hard power. When the Gaddafi regime fell, grateful Libyans visibly waved the Qatari flag side by side with the pre-Gaddafi Libyan flag and those of other NATO members (Roberts 2011).

Soon after Gaddafi's fall, the NTC took over and relocated its headquarters to Tripoli. Then came largely democratic elections, which favoured moderates and seculars over Islamists in the formation of the first elected government and the post-revolutionary constitution. Yet the country was far from a showcase of externally assisted Arab Spring. Within a year, it became clear that Libya was far from saved, despite a relatively speedy revival of the energy sector. The new leadership, among other things, failed to consolidate its power, refurbish institutions of state, create the appropriate conditions for a vibrant civil society, and rebuild a scared nation. Haunted by the horrors of the civil war, AQ-affiliated extremist groups, allegedly the Ansar al-Sharia, managed to target the American consulate and murder American ambassador Chris Stevens in Benghazi – a chilling reminder to the West of the lessons of blowback.[6] Despite an initial outcry against militias and attempts by the government to rein in extremist groups, a wobbly internal security apparatus prevented the Libyan leadership from decisively reining in Ansar al-Sharia and resolving a whole host of security challenges, including a potential backlash from Gaddafi loyalists, who have been incensed by the manner in which their previous leader was captured and killed by rebels, but also how they have been marginalized and targeted under the new system (Eljarh 2013). The inability of the elected Libyan government, so far, to disarm former rebels so as to form a national army, and rein in many reported cases of human rights violations, vengeance killings and wanton vigilantism by armed rebels, is another major problem. Adding to this was the potential resurgence of extremist elements, namely Al-Qaeda in the Islamic Maghreb (AQIM), that could exploit the security vacuum in the country, especially in light of the extremist insurgency in Mali and the ramifications for Algeria's volatile and hydrocarbon-rich southern territories. Another problem is the resurgence in secessionist sentiments, with a renewed sense of rivalry and conflict between Benghazi and Tripoli over the two fundamental issues of oil distribution and political autonomy/representation. Despite seculars' nominal ascendancy in the first elected parliament, the Islamist groups, including the Libyan Muslim Brotherhood, made significant strides in capacity-building, electoral campaigning and political messaging, with reports of Islamists even influencing the selection of the prime minister and the cabinet from behind the scenes (Fitzgerald 2013).

Overall, the country remains vulnerable to human rights violations and even mass atrocities, unless the new Libyan regime consolidates the democratic gains of the bloody and prolonged revolution. The country has one crucial advantage over other post-revolutionary Arab countries: its immense hydrocarbon wealth. But what is important is how the new regime can efficiently and expediently translate its fiscal capacity into institutional strength by delivering on its promises of security, social justice and speedy economic recovery.

The slow-motion death of a nation

In the wake of the Arab Spring, Syria seemed to be partially immune. The regime enjoyed a unique set of assets and favourable conditions, which could have – at least theoretically – prevented an outright popular revolution. For decades, the Syrian regime's pan-Arabist 'vanguardism' enjoyed particular prestige and support among the Arab constituency. The Syrian leader, Bashar Al-Assad, previously seen as a reformer, used to be called '*Mahboob*' (beloved) by the Syrian people, while enjoying the status of being among the most popular Arab leaders in the previous decade, especially for his pivotal role in the so-called Axis of Resistance. He also signalled a break from the past, beginning with his withdrawal from Lebanon after the 2005 Cedar Revolution, which carried some promise of favourable changes at home. The Syrian regime, in contrast to many of its Arab allies, was also effective in presenting itself as a bulwark of national unity, secularism and tolerance, despite the country's diverse sectarian make-up. Historically, Syria's quasi-socialist economic system, which outlasted most of its Arab peers, also created the conditions which prevented the emergence of the kind of abject and widespread poverty that characterized other Arab countries from Yemen to Egypt. A largely depoliticized civil society – in a state of hibernation – also increased the viability of a seemingly intact, entrenched and coherent police state. All these factors gave an impression that the regime could get its act together and prevent the kind of popular uprising which would turn out to be the bloodiest of all Arab Spring revolutions. Shockingly, the country has not only witnessed massive, passionate and sustained protests across the nation, but it has also gradually moved towards a state of civil war and internal disintegration (International Crisis Group 2011).

The original sin What began as largely peaceful protests advocating political rights and a democratic opening evolved into a full-scale civil war, threatening to tear the rich tapestry of the Syrian nation apart, mainly because of the regime's violent crackdown and sheer incompetence: it severely mishandled protests, using excessive force instead of genuine political dialogue to enable gradual but irreversible reforms. It all stemmed from the regime's basic misreading of the situation as a temporary noise, which could be silenced by business-as-usual intimidation tactics. It was precisely this inflexibility and hubris which contributed to the intensification and militarization of popular uprisings across the country, while structural preconditions (i.e. economic stagnation and political ossification) provided the foundation upon which protests were envisioned, mobilized and strengthened over time. Assad initially introduced some cabinet reshuffles, and hinted at a national dialogue with opposition groups, but without (a) halting the campaign of intimidation and (b) reaching out to the broader spectrum of the opposition, meaning there was little chance of any breakthrough. By imposing an information blackout, the regime sought to avoid the watchful gaze of the international community, while its dismissal of mass opposition forces as 'terrorists' and traitors was a calculated move to discredit legitimate calls for a political opening. The bombardment and constant shelling of Homs in early 2012, widely covered by international media, arguably constituted the beginning of Assad's regional and international isolation, forcing the likes of Russia and China to come to his rescue in full force. When the uprisings spread to northern areas, encompassing large swathes of Aleppo, Syria's commercial hub, and border towns with Turkey (and later with Jordan in the east), the regime reportedly resorted to aerial attacks and massive bombardments to deny strategic gains to the rebels (International Crisis Group 2012a).

In response to the regime's blanket use of military force, the so-called Free Syrian Army (FSA) – initially a small group of army defectors mainly sponsored by the Sunni powers of Turkey, Qatar and Saudi Arabia – hand in hand with elements within the exiled opposition, called for external intervention (i.e. the imposition of a 'no-fly zone' in rebel-captured and/or border areas) and espoused an armed rebellion. Soon, the FSA evolved into a loose collection of volunteer, multi-ethnic armed brigades, largely composed of Sunni personnel. Within the first year, the rebels were hammered by the regime's decisive superiority in conventional weaponry. But as the conflict dragged on, AQ-affiliated groups, notably the veterans of the Sunni insurgency against the US and Shia leadership in Iraq, as well as other Salafi radical groups, joined the armed uprising against what they perceived as an 'infidel' Baathist regime. First came a string of bombings in Damascus in late 2011, leading to the death of dozens of innocent civilians. But the decisive operational and psychological blow to the regime came in mid-2012, with the assassination of Syria's top security officials, notably defence minister Dawoud Rajha and his deputy, Assef Shawkat (Assad's brother-in-law), which precipitated high-profile defections within the Syrian regime, beginning with various top diplomats across the Arab world and the West, followed by Brigadier General Manaf Tlass, Prime Minister Riad Hijab (August 2012), and most recently Brigadier General Mohammed Nour Ezzedeen Khallouf (March 2013), the army's chief of supplies and logistics, prompting Assad to desperately plead for support, most especially from emerging powers (Barnard 2013). Radical extremists fought alongside and infiltrated the FSA, with groups such as Jubat al-Nusra emerging as the most lethal enemies of the regime. Popular and effective, the radical groups attracted more volunteers and began sidelining more secular elements within the FSA, while imposing sharia in areas under their control. What followed was a series of massacres and brutal acts against supposed regime sympathizers in areas under the rebels' control (International Crisis Group 2012b). As a result, the regime was able to cash in on sectarian fears among varying minority groups such as Christians and Alawites, which stood by the regime, fearing the emergence of a Sunni-dominated sectarian regime, while the Kurdish groups in the oil-rich north-eastern regions tried to distance themselves from the uprisings in a bid to optimize a historic chance of self-autonomy, notwithstanding reports of tactical coordination between FSA and Kurdish factions.

Eventually, rebel factions turned on each other, with the two most prominent groups, the moderately Islamist Farouq Brigade and the radical Jubhat al-Nusra, engaging in open warfare (Kotsev 2013). Suddenly, it became a battle within the Syrian uprisings, portending a potentially disastrous post-Assad situation. In order to consolidate their operational gains, coordinate their efforts and sideline radical elements to secure financing and logistical support from abroad, in December 2012 the more moderate rebel factions formed a bottom-up Supreme Military Command (SMC), a thirty-member unified command structure composed of the top field commanders, tasked with syncing the FSA's macro-operations (O'Bagy 2013).

Meanwhile, both the civilian opposition and the international community failed to arrive at a consensus on how to move forward, as the uprisings transformed into a conflict moving according to its own logic. In the absence of a coherent, legitimate and effective civilian opposition, the military stalemate dragged on, with armed rebels actually determining the course of the revolution.

When all fall down Facing a humanitarian tragedy of historical proportions, with more than 90,000 people killed, 4 million people internally displaced, and more than a million registered Syrian refugees, neither the Syrian opposition nor the international community got its act together (Al Jazeera 2013). As the conflict dragged on, the case of intervention in Libya (and its chaotic aftermath), instead of serving as a strong precedent, injected a deep sense of isolationism in Washington and elsewhere, and emboldened Syrian allies to block any sort of intervention on the grounds that it could be again stretched into a regime-change campaign by NATO. Lacking the hydrocarbon riches of Libya, enjoying external support, and having a more powerful military, the Syrian regime was in every respect a whole new ball game for the West, discouraging any form of overt military intervention.

Interestingly, the main proponent of intervention was the GCC, especially Qatar. In September 2012, Qatar's Emir Sheikh Hamad bin Khalifa Al Thani called for a 'boots on the ground' Arab military intervention in Syria, stating: 'It is better for the Arab countries themselves to interfere out of their national, humanitarian, political and military duties, and to do what is necessary to stop the bloodshed in Syria' (Lynch and Gearan 2012). The following year, when Qatar hosted the Arab League in March, Qatar's prime minister and foreign minister, Sheikh Hamad bin Jassim Al Thani, called for an Arab league 'to preserve security'. Of course, Turkey's calls for a NATO-led imposition of a no-fly zone reinforced attempts at organizing a regional 'solution' (Reuters 2013b).

While a military intervention faces many obstacles, reports suggest that the GCC powers and Turkey, along with the CIA, have been the backbone of the armed rebellion, providing much-needed ammunition, logistics, intelligence and training. Reportedly, through Jordan and Turkey, the Sunni powers were also able to facilitate the defection of top regime insiders and supply increasingly advanced armaments such as Rak-12, especially from Croatia, which tipped the balance of power increasingly in favour of the rebels in early 2013. For years, the FSA had desperately sought a range of advanced weaponry (e.g. anti-aircraft weapons such as the 9K38 Igla, 122 mm and 120 mm guns, as well as guided mortar rounds, anti-tank guided missiles and RPG 29s, etc.) to neutralize the regime's military edge.[7] Fearing that the weapons could end up in the hands of the wrong people, the West officially restricted itself to non-lethal aid, despite a push within Washington as well as Britain and France to arm the rebels, while stealthily the CIA undertook a vetting process to ensure that what weapons were supplied went to the more moderate elements (Chivers and Schmitt 2013; Hudson 2013a). But by mid-2013, the Obama administration had succumbed to growing pressure for intervention. Immediately after the high-profile defeat of rebel forces by the Assad regime and Hezbollah fighters in the strategic town of Qusayr on the Lebanon–Syria border, which was swiftly accompanied by the ascent of 'liberal hawks' Susan Rice (now National Security Advisor) and Samantha Power (now US ambassador to the UN), Washington agreed to provide arms to the rebels, but stopped short of a more overt military intervention, owing primarily to the reluctance of the defence establishment (Lubold 2013). Most likely, the decision will either deepen the military stalemate and/or slowly propel Washington towards direct intervention – undermining hopes for a peaceful settlement any time soon.

Beyond the FSA, Qatar is said to have been influential owing to its ties with the Syrian Muslim Brotherhood, the major force within the Syrian opposition and the leading opponent of the Assad regime for decades[8] (Daily Star 2013). Facing tremendous internal divisions, the exiled opposition has been greatly dependent on external support to retain some degree of relevance and political life. When the Syrian National Council (SNC), supposedly an amalgamation of various opposition elements, failed to secure institutional supervision over the FSA, and suffered internal fragmentation owing to policy disagreements over the issue of external intervention, in late 2012 Qatar and the USA facilitated the creation of a broader umbrella opposition group, the National Coalition for Syrian Revolutionary and Opposition Forces, with moderate Islamist Moaz al-Khatib elected as its leader. In this sense, Qatar and the USA arrived at an agreement to dispel concerns regarding the lack of representation as well as the dominance of the Syrian Brotherhood. The FSA and various opposition factions largely welcomed al-Khatib, but his subsequent attempt in February 2013 to negotiate the peaceful exit of Assad, with Vice-President Farouk Al-Sharaa as a transition leader, failed to gain traction. In retrospect, his effort to secure a peaceful, political solution suffered a similar fate as earlier attempts, notably those by UN special envoy Kofi Annan, and later Lakhdar Brahimi, as well as Syrian deputy prime minister Qadri Jamil, who reportedly sought to negotiate the exit of Assad with Russian help in August 2012. With so much blood spilled on the soil of Syria, compounded by a proxy war among external powers supporting opposing sides, every attempt at political compromise was vetoed by hardliners on both sides arguing that victory was in reach. Indignant at constant meddling and lack of concrete support from external powers, al-Khatib offered his resignation in March 2013, shortly after the election of Texas-based business executive Ghassan Hitto as interim prime minister of the Syrian government in exile – a man said to have close ties with both Qatar and the Brotherhood[9] (Chulov 2013). With continuous infighting within the opposition and the UNSC, the war on the ground pushed forward, further tearing down the fabric of the Syrian nation, with no end to violence in sight – even when Assad falls/abdicates.

The reign of terror

The military intervention in Libya and the disintegration of Syria into a vicious battlefield – pitting various local and international interests against each other – have created new havens of terror and instability at the heart of the Middle East. By some estimates, up to 10 per cent of rebels in Syria are composed of foreign jihadi fighters, including the oft-mentioned Phoenix native Eric Harroun (Hudson 2013b). They share one mission: toppling Assad and confronting the so-called Shia crescent, a vast collection of peoples belonging to the minority Muslim sect. In this regard, recent years in particular have witnessed a spike in extremist attacks against Shia minorities across the greater Middle East, ranging from eastern Afghanistan and Pakistan all the way to Bahrain, Yemen, Syria and Lebanon – resembling the vicious cycle of sectarian war in post-Saddam Iraq, which has entered a new stage of confrontation during Nouri al-Malaki's second term (Murphy 2013).

Baghdad has been particularly alarmed by the Syrian crisis, and the impending downfall of Assad, precisely because the Shia leadership – supported by Iran – is facing a concerted Sunni opposition, backed by the GCC. Even Iran, the most powerful Shia-led power, has experienced an upswing in its domestic Sunni insurgency, especially in the Sistan-Baluchistan province, claiming the lives of top Revolutionary Guards in recent years. An intensifying Sunni–Shia rivalry has also affected the Kurdish minority, with various Kurdish factions in Iraq and Syria adopting opposing patrons and allies, some in Tehran and Damascus, others in Ankara and the GCC. The sectarian flames have also undermined Iran's attempts to build enduring alliances with post-revolutionary, populist leaderships in places such as Egypt, while Tehran–Ankara ties have been severely undercut by growing disagreements over the Syrian crisis, as well as factional wars within Iraq's political system.

In addition to a pan-regional slide towards sectarian warfare, the Syrian refugee crisis is placing tremendous pressure on the finite resources of already fragile neighbouring countries, raising the possibility of a new civil war and/or political upheaval. Jordan, where half of the population is of Palestinian origin, suffered a bloody civil war in 1970 as a result of a power struggle between the Palestinian and the indigenous leadership. Shortly after the deportation of the Palestinian leadership from Jordan, the Palestinian refugee crisis spilled over into Lebanon, precipitating a decades-long civil war among various factions. No wonder both Amman and Beirut, in recent months, have constantly begged for regional and international support to avoid an explosive demographic challenge, especially given the dearth of global funding to cope with the humanitarian crisis. Facing threats of reprisal from Damascus in response to (a) the entry of rebels through Lebanese territories and (b) the pro-opposition stance of Major General Ashraf Rifi, head of Lebanon's internal security forces, a heated disagreement erupted between Lebanon's consensus leader, Prime Minister Najib Mikati, and the powerful Hezbollah group, which, in turn, led to the collapse of the government in March 2013, plunging the country into ever greater uncertainty (Kenner 2013). In Jordan, King Abdullah – facing a rising tide of discontent and an influential Jordanian Muslim Brotherhood – was forced to consider a $2 billion conditional IMF loan – imposing policies similar to those that have left Jordan and other Arab states in a development debacle – and a new oil deal with Iraq's Shia leadership, allowing Amman to simultaneously rein in a fuel crisis as well as pressure the GCC to honour its earlier financial pledges lest Jordan fall into Iraq's embrace (Sky 2013). In addition to cabinet reshuffles, the incarceration of former Jordan intelligence chief Mohammad al-Dahabi on charges of corruption, and the firing of prime minister Marouf al-Bakhit at the onset of the Arab Spring, the Hashemite kingdom stepped up its 'reform game' to appease external critics and project democratic reform. In January 2013, Jordan undertook supposedly game-changing parliamentary elections, which (theoretically) would give birth to a new government and prime minster elected in consultation with (but not directly appointed by) the king. The problem was that the elections were boycotted by the opposition, who claimed that amendments to the electoral law were not sufficient to redress a highly skewed electoral landscape, which has favoured regime supporters such as tribal leaders at the expense of legitimate opposition parties in recent decades. Moreover, the 'newly elected prime minister' saw the reinstallation of Abdullah an-Nsour, who has occupied the post since his appointment by the king in October 2012, making him the fifth and sixth post-Arab Spring prime minister (Abu-Rish 2013). In Morocco, the monarchy, despite symbolic reforms such as apologizing for the crimes of its predecessors, intelligently placed itself above the fray by injecting the PJD into the heart of the country's structural economic and political issues, conveniently shifting the blame to the Islamist prime minister whenever problems arise.

Despite an almost universal outcry against IFIs, populist Islamist parties across the Arab world have, as in Jordan, considered IMF loans, which obviously accompany a package of neoliberal reforms, focused on privatization and rolling back of state subsidies. While Morocco's PJD negotiated a $6.2 billion liquidity line from the IMF to cope with the country's myriad economic challenges, both Ennahda in Tunisia and FJP in Egypt have considered $1.78 and $4.8 billion loans from the same IFI, respectively. The controversial loans come amid an impending current account crisis in Egypt, which is threatening the import of food and other basic commodities, while Tunisia struggles to create enough jobs and growth to keep protesters at bay, and maintain a fragile coalition government in power. Continuing uncertainties in the Eurozone, traditionally the Arab world's top trading partner, have placed growing pressure on exporters, tourism, real estate and other sectors dependent on European capital, tourists and investments. An indecisive election in Italy, coupled with a new banking crisis in Cyprus, have done little to raise business confidence and sovereign credit rating among troubled economies, placing more pressure on countries such as Germany, currently in the middle of crucial elections, to expand the increasingly unsustainable rescue packages in place.

Yet the economic troubles of ATCs also have a lot to do with political troubles at home. What we witness in places such as Egypt and Tunisia could be surmised as examples of 'majoritarian democracy and its discontents': plurality-based ruling Islamist parties enjoying momentary dominance in the parliament and the executive office, but lacking enough mandate and political capital to effectively govern. This problem is particularly acute in the case of Egypt, where President Morsi and the Muslim Brotherhood astutely outmanoeuvred both the liberal opposition and the military to consolidate control over the interior ministry, parliament and the state media, while playing a decisive role in drafting the post-revolutionary constitution. In a country beset by rumours of coups and sabotage, there isn't much trust to go around. So when Morsi – claiming that he was simply pre-empting his opponents – pushed for seemingly authoritarian measures, ranging from decrees invoking presidential immunity from judicial prosecution to mass appointment of allies to top state positions, there was an unprecedented backlash, prompting massive protests organized by an increasingly unified and determined opposition under the guidance of the NSF. Caught in the middle, the Egyptian military has so far prioritized national security, often toeing Morsi's line.

Aside from securing the 'tactical' support of the armed forces, the Brotherhood – after displaying considerable pragmatism in its foreign policy – also enjoys a measure of support from external powers, including Washington and the GCC. While Washington has banked on Morsi's support to retain the Israeli–Arab status quo, the GCC states have lavished financial assistance on Cairo to gain leverage over the Brotherhood, especially in light of Iran's overtures towards the new Egypt. Realizing the strategic significance of aiding democratic reforms in the Arab world, the Group of 8 (G8) pledged around $80 billion in assistance in 2011 (Basheer 2011). Emerging powers, namely Brazil, Russia, China, Turkey, Indonesia, South Africa and India, hardly made any substantial commitments. The May 2011 Deauville meeting, which pledged $40 million in aid, was a purely Western event. However, as the economic woes of the West continued, and the Arab world plunged into renewed uncertainty, the $80 billion pledge largely failed to materialize. Ironically, much of the development assistance – supposedly for smooth and managed democratic transition – is coming from the GCC. For Egypt, in addition to $10 billion in investments, Qatar has offered $500 million in direct assistance, while the UAE and Saudi Arabia have offered $3 billion and $500 million in assistance, respectively (Reuters 2011b).

By early 2013, Qatar had become the largest source of soft loans and emergency cash deposits, amounting to $8 billion (ANSAMed.it 2013). With almost $2 trillion in SWFs, the GCC holds undisputed leverage over vulnerable Arab states as well as Western powers reeling

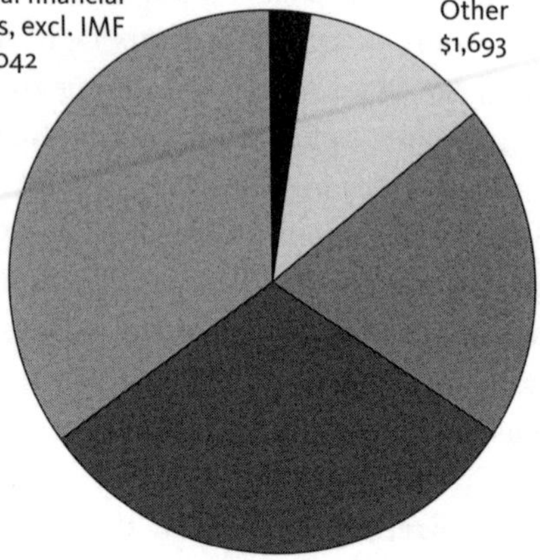

7.1 Breakdown of external aid to ATCs and Jordan (2012) (*source*: IMF 2012)

from domestic economic woes. With European banks deleveraging and bond markets shunning shaky ATCs, the post-revolutionary governments are increasingly dependent on IFIs and the GCC for external financing (see Figure 7.1).

But the GCC's influence isn't confined to its financial prowess. The emergence of Salafi-Wahhabi forces – who trace their ideological and financial roots to the GCC – is another factor that has affected the Arab Spring. After a long period of shunning elections and secular politics in favour of grassroots activities with an ultra-conservative agenda, the Salafi groups have joined the fray (McCants 2013). In Egypt, the Salafi groups constitute the second-largest parliamentary bloc, playing a decisive role in the drafting of the post-revolutionary constitution. In the absence of a working relationship between the Brotherhood and liberal opposition elements, the sheer dominance, both within elected institutions as well as civil society, of Salafi groups meant that they could swing the Muslim Brotherhood farther to the right in terms of legislation and actual policy implementation. As a result, the moderate political wing of the Muslim Brotherhood has increasingly lost influence to the more hardline organizational wing, which has espoused a much more doctrinaire Morsi presidency (McCants 2012). In Tunisia, the Ennahda party (a) supported measures directed at establishing a 'strong parliament' to prevent executive abuse, (b) blocked the integration of Salafi groups into the political process, and (c) sought the political support of liberal-secular coalition partners such as the Congress for the Republic (CPR) and the Democratic Forum for Labour and Liberties (Ettakatol) (Fish and Michel 2012; McCants 2012). But the Salafi groups have nonetheless stepped up their efforts to undermine both secular and moderate Islamist factions, culminating in the assassination of prominent secularist Shoukri Belaid in February 2013 by allegedly radical elements. Consequently, the ruling coalition collapsed, and massive protests erupted, with the country drenched in greater political and economic uncertainty (Aliriza 2013). Prior to the incident, Tunisia was already a site of growing political violence, featuring occasional clashes between the government and Salafi groups, Salafi attacks on the US embassy and alcohol sellers, and partisan confrontations between Islamists and secular groups such as the Tunisian General Labour Union (UGTT) (McCants 2012; Aliriza 2012). The post-Saleh Yemen, meanwhile, transformed into a fertile ground for extremism, with both AQ affiliates and Gulf-supported Salafi groups doing their share to block the emergence of a stable, secular democracy. Add to this the fact that the state, under the transitional leadership of President Abdu Rabu Mansour Hadi, despite his earlier successful operations against AQ-affiliated groups in Abiyan Province in 2012, is struggling to establish a unified chain of command among the heavily tribal security forces, and rein in secessionist sentiments, which threaten to cause Yemen to disintegrate (again).

'As I departed the Middle East after a month of travels, I reflected on how – for many of those living under the monarchies – the Arab Spring was not viewed as a movement toward greater freedom and democracy, but rather as the breakdown of society into violence and chaos,' Yale academic Emma Sky (2013) wrote two years into the Arab Spring, reflecting on Arab monarchies' ability to stave off similar democratic uprisings. As Sky intelligently observes, people across the kingdoms, from Saudi Arabia to Oman, and Jordan, were more concerned with corruption, transparency, jobs, income and good governance than political freedom. The horrors of the Libyan and Syrian revolutions may have played an important role in blunting an urge for outright democratic revolution – which may also explain why Algeria – recalling its bloody civil war in the 1990s – has also withstood the Arab Spring, so far, despite the lack of any substantial reform towards democracy and alleviation of massive youth unemployment.

The Arab uprising took a more dangerous turn when, a year into his presidency, Morsi managed to alienate all relevant domestic and international actors, culminating in massive rallies and a military coup that toppled his government in early July. His downfall was accomplished through the tactical alliance of the liberal opposition, the military, and external actors such as Saudi Arabia, which always harboured deep suspicion towards the Brotherhood and their designs in the Persian Gulf Sheikhdoms.

By refusing to sincerely engage the liberal opposition, Morsi managed to unify them, albeit momentarily, under the NSF. As opposition-led rallies intensified, Morsi faced greater political uncertainty, which in turn worsened the climate of economic insecurity. Given his weak, tentative hold on the security apparatus, especially the Interior Ministry, Morsi had little power to impose stability. Deadlock in negotiations with the IMF postponed the infusion of much-needed capital, adding further to declining investor confidence. A leadership change in Morsi's main external patron, Qatar, was far from reassuring.

Most importantly, from the perspective of the Egyptian military, which held a direct stake in the Egyptian economy, Morsi's inability to revive the economy was seen as undermining their interests. In addition, Morsi was also perceived to have violated another implicit agreement between his government and the military by meddling in foreign policy and national defence issues – the two main prerogatives of the Egyptian military since the 1952 Free Officers' Coup.

Towards the end of his reign, Morsi took a more explicit position on foreign policy issues, namely calling for jihad against the Assad regime in Syria and threatening Ethiopia over a dam project in the Nile, while facilitating the infiltration of the security apparatus by his supporters. For external actors such as Saudi Arabia and UAE, who maintained strong ties with Hosni Mubarak and the Egyptian military in recent decades, a military-ruled Egypt was the closest that they could get to achieving 'Mubarakism without Mubarak'.

Salafi groups, meanwhile, also sniffed a new opportunity to outflank their less radical Islamist competitors by turning against Morsi. So when hundreds of thousands of protesters, inspired by the Tamarod Movement, sought the downfall of Morsi and occupied Tahrir Square, the stage was set for the military to step in, with GCC powers providing up to $12 billion for the post-Morsi government.[10] What followed was violent clashes between the military and the Muslim Brotherhood supporters, a crackdown on the Brotherhood's leadership, and renewed fears of a civil war in Egypt, pitting the brotherhood against supporters of the July coup.

8 | WHERE DO WE GO FROM HERE? FINDING THE TRUE PATH TO AN ARAB SPRING

> When the facts change, I change my mind. What do you do, sir? (John Maynard Keynes)

Despite all their troubles, and collective expressions of cynicism, people in the ATCs still envision a better future. According to a Gallup (2012a) poll, an overwhelming majority of people in Tunisia, Libya, Yemen and Egypt expect a better future. For instance, expectations of better security and safety breached 70 per cent, while in terms of the economy it stood at above 60 per cent. Another Gallup (2012b) poll suggested that in places such as Egypt, Yemen and to a certain degree Libya, a considerable proportion of society favours the implementation of sharia as the only source of legislation, with women and men showing similar levels of preference. To be sure, this explains the ability of Islamist parties in places such as Egypt – and Yemen – to push through more conservative post-revolutionary constitutions. Yet there was an interesting related finding: men with higher expressions of religiosity and a better economic standing had a more favourable view of women's rights (e.g. the female right to initiate divorce).

While the polls suggest that Islam will continue to play a pivotal role in post-revolutionary societies, they also underline the importance of socio-economic development and an overall sense of economic stability among citizens. Though liberal-democratic forces – the backbone of the initial stages of uprisings – may have a legitimate case to make against perceived post-revolutionary drifts towards illiberal governance, the fundamental issue facing the Arab world, especially the ATCs, is the establishment of a state that combines social development and democratic freedom, something along the lines of NICs in the East, Latin American centre-left parties in the South, and Nordic social-democratic states in the West. The high rates of inequality in libertarian economies, so-called liberal market economies (LMEs), such as the USA, suggest that formal constitutional political democracy is by no means a guarantee of actual freedom and ability to participate as a full member of the polity (Meyer and Hinchman 2007). Among developing countries, states such as the Philippines – with stellar levels of political freedom and economic growth co-existing with one of the region's worst rates of poverty and inequality – should serve as a cautionary tale for those who narrowly push for liberal-political democracy, without recognizing the (theoretical and actual) shortcomings of libertarian economic systems, which breed inequality, fuel inter-class tensions, and undermine the key component of a civic-democratic culture: social capital and solidarity. The key to the ATCs' development, whether under Islamist parties or a broad-based political coalition, lies in establishing a strong developmental state, and engaging new, favourable trading arrangements. Transcending capitalism may be a highly utopian objective at this point, but establishing productive and successful coordinated market economies (CMEs) under economic globalization is possible[1] (Sandbrook et al. 2007; Meyer and Hinchman 2007: 136–59). This is the only way to achieve diversified, sustainable and inclusive economic growth among the ATCs, and the wider region.

In their best-selling book *Why Nations Fail*, economists Acemoglu and Robinson have developed an elaborate but parsimonious theory on how national development is heavily tied to institutional attributes: 'Extractive/absolutist institutions', built on autocratic-arbitrary governance and monopolies, generate wealth and power, albeit in an unsustainable fashion, for a narrow minority at the expense of the general population and national development, while 'inclusive/pluralistic' institutions, anchored by accountable governance, rule of law and competitive markets, ensure inclusive and sustainable growth for society as a whole. More specifically, the authors look at how political and economic institutions are heavily intertwined. Thus, democratic governance and sustained economic development go hand in hand.

Throughout its modern history, the Arab world, plagued by extractive institutions benefiting a narrow, elite group, has seen one elite group replacing another, without a fundamental transformation in the institutional make-up of society. In the absence of a shift in the balance of forces between the power elite and broader society, each 'critical juncture' (e.g. the collapse of the Ottoman Empire, the end of colonialism and the advent of economic globalization) simply saw the reinforcement of prior extractive institutional practices. As Acemoglu and Robinson aptly observe, without oil wealth, the region as a whole, and petro-states especially, would have been at par with poorer countries in other developing regions such as Latin America. And despite huge oil windfalls, the Arab region is richer than it is developed.

At this critical juncture of the Arab uprisings, the region has a new opportunity to not only push for democratization and more inclusive political institution, but also espouse a new development paradigm that translates contingent political opening into inclusive economic regimes.

The developmental state deficit

If one looks at the composition of many Arab economies, ranging from Egypt and Syria to Tunisia and Jordan, low- to medium-end service-oriented sectors predominate. By global standards, the share of industrial manufacturing and high-end technological production is dismal (see Table 8.1). As experts such as Harvard economist Dani Rodrik (2011) correctly point out, the problem with over-reliance on the service sector, especially in developing countries with a relatively small middle class and a large low-income population, is twofold: (1) most well-paying jobs in the service sector are accessible to only a minority of highly educated individuals, while external shocks – from security problems to financial bubbles – can easily disrupt sectors such as real estate, tourism and financial services; and (2) manufacturing, unlike services, allows for 'unconditional convergence' in productivity levels; upward mobility in the production chain (from light to heavy manufacturing); and optimization of economies of scale, therefore providing secure and well-paying jobs for an increasing proportion of the workforce. Manufacturing-based economies can better cope with external shocks, because they can shift to domestic consumption to generate growth (since as a result of better employment conditions a more sizeable domestic market has been created).

TABLE 8.1 Main characteristics of the region (2000–07)

	Workers' remittances (% of GDP)	Food imports (% of merchandise imports)	Fuel exports (% of merchandise exports)	International tourism, receipts (% of total exports)	Manufactures exports (% of merchandise exports)	Openness*	Unemployment, total (% of total labour force)
East Asia & Pacific	1.39	4.97	7.46	5.96	79.65	77.10	4.55
Latin America & Caribbean	1.66	7.23	17.51	6.38	55.35	44.59	9.19
Arab region	6.97	16.84	56.32	14.13	24.47	87.89	12.36
Sub-Saharan Africa	1.71	11.63	36.98	8.28	31.85	65.76	–

Note:* Exports + imports/GDP
Source: Drine (2009) (with permission)

The problem in the Arab world is that economic liberalization has shifted resources, both labour and capital, towards short-term-oriented, profit-generating economic activities, which do not generate sufficient and quality employment opportunities for the general populace. The subsequent over-reliance on a few service sectors led to high levels of unemployment and even more underemployment among many Arab countries, which lacked inclusive economic growth. In short, the Arab economies are structurally imbalanced, preventing the full optimization of domestic resources and external opportunities for the benefit of the larger population on a sustained scale. It is precisely for this reason that the Arab region compares poorly to other major developing regions in terms of key economic indicators, despite their relative 'openness' to international trade and investments (see Table 8.1).

If one looks at history, all successful industrialized countries owe their economic miracles to large-scale manufacturing under the guidance of a decisive developmental state, which judiciously used industrial and trade policies to prop up domestic industrial capacity, facilitate technology transfer, and expand as well as deepen export markets.[2] In the twentieth century, successful late-developing countries either created large-scale supply chains similar to those in the industrial West (e.g. Japan and South Korea), or, especially in the case of industrial latecomers, simply integrated into existing pan-regional and global production chains (e.g. Thailand and China). As Geneva-based economist Richard Baldwin (2013) argues, successful developing countries were able to optimize the seismic shifts in modes of industrialization, largely enabled by the advent of business and industrial offshoring as well as subsequent developments in information technology:

> The radically different impact of this globalisation is due largely to its very different nature. When firms offshore production stages they must also offshore their firm-specific managerial and technical know-how ... [Thus] developing nation factories can, within months, export world-class manufactured goods – a feat that used to take decades when nations had to build up an industrial base before they became globally competitive (think US, Japan,

Germany and South Korea). The final big change was the way offshoring killed import substitution.

The impact on other ISI-oriented developing countries, Baldwin (ibid.) argues, was severe, as recipients of offshore factories – and new members of already established pan-regional supply chains – became 'hypercompetitive' overnight. As a result, they were able to rapidly move up the value chain and close in on Western economies in terms of increasingly high-end manufacturing, while displacing their less-integrated peers in Arab and Latin American regions. Clearly, the kind of 'integration' we are talking about here is not the simplistic and narrow form of trade and capital liberalization prescribed by the IFIs, but instead a judicious and strategic state-led effort to maximize the new opportunities in the global economy. After all, countries such as China have hardly been paragons of economic openness, while other NICs astutely utilized a combination of trade barriers, industrial policies based on 'reciprocal mechanisms' – strict performance-based state support for strategic economic sectors – and favourable technology-transfer schemes with foreign companies, and privileged access to Western markets through the negotiation of exclusive trading agreements. Nonetheless, as Dani Rodrik (in El-Erian 2008: 105) argues in *One Economics, Many Recipes*, successful developing countries utilized not a 'one size fits all' approach, but instead an eclectic combination of 'best practices' tuned to domestic circumstances. Despite some crucial similarities, for instance the emphasis on technology transfer, R&D and reciprocal mechanisms to ensure upward movement in the manufacturing ladder, the NICs themselves adopted divergent strategies: focusing on large-scale subsidies and policy support to national champions (as in Korea), cultivation of cutting-edge production by a myriad of dynamic small and medium-sized enterprises (as in Taiwan), and heavy investment in world-class infrastructure and adoption of best business practices to become a regional production, travel, services and financial hub (as in Singapore and to a certain degree Hong Kong). Their success was hardly based on the IFIs' narrow notion of integration, which emphasizes capital liberalization (encouraging risky 'hot money inflow'), FDIs (without clear stipulations on ensuring technology transfer) and trade openness (without considering the resilience of domestic producers to withstand the barrage of subsidized goods from more advanced countries) (Lall 2004). The NICs, and other successful developing economies, 'created' their national comparative advantage by moving up the ladder of production, whereby they amassed, albeit gradually, domestic capital for high-end manufacturing through gains from labour-intensive activities in the initial stages of economic take-off (Chang 2005).

It must be also noted that these economies were able to optimize more permissive and favourable external conditions to the best of their abilities. As economist Mohammad El-Erian (2008: 105) puts it, 'There are many challenges [developing countries] must overcome, including that of managing success domestically and of having the international system accommodate their success in an orderly fashion.' Many of them were also able to use strategic and political shortcomings to extract favourable trading agreements from Western powers for *national* development. As 'front-line' states, countries such as South Korea and Taiwan – facing the communist threat from the Soviet Union and China – were able to attract strategic, technological and economic support from Washington, while also benefiting from the post-war boom in places such as Japan. In the case of Singapore, a Chinese-majority city-state amid a Malayan neighbourhood, the leadership, under the watchful guidance of Lee Kwan Yu, constantly used the pretext of external threats to consolidate domestic power and push for national development. Later, the leadership was also able to utilize its strong ties with both Washington and Deng-era China to project Singapore as a locus of regional cooperation, integration and trade – a bridge between opposing poles.

In contrast, most Arab leaders used their strategic importance – whether with respect to hydrocarbon trade or Cold War rivalries – to consolidate domestic autocratic regimes, crack down on opposition, and engage in a mindless military build-up without strong economic foundations. Thus, the difference between Arab states and the NICs does not lie in democratic institutions per se, since the latter (with the exception of Hong Kong) were all autocratic during the initial stages of development. Nor is it a question of 'patriotism', since the likes of Gamal Abdel-Nasser were the beating heart of anti-imperial, anti-Western Arab self-sufficiency. The answer lies largely in how the NICs' leadership adopted the right economic strategies to make the best out of their circumstances. In short, they had the right economic paradigm in mind. When economic globalization commenced, many NICs were already in a strong position to benefit from new opportunities in the global market, while picking and choosing (given their relatively strong leverage with the IFIs as well as astute economic diplomacy) which pro-market reforms to follow. The 1997/98 Asian financial crisis (AFC) gave the IFIs some room to 'discipline' NICs such as South Korea, which led to the dissolution of monopolistic and corrupt age-old national champions (the so-called 'chaebols'), but the leadership in these nations did not follow simplistic libertarian economies, nor did the fundamental structure of these economies alter. There were some readjustments and 'house cleaning' here and there, but age-old economic paradigms inspired a dynamic push towards even more productive economics in the twenty-first century. For instance, South Korea's economy – despite the post-AFC structural reforms – is still dominated by electronics and manufacturing giants, ranging from Samsung and LG to Hyundai and Kia, while Taiwan's SMEs and Singapore's educational institutions are at the forefront of R&D and cutting-edge production (Sharma 2011).

It is precisely this balanced form of economic development, with 'optimized' levels of economic openness, which explains the high levels of social cohesion, human capital and political stability across the NICs. Some, such as Taiwan and Korea, emerged as beacons of democracy in the region, while others, such as Singapore – while falling short of a democratic transition – have built a highly educated society and a vibrant private sector, which has constantly pushed for open and transparent *governance* – arguably, a crucial step in the direction of a more democratic government some time in the future.

Rapid industrialization, despite the short-term pressure on labour, led to an increase in the number of workers with stable and relatively well-paying jobs. The result was the simultaneous emergence of a consumer society and a rapid increase in productivity levels, which, in turn, helped to improve the country's overall competitiveness and output.[3] This was not the case in the Arab world. That is why none of the Arab countries has climbed up to join the ranks of OECD members. Oil-rich Arab countries were successful only in matching income levels in the OECD. In the Middle East, all the major industrial powers are non-Arab. In heavy manufacturing and steel production, Iran and Turkey are the regional giants.[4] In high-tech manufacturing, Israel dwarfs all its neighbours.[5]

What proponents of economic globalization tend to overlook is how the developmental role of the state is indispensable to sustain social development and economic growth in underdeveloped markets. Arab autocrats and their cadre of neoliberal technocrats ignored this crucial economic lesson. Time and again, development economists have emphasized the state's role in providing – through subsidies – the managerial and technological capabilities, implants of minimum efficient scale and distribution networks to create economic opportunities in the industrial sector for investment and growth, even under prevailing international trading regimes (Amsdem 2005). The state is also crucial in overcoming the inherent vulnerabilities of markets, especially in developing countries; it is not only about dealing with imperfect competition (crony capitalism) and environmental externalities, but also the state's indispensable role in (a) managing information externalities, whereby private firms are not cognizant of investment opportunities within the economy, and (b) coordinating externalities, whereby the private sector will not invest in the economy unless 'factor markets' and necessary downstream and upstream industries as well as basic infrastructure are available. Unfortunately, owing to aggressive and misguided economic liberalization programmes, which encouraged state withdrawal, many Arab countries were deprived of any significant 'development policy space' (Gallagher 2005: 62–85). But, instead of helping the state to become a much more nimble and progressive agent of development, economic globalization sought to outsource development to the 'private' sector. The problem was that the private sector in its true sense – the independent, entrepreneurial class outside the clutches of the state – was either non-existent or weak and limited. It was by no means ready to pick up where Arab socialism left off.

Arab socialism was hardly an effective developmental model, not because it was state-led per se, but mainly because it – and the ruling elite for that matter – lacked an appropriate policy paradigm to ensure sustainable industrialization and judicious integration into international markets. In developmental terms, Arab regimes opened up where they should have been more judicious, conservative and strategic minded: acquiescing to trade and capital account liberalization; implementing suboptimal, non-transparent privatization of state assets; and pursuing low-value-added, export-oriented production with low employment gains for the general population. In the same breath, they remained enclosed, autocratic and indolent where they should have been more transparent, accountable and nimble: developing national champions en route to establishing a more favourable national comparative advantage; implementing optimal industrial targeting, reciprocal mechanisms and population management schemes; allowing for and supporting the emergence of an independent, vibrant entrepreneurial class; and reining in endemic corruption, especially when it hurts productivity, undermines strategic economic investments, and sustains patronage networks to the detriment of integrating competitive economic agents and investing in the human capital of the general population.

But one fundamental problem with the state-led socialism of post-colonial Arab states (and their successors) was the absence of so-called 'reciprocal mechanisms': performance-based, results-oriented strategic state support for targeted industries, ensuring constant quality improvement, higher-value-added production, and maximization of economies of scale, factors that have played a critical role in the economic take-off of NICs and more advanced emerging economies in recent decades (Kumar 2005). In contrast, the Arab autocrats had little 'economic rationale' behind their policies, with state resources largely feeding personalized patronage systems (see Chapter 3).

It is not only about production efficiency and industrial output. While lower tariffs and taxes might entice low-end manufacturing investments and 'money inflow', building an advanced industrial economy – en route to a knowledge economy in the future – necessitates the attraction of high-quality 'greenfield' investments with the aim of building a large-scale, high-value-added production base. But this would, obviously, necessitate a highly educated and skilled working force, dynamic labour markets underpinned by capital–

labour synchronicity, and a state committed to R&D. Yet all of these are only possible with a favourable socio-political context. Development becomes difficult, if not impossible, when there is widespread inequality and poverty, which, in turn, undermines political stability and social cohesion. This is precisely why the Arab states should focus on redistributive justice and population management (Sandbrook et al. 2007).

In his book *Commonwealth*, Jeffrey Sachs (2009) raised the highly important issue of 'youth bulge', whereby a large proportion of the population depends on a small adult, productive population. The Arab world's youth bulge, following Sachs' analysis, created a situation whereby a tiny productive population had to sustain the needs of most of the population as a whole, while limited resources did not translate into proper training, nourishment and improvement of a huge youthful population, therefore creating a cycle of poverty, low productivity and intergenerational high fertility rates. As the Arab Spring demonstrates, a huge youth bulge creates high levels of unemployment and deep-flowing disenchantment and frustration, increasing the probability of political chaos, riots and instability, which could, in turn, contribute to a cycle of poverty and economic stagnation. This is precisely why the ATCs should pay close attention to the population policy. As Sachs notes, the problem is that in many countries the introduction of modern medical technology wasn't followed by a check on fertility rates. Therefore, the introduction of voluntary means of fertility reduction as well as the availability of maternal and childcare facilities could substantially reduce infant mortality, and undercut the incentive for high fertility rates. In the long run, the improvement in the overall economic conditions – partly due to population stabilization – could facilitate not only industrialization, but also improvements in social security, encouraging parents to have fewer children as a guarantee of their old-age security and household productivity.

All NICs, along with China and new emerging economies such as Indonesia, used population management measures in order to create a stable balance between population growth and resource availability. The result has been a smooth demographic transition, an economic miracle, high levels of labour productivity, and a competitive human resource base. With a strong population policy, these countries were able to introduce economic dynamism by focusing on the development of their human resources and optimization of their agricultural and natural base for purposes of industrialization and technological growth. For the NICs – and later in places such as China, Indonesia and Vietnam – the development of human capital was not confined to investment in education and health per se; there was also a conscious effort to increase labour productivity and individual living standards by looking at ways to prevent an unsustainable youth bulge. Population management was a key pillar of their development strategies, ensuring a balanced demographic growth that would not overstretch state finances, escalate unemployment rates and undermine the productivity gains of earlier generations. This came on the back of (or coupled with) relatively successful and egalitarian land reform programmes in places such as Taiwan, which ensured a measure of rural productivity and equitable growth, preventing the perpetuation of feudal-like economic systems that have shackled economic potential as well as social cohesion in many other developing countries. Rising individual living standards, better conditions in the rural areas and proactive state efforts to provide 'family planning' programmes for vulnerable sectors enabled them to avoid the sort of population explosion experienced in other developing countries, whereby large cities – stretched to their limits in terms of infrastructure and the provision of welfare services – are inundated by people escaping grinding rural poverty, with both the farming and the urban poor population responsible for high birth rates beyond the absorption capacity of the overall economy. Having achieved demographic stability, these states were able to focus more on capital deepening rather than capital widening, since they could invest in the quality of infrastructure and human resources rather than merely catching up with growing demand for services. The Arab world doesn't need to go far to find inspiration: Middle Eastern countries such as Iran have been responsible for one of the most successful programmes pertaining to population management, and also adult and female literacy, helping, over time, the country to stabilize its demographics and – despite international isolation – build one of the most educated and scientifically literate countries in the region and beyond[6] (Sachs

2009; World Bank country report). Another important social issue, with huge economic ramifications, is the integration of women into the workforce, which, historically, has been accompanied by higher levels of economic productivity and demographic stabilization (Meyer and Hinchman 2007).

Finally, there is the issue of alternative trading arrangements. As Sally (2008), Baldwin (2013) and Altman (2013) have argued, the WTO – hamstrung by inflexible rules, internal squabbles and a fatal deadlock under the Doha Round – has become irrelevant (and almost dead) in the new global economy, where supply-chain trade – as opposed to service- and commodity-based trade – and regional trading agreements are becoming the new norm. This is particularly relevant in the case of ATCs, precisely because, as Malik and Awadallah (2011: 8–9) argue, the region has a dismal level of intra-regional trade, barely surpassing the 1960 rate of 10 per cent, despite having one of the most favourable geographical profiles in the world (e.g. wide coastlines, long land borders, and proximity to global trade centres).

The Arab Spring, therefore, not only represents a widespread yearning for democracy and political freedom, but also reflects the depth of economic challenges, which are rooted in a misguided development paradigm that has failed to provide sustainable and inclusive growth for the majority. Thus, in order to understand the Arab revolutions and credibly analyse their trajectory, one should incorporate a better understanding of their economic dimension. What this book, and especially this chapter, has argued is that the success of the Arab Spring is heavily tied to the ability of post-revolutionary government to adopt appropriate economic policies to redress the great divide between the minority elite and the majority of the population, especially women. Given the neoliberal bent of elements within the new post-revolutionary leadership (see Chapter 5), compounded by growing anxieties over their alleged conservative rollback of civil liberties for minorities and serious short- to medium-term macroeconomic imbalances, it is far from clear whether the Arab Summer will usher in a much-needed push towards developmental policies directed at sustained poverty alleviation; reinvigorating strategic industries in the manufacturing and agricultural sectors to address high unemployment rates; developing a coherent population management policy to address the huge youth bulge; and revamping earlier measures designed to enhance regional economic integration, especially in light of growing geopolitical uncertainties due to the Syrian crisis and rising tensions in the Persian Gulf.

NOTES

1 A brave new Middle East

1 Arab Spring: Wikiquote, en.wikiquote.org/wiki/Arab_Spring.

2 Notwithstanding the argument that economic globalization came in response to structural problems emanating from internal contradictions within the state-led Keynesian capitalism – compounded by US imperialistic adventures in places such as Vietnam and the Middle East.

3 In more specific terms, economic globalization's development paradigm rested on the following pillars: the proper functioning of (real and financial) markets, and the protection of private property rights, while relegating 'welfare' responsibilities to the private sector, but retaining token safety nets to maintain social cohesion as well as ameliorate the impact of reforms and at times crises; a reduction in both conventional (tariff) and unconventional (non-tariff) barriers to trade followed by a gradual move towards capital account liberalization, primarily to encourage foreign direct investments and foreign portfolio investments; restructuring of the domestic economy in the direction of export-oriented industrialization and export-market/import-dependent growth; gradual withdrawal of the state from the national economy in exchange for growing private sector participation in all key aspects of the economy; securing macroeconomic stability, through fiscal discipline (i.e. budget deficit reduction) and monetary 'restraint' (i.e. inflation and interest rates targeting); reorientation of industrial policy, through the abolition of interventionist macro-industrial management, and parallel effort at specialization of production under a comparative advantage framework.

4 For discussions on Iran's constitutional movement see Ansari (2006) and Abrahamian (2011). On Turkey's 1908 revolution, see Zurcher (1993).

2 The anti-development state

1 George Owell quotes, www.george-orwell.org/l_quotes.html.

3 The advent of economic globalization

1 Fordism was an era of fixed capital mobility, where states predominantly relied on expansion of domestic markets to sustain economic growth. Large-scale, standardized manufacturing (Fordism) led to high levels of employment and sustained sources of income for the majority. Both labour and capital were mutually sustaining each other.

2 For a more detailed profile of Friedman's intellectual background and thoughts, see Nasar (2011: 354–72).

3 This was the genesis of 'supply-side economics', embraced by Reagan's and Thatcher's administrations in the early 1980s. After decades of demand-side economic planning, a response to the vagaries of the Great Depression in the inter-war period, the focus now shifted to prioritizing the supply side of economic activity.

4 globalization.kof.ethz.ch/.

5 Egypt was even considered one of

the hottest emerging economies in the world, part of the CIVETS (Colombia, Indonesia, Vietnam, Egypt, Turkey, South Africa), while global financial institutions characterized Tunisia as a trailblazer Arab country in free trade and economic liberalization.

6 See data from the International Monetary Fund, the World Bank and the CIA *World Factbook*.

7 Note the important role played by the Egyptian and Tunisian armies in ensuring a relatively smooth transition in the wake of Ben Ali and Mubarak's fall.

4 The Great Recession

1 John Maynard Keynes: Wikiquote, en.wikiquote.org/wiki/John_Maynard_Keynes.

2 There was, however, a strategic logic behind this upward, encouraging trend in agricultural production. In light of the fierce ideological rivalry between the USA and the Soviet Union, the West saw the need to deal with widespread poverty in large developing countries head-on lest the latter fall into the 'abyss' of violent anti-capitalist communist revolutions, such as were sweeping across Indochina, South America, Asia and Africa. The introduction of the so-called 'Green Revolution' to developing nations – from India to Mexico and the Philippines – from the 1940s to the 1970s heralded a new era of optimism, in which the fruits of cutting-edge science combined with the efficiency-maximizing methods of modern capitalism. The US government, in conjunction with private institutions such as the Rockefeller and Ford foundations, supported efforts by agricultural scientists to increase per hectare yield and crop resistance, as well as overall food production in many poor agricultural areas. Despite unparalleled growth in the human population, modern agricultural practices allowed for even higher levels of increases in per capita food production. The result was a global expansion in food production and the conversion of idle and/or forested lands into large-scale agro-industrial sites.

3 'World Bank neglects African farming, study says', *New York Times*, 15 October 2007.

4 Aditya Chakrobortty, 'Secret report: biofuels caused food crisis', *Guardian*, 3 July 2008.

5 Based on a 2008 United Nations report: 'the annual food import basket in LDCs cost more than three times that of 2000, not because of the increased volume of food imports, but as the result of rising food process' (UN in Bello 2009).

5 The new power brokers

1 In between there were of course those who developed a 'hybrid' body of thought by combining socialism with Islamism or liberalism with Islamism. Later in the twentieth century, for instance, Dr Ali Shiati would introduce a form of ideology that combined socialism and Islamism. Meanwhile, Iranian reformist thinkers, from Abdolkarim Soroush and Mir Hossein Mousavi to Muhammad Khatami and Zahra Rahnavard, combined liberal and Islamic thought.

2 For a discussion of Islamist criticism of secularism and liberal democracy, see Rubin (2003).

3 Fundamentally, there are no inherent incompatibilities between monotheist religions, the Judaeo-Christian-Islamic traditions, and democratic politics: the expression of popular sovereignty through regular elections. Perhaps the main distinction is between certain forms of Islam and Christianity, existing under specific socio-political conditions. For instance, if one looks into history, we find that the Catholic Church played a critical role in

the politics of European societies. The Reformation movement and the Thirty Years War were indeed a response to the power of the Church – and its purported abuse of it – as the central arbiter of European socio-political affairs in the Middle Ages. Throughout the Renaissance period, there was clear friction between the secular prince – backed by liberals and the bourgeoisie – and the Church, as they jostled for the temporal and spiritual dominions of Europe, trying to assert jurisdiction over conflicting realms of influence. The struggle, especially after the Treaty of Westphalia (1648), was eventually won by the monarchs, paving the way for the rise of modern, secular European nation-states over the succeeding centuries.

6 Gulf exceptionalism

1 Brainyquote, W. E. B. Du Bois, www.brainyquote.com/quotes/quotes/w/webdubo388223.html.

2 This pertains to the inexorable deterioration in non-oil sectors due to currency appreciation as a result of booming hydrocarbon exports; it is based on the experience of the Netherlands after the country stepped up its natural gas exports after major discoveries in the post-Second World War period.

7 Peering into the abyss

1 Brainyquote, Martin Luther King, Jr: www.brainyquote.com/quotes/topics/topic_hope.html.

2 One must also consider the fact that major tribes in eastern Libya, especially in Benghazi, had always had an uneasy relationship with Gaddafi. This explains why Benghazi was the site of a major revolutionary backlash, and eventually the host of the National Transitional Council government.

3 For a succinct discussion of the Libyan intervention, see Dunne (2011).

4 Some reports suggested that Gaddafi sponsored assassination plots against the Saudi king, Abdullah.

5 The imposition of a no-fly zone was followed by a dramatic increase in casualties. Prior to the imposition of UN Resolution 1973, an estimated thousand people had been killed. By the end of the Libyan revolution, around thirty thousand individuals may have been killed.

6 The roots of the concept date back to the anti-Soviet campaign in Afghanistan, whereby Western-backed jihadi groups eventually ended up targeting their patrons: the West, Saudi Arabia and Pakistan.

7 For an excellent piece on experts' assessment of weapons sought by the rebels, and their individual pros and cons, see Hudson (2013a).

8 After the defeat of the FSA in the battle of Qusayr (June 2013), Saudi Arabia, annoyed and alarmed by Qatar's growing ties with more extremist elements within the FSA, took the reins by exercising more direct control over the funding and organization of the armed opposition; the decision was also supported by Washington, increasingly concerned about the proliferation of extremist elements and the military weakness of the FSA.

9 As a Kurdish Syrian, Hitto was also expected to win Kurdish support against Assad. Later, al-Khatib reluctantly agreed to attend the Arab League summit in Qatar as the leader of the Syrian state, which was followed by the inauguration of the Syrian opposition's first embassy, in Doha, prompting speculation about his reinstatement.

10 F. MacDonald and D. El Baltaji, 'Kuwait Egypt Aid Pushes Gulf Pledges to $12 billion in 24 hours', Online: http://www.bloomberg.com/news/2013-07-10/kuwait-egypt-aid-pushes-gulf-pledges-to-12-billion-in-24-hours.html (10 July 2013).

8 Where do we go from here?

1 For instance, Sandbrook et al. (2007) have analysed how social-democratic states such as Mauritania, Costa Rica, Kerala and to a certain degree Chile were able to prosper and maintain their welfare-progressive policies even under conditions of economic globalization, albeit with some modifications and compromises. Meyer and Hinchman (2007) have analysed how Sweden, Denmark and the Netherlands were not only able to retain their welfare foundations, but also successfully make necessary adjustments under the pressure of globalization for economic competitiveness.

2 For discussions on developmental state models, see Gallagher (2005); also Lee and Yamazawa (1990); Kiely (2007).

3 On the emergence of consumer society, see Ferguson (2011). On the experience of industrialization in the West, see Chang (2005) and Gallagher (2005).

4 For instance, see the 2010 world crude steel production rankings from the World Steel Association.

5 For instance, see OECD (2013): 'Statistical analysis of science, technology, and industry'.

6 Despite huge criticisms of Iran and its flailing economy, many Arab intellectuals and leaders, especially among ATCs, have praised Iran for its scientific achievements, despite the international sanctions. Turkey may have been touted as a potential model, but there are some best practices to be adopted from other neighbours like Iran, which have sought stronger cultural, education and scientific ties with post-revolutionary Arab states. In fact, Iran has a higher Human Development Index (HDI) score than countries such as Turkey and Brazil.

REFERENCES

Abdel Fatah, M. (2009) 'Impact of Arab Human Development reports', carnegie endowment.org/2009/09/09/impact-of-arab-human-development-reports/fih9.

Abdo, G. (2013) 'Bahrain's closed doors', mideast.foreignpolicy.com/posts/2013/01/24/bahrains_closed_doors, 24 January.

Abrahamian, E. (2011) 'Mass protests in the Iranian Revolution, 1977–79', in A. Roberts and T. Garton Ash (eds), *Civil Resistance and Power Politics*, Oxford: Oxford University Press.

Abu-Rish, Z. (2013) 'Romancing the throne: the New York Times and the endorsement of the authoritarian Jordan', www.jadaliyya.com/pages/index/9949/romancing-the-throne_the-new-york-times-and-the-en, 3 February.

Acemoglu, D. and J. Robinson (2012) *Why Nations Fail: The Origins of Power, Prosperity and Poverty*, New York: Random House.

Aggestan, K. et al. (2009) 'The Arab state and neo-liberal globalization', in L. Guazzone and D. Pioppi (eds), *The Arab State and Neo-liberal Globalization: The Restructuring of State Power in the Middle East*, Reading: Ithaca.

Ajami, F. (2012a) 'Five myths about the Arab Spring', www.washingtonpost.com/opinions/five-myths-about-the-arab-spring/2011/12/21/gIQA32TVuP_story.html, 13 January.

— (2012b) 'The Arab Spring at one', www.foreignaffairs.com/articles/137053/fouad-ajami/the-arab-spring-at-one, March/April.

Akhtar, S. (2011) 'Food security in the Arab world: price volatility and vulnerabilities and the World Bank response', web.worldbank.org/WBSITE/EXTERNAL/TOPICS/EXTHEALTHNUTRITIONANDPOPULATION/0,,contentMDK:22864816~menuPK:2643791~pagePK:64020865~piPK:149114~theSitePK:282511,00.html, March.

Al-Akhbar (2013) 'Saudi king moves son one step closer to succession', english.al-akhbar.com/content/saudi-king-moves-his-son-one-step-closer-throne, 2 February.

Aliriza, F. (2012) 'The revolution in Tunisia stalls', www.foreignpolicy.com/articles/2012/09/20/the_revolution_in_tunisia_stalls, 20 September.

— (2013) 'A murder in Tunis', www.foreignpolicy.com/articles/2013/02/06/a_murder_in_tunis_belaid_assassination, 6 February.

Al Jazeera (2012) 'The Brotherhood and Mubarak', www.aljazeera.com/programmes/aljazeeraworld/2012/05/2012517131828948619.html, 24 May.

— (2013) 'UN warns of humanitarian tragedy in Syria', www.aljazeera.com/news/middleeast/ 2013/02/20132200453451511.html, 20 February.

Al-Kuraysi, S. (n.d.) 'Dr Yusuf Al-Qaradawi and democracy', islam-basic.blogspot.com/2010/12/dr-yusuf-al-qaradawi-and-democracy.html.

Almond, M. (2011) 'Arab governments alarmed by crackdown on British Summertime protests', markalmondoxford.blogspot.com/, 9 August.

Al-Omran, A. (2013) Saudi activists

silenced and the US is silent', mideast.foreignpolicy.com/posts/2013/03/11/saudi_activists_silenced_and_the_us_is_silent, 11 March.

Al-Qassemi, Sultan S. (2011) 'How Saudi Arabia and Qatar became friends again', www.foreignpolicy.com/articles/2011/07/21/how_saudi_arabia_and_qatar_became_friends_again?page=full, 21 July.

— (2012a) 'Breaking the Arab news', www.foreignpolicy.com/articles/2012/08/02/breaking_the_arab_news?page=full, 2 August.

— (2012b) 'Morsi's win is Al Jazeera's loss', www.al-monitor.com/pulse/originals/2012/al-monitor/morsys-win-is-al-jazeeras-loss.html, 1 July.

— (2013) 'Qatar's Brotherhood ties alienate fellow Gulf states', www.al-monitor.com/pulse/originals/2013/01/qatar-muslim-brotherhood.html.

Altman, D. (2013) 'Trade coalitions of the willing', www.foreignpolicy.com/articles/2013/03/18/trade_coalitions_of_the_willing_barack_obama?page=full, 18 March.

Amsdem, A. (2005) 'Promoting industry under WTO law', in K. Gallagher (ed.), *Putting Development First: The Importance of Policy Space in the WTO and International Financial Institutions*, London: Zed Books.

Anderson, L. (2011) 'Demystifying the Arab Spring', *Foreign Affairs*, 90: 2–7.

Anderson, P. (2011) 'On the concatenation in the Arab world', www.newleftreview.org/?view=2883, 2 April.

ANSAMed.it (2013) 'Egypt: Qatar grants another 3 billion dollars', www.ansamed.info/ansamed/en/news/nations/egypt/2013/04/10/Egypt-Qatar-grants-another-3-billion-dollars_8529973.html, 10 April.

Ansari, A. (2006) *Confronting Iran: The Failure of American Foreign Policy and the New Great Conflict in the Middle East*, New York: Perseus.

Anwar, D. (2010) 'Foreign policy, Islam and democracy in Indonesia', *Journal of Indonesian Social Sciences and Humanities*, 3: 37–54.

Aras, B. and O. Caha (2003) 'Fethullah Gulen and his liberal "Turkish Islam" movement', in R. Barry (ed.), *Revolutionaries and Reformers: Contemporary Islamist Movements in the Middle East*, New York: State University of New York Press.

Aristotle (1946) *The Politics of Aristotle*, trans. E. Barker, Oxford: Oxford University Press.

Bahrain Centre for Human Rights (2013) 'Bahrain: solidarity protests for HRD Nabeel Rajab around the world, but attacked in Bahrain; Said Yousif Al-Muhafdha arrested', www.bahrainrights.org/en/node/5689, 26 March.

Baldwin, R. (2013) 'The WTO and the global supply chains', www.eastasiaforum.org/2013/02/24/the-wto-and-global-supply-chains/.

Banks, J. and E. Hanushek (eds) (1995) *Modern Political Economy: Old Topics, New Directions*, New York: Cambridge University Press.

Barnard, A. (2013) 'Assad issues a worldwide plea as a top Syria general defects', www.nytimes.com/2013/03/17/world/middleeast/syria-updates.html?_r=0, 18 March.

Basheer, M. (2011) 'G8 commits $80 billion to Arab Spring democracy', www.voanews.com/english/news/middle-east/G8-Commits-80-Billion-to-Arab-Spring-Democracy--130242553.html, 20 September.

BBC (2011) 'UAE arrests democracy activists', www.bbc.co.uk/news/world-middle-east-13043270.

Bedirhanoglu, P. (2007) 'The neoliberal discourse on corruption as means of consent building: reflection from post-crisis Turkey', *Third World Quarterly*, 28(7): 1239–54.

Behrendt, H. and N. Kamel (2009) 'The impact of financial and economic crisis on Arab states', www.ilo.org/public/english/support/lib/financial crisis/download/impact_english.pdf, April.

Beinin, J. (2009) 'Neo-liberal structural adjustments, political demobilization, and neo-authoritarianism in Egypt', in L. Guazzone and D. Pioppi (eds), *The Arab State and Neo-liberal Globalization: The Restructuring of State Power in the Middle East*, Reading: Ithaca.

Bello, W. (2000) 'The future of global economic governance', www.unu.edu/millennium/bello.pdf, May.

— (2003) *Deglobalization: Ideas for a New World Economy*, London: Zed Books.

— (2009) *Food Wars*, London: Verso.

Bello, W. and J. Heydarian (2010) 'Climate change: shifting paradigms: moving away from global capitalism', *World Geography: Understanding a Changing World*, ABC-CLIO, September.

Bello, W. et al. (1982) *The Development Debacle: The World Bank in the Philippines*, Birmingham: Third World Publications.

Berman, S. (2013) 'The promise of the Arab Spring', www.foreignaffairs.com/articles/138479/sheri-berman/the-promise-of-the-arab-spring, January/February.

Beyerle, S. and A. Hassan (2012) 'Popular resistance against corruption in Turkey and Egypt', in M. Stephen (ed.), *Civilian Jihad*, New York: Palgrave.

Bosetti, G. (2011) 'Liberal democracy and Islam: Abdolkarim Soroush', www.resetdoc.org/story/00000021632, 13 June.

Bremmer, I. (2013) 'Risk #3: Arab Summer', eurasia.foreignpolicy.com/posts/2013/01/14/risk_3_an_arab_summer, 14 January.

Carlos, H. (2009) 'Political mass mobilization against authoritarian rule: Pinochet's Chile, 1983–88', in A. Roberts and T. Garton Ash (eds), *Civil Resistance and Power Politics*, Oxford: Oxford University Press.

Carothers, T. (2011) 'Egypt and Indonesia', www.tnr.com/article/world/82650/egypt-and-indonesia, 2 February.

Chang, H.-J. (2005) 'Kicking away the ladder: "good policies" and "good institutions" in historical perspective', in K. Gallagher (ed.), *Putting Development First: The Importance of Policy Space in the WTO and International Financial Institutions*, London: Zed Books.

Chatriwala, O. (2011) 'What Wikileaks tells us about Aljazeera', www.foreignpolicy.com/articles/2011/09/19/what_wikileaks_tells_us_about_al_jazeera.

Chivers, C. J. and E. Schmitt (2013) 'Arms airlift to Syria rebels expands, with aid from CIA', www.nytimes.com/2013/03/25/world/middleeast/arms-airlift-to-syrian-rebels-expands-with-cia-aid.html?pagewanted=all&_r=0, 24 March.

Cho, D. (2008) 'A few speculators dominate vast market for oil trading', *Washington Post*, 21 August, www.washingtonpost.com/wp-dyn/content/article/2008/08/20/AR2008082003898.html.

Chulov, M. (2013) 'Moaz al-Khatib's resignation plunges Syrian opposition into chaos', www.guardian.co.uk/world/2013/mar/24/moaz-al-khatib-resignation-syrian-opposition, 24 March.

Cohen, B. (2003) 'Monetary governance

in a globalized world', in R. Goddard et al. (eds), *International Political Economy: State Market Relations in a Changing Global World*, Basingstoke: Palgrave Macmillan.

Constable, P. (2007) 'Divisive scholar draws parallels between Islam and democracy', www.washingtonpost.com/wp-dyn/content/article/2007/04/10/AR2007041001509.html?hpid=sec-religion?hpid=sec-religion, 11 April.

Cook, S. (2013) 'What is Egypt?', www.foreignpolicy.com/node/1422913?page=full, 1 March.

Crossette, B. (2002) 'Study warns of stagnation in Arab societies', www.nytimes.com/2002/07/02/international/middleeast/02ARAB.html, 2 July.

Dahl, R. (1956) *A Preface to Democratic Theory*, Chicago, IL: University of Chicago Press.

— (1989) *Democracy and Its Critics*, New Haven, CT: Yale University Press.

Daily Star (2013) 'Syria's Muslim Brotherhood: influential, organized, but mistrusted', www.dailystar.com.lb/News/Middle-East/2013/Apr-04/212490-syrias-muslim-brotherhood-influential-organized-but-mistrusted.ashx, 4 April.

Dash, K. (2003) 'The Asian economic crisis and the role of IMF', in R. Goddard et al. (eds), *International Political Economy: State Market Relations in a Changing Global World*, Basingstoke: Palgrave Macmillan.

Davutoglu, A. (2011) 'Naturalizing the flow of history', www.aljazeera.com/indepth/opinion/2011/03/201131675653423697.html, 16 March.

Diamond, L. (1999) *Developing Democracy: Toward Consolidation*, Baltimore, MD, and London: Johns Hopkins University Press.

— (2010) 'Why are there no Arab democracies?', *Journal of Democracy*, 21(1): 93–104.

Diouf, J. (2009) 'Food security in the Arab world', www.fao.org/about/director-gen/statements2009/58338/en/, January.

Dreyer, C. (2010) 'A call for Muslims in the West to serve their societies', en.qantara.de/A-Call-for-Muslims-in-the-West-to-Serve-Their-Societies/8400c8469i1p162/, 11 November.

Drine, I. (2009) 'Impact of the global economic crisis on the Arab region', www.wider.unu.edu/publications/newsletter/articles/en_GB/05-06-2009/, 5 June.

Droz-Vincent, P. (2007) 'From political to economic actors: the changing role of Middle Eastern armies', in O. Schlumberger (ed.), *Debating Arab Authoritarianism: Dynamics and Durability in Nondemocratic Regimes*, Stanford, CA: Stanford University Press.

Dunne, T. (2011) 'Libya and state intervention', *APC R2P Brief*, 1(1).

Economist (2002) 'Arab development: self-doomed to failure', www.economist.com/node/1213392, 4 July.

— (2011) 'The rise of Qatar: pygmy with the punch of a giant', www.economist.com/node/21536659.

— (2012a) 'Arab Spring economies: unfinished business', www.economist. com/node/21546018, 4 February.

— (2012b) 'Kuwait's elections: giving democracy a bad name', www.economist.com/blogs/pomegranate/2012/12/kuwaits-election, 6 December.

Economist Intelligence Unit (2009) 'The GCC in 2020: outlook for the Gulf and the global economy', graphics.

eiu.com/marketing/pdf/Gulf2020.pdf, March.

EIA (Energy Information Administration) (2013) 'Sanctions reduced Iran's oil exports and revenues in 2012', www.eia.gov/todayinenergy/detail.cfm?id=11011, April.

Eickelman, D. (2003) 'Inside the Islamic Reformation', in R. Barry (ed.), *Revolutionaries and Reformers: Contemporary Islamist Movements in the Middle East*, New York: State University of New York Press.

El-Dahshan, M. (2013) 'Don't overlook Bahrain, it's a matter of life and death', transitions.foreignpolicy.com/posts/2013/03/28/don_t_over look_bahrain_it_s_a_matter_of_life_and_death, 28 March.

El-Erian, M. (2008) *When Markets Collide: Investment Strategies for the Age of Global Economic Change*, New York: McGraw Hill.

Eljarh, M. (2013) 'Ansar Al-Sharia returns to Benghazi', transitions.foreign policy. com/posts/2013/03/08/ansar_al_sharia_returns_to_benghazi, 25 March.

Esposito, J. and J. Voll (2001) 'Islam and democracy', www.artic.ua.es/biblioteca/u85/documentos/1808.pdf, November/December.

European Investment Bank (2012) 'Mobilizing the potential of GCC Sovereign Wealth Funds for Mediterranean partner countries', www.eib.org/attachments/country/femip_study_potential_of_gcc_sovereign_wealth_funds_en.pdf.

Farhi, F. (2012) 'Tehran's noise is all bluster', www.nytimes.com/roomfordebate/2012/05/29/nudging-bahrain-without-pushing-it-away/tehrans-noise-is-all-bluster, 30 May.

Ferguson, N. (2011) *Civilization: The West and the Rest*, London: Penguin.

Fish, S. and K. Michel (2012) 'What Tunisia did right', www.foreignpolicy.com/articles/2012/11/02/what_tunisia_did_right, 15 December.

Fisk, R. (2005) *The Great War for Civilization: The Conquest of the Middle East*, New York: Knopf.

Fitzgerald, M. (2013) 'Introducing the Libyan Muslim Brotherhood', mideast.foreignpolicy.com/posts/2012/11/02/introducing_the_libyan_muslim_brotherhood, 5 January.

Foucault, M. (1995) *Discipline and Punish*, New York: Vintage.

Friedman, T. (2004) 'Holding up Arab reform', www.nytimes.com/2004/12/16/opinion/16friedman.html, 16 December.

Fukuyama, F. (1983) 'The end of history?', www.wesjones.com/eoh.htm, Summer.

— (1992) *The End of History and the Last Man*, New York: Free Press.

— (2009) 'Iran, Islam and the rule of law', online.wsj.com/article/SB10001424052970203946904574300374086282670.html, 27 July.

— (2012) 'Acemoglu and Robinson on why nations fail?', blogs.the-american-interest.com/fukuyama/2012/03/26/acemoglu-and-robinson-on-why-nations-fail/, 26 March.

Gallagher, K. (ed.) (2005) *Putting Development First: The Importance of Policy Space in the WTO and International Financial Institutions*, London: Zed Books.

Gallup (2002) 'Arabs favor Al-Jazeera over state-run channels for world news', www.gallup.com/poll/7210/arabs-favor-aljazeera-over-staterun-channels-world-news.aspx.

— (2012a) 'Opinion briefing: Arab nations differ on uprisings' upside', www.gallup.com/poll/157400/opinion-briefing-arabs-doubt-benefits-uprisings.aspx.

— (2012b) 'Arab women and men see

eye to eye on religion's role in law', www.gallup.com/poll/155324/arab-women-men-eye-eye-religion-role-law.aspx.

Gause, G. (2011) 'Why Middle Eastern Studies missed the Arab Spring: the myth of authoritarian stability', www.foreignaffairs.com/articles/67932/f-gregory-gause-iii/why-middle-east-studies-missed-the-arab-spring, July/August.

GlobalPost (2013) 'Qatar-backed group buys luxury London hotel', www.globalpost.com/dispatch/news/afp/130328/qatari-backed-group-buys-luxury-london-hotel, 28 March.

Goddard, R. (2003) 'The International Monetary Fund', in R. Goddard et al. (eds), *International Political Economy: State Market Relations in a Changing Global World*, Basingstoke: Palgrave Macmillan.

Goldstone, J. (2011) 'Understanding the revolutions of 2011', *Foreign Affairs*, 90: 8–16.

Gore, C. (2003) 'The rise and fall of the Washington Consensus as a paradigm for developing countries', in R. Goddard et al. (eds), *International Political Economy: State Market Relations in a Changing Global World*, Basingstoke: Palgrave Macmillan.

Greenwald, G. (2012) 'The growing Iranian military behemoth', www.salon.com/2012/02/04/the_growing_iranian_military_behemoth/, 4 February.

Gresser, E. (2011) 'Doha: heading for failure?', www.eastasiaforum.org/2011/05/07/doha-heading-for-failure/, 7 May.

Guardian (2011) 'Women have emerged as key players in the Arab Spring', www.guardian.co.uk/world/2011/apr/22/women-arab-spring, 22 April.

Gumuchian, M. (2011) 'Saif al-Islam Ghadaffi: the "Michael Corleone" of Libya', news.nationalpost.com/2012/04/11/the-michael-corleone-of-libya/, 12 April.

Habibi, N. (2009) 'The impact of the global economic crisis on Arab countries: a year-end assessment', www.brandeis.edu/crown/publications/meb/MEB40.pdf, December.

Hafez, M. (2008) 'World Investment Report 2008', www.oecd.org/dataoecd/30/59/41865366.pdf, March.

Hamid, S. (2011a) 'The rise of the Islamists', www.foreignaffairs.com/articles/67696/shadi-hamid/the-rise-of-the-islamists, May/June.

— (2011b) 'A new security strategy, but not necessarily a new GCC', www.thenational.ae/thenationalconversation/comment/a-new-security-strategy-but-not-necessarily-a-new-gcc, 16 May.

Hashem, A. (2012) 'The Arab spring has shaken Arab TV's credibility', www.guardian.co.uk/commentisfree/2012/apr/03/arab-spring-arab-tv-credibility, 3 April.

Hassan, A. and S. Beyerle (2009) 'Popular resistance against corruption in Turkey and Egypt', in M. Stephan (ed.), *Civilian Jihad: Non-Violent Struggle, Democratization, and Governance in the Middle East*, New York: Palgrave.

Hassan, H. (2013) 'Syria is now Saudi Arabia's problem', www.foreignpolicy.com/articles/2013/06/06/syria_is_now_saudi_arabias_problem, 6 June.

Henderson, S. (2013) 'Regime change in Qatar', www.foreignpolicy.com/articles/2013/06/14/regime_change_qatar, 14 June.

Hertog, S. (2011) 'The costs of counter-revolution in the GCC', mideast.foreignpolicy.com/posts/2011/05/31/the_costs_of_counter_revolution_in_the_gcc, 31 May.

Heydarian, R. J. (2011) 'Arab Spring, Turkish Summer?', www.fpif.org/articles/arab_spring_turkish_summer, 16 May.

Hudson, J. (2013a) 'The weapons that could change the game in Syria', blog.foreignpolicy.com/posts/2013/03/15/the_weapons_that_could_change_the_game_in_syria, 15 March.

— (2013b) 'Foreigners make up a tiny fraction of the Syrian opposition', blog.foreignpolicy.com/posts/2013/04/02/foreigners_make_up_a_tiny_fraction_of_the_syrian_opposition, 2 April.

Human Rights Watch (2012a) 'World Report 2013: Bahrain', www.hrw.org/world-report-2012/world-report-2012-bahrain.

— (2012b) 'World Report 2013: Kuwait', www.hrw.org/world-report-2012/world-report-2012-kuwait.

— (2013) 'World Report 2013: Oman', www.hrw.org/world-report/2013/country-chapters/oman.

Hussain, K. and A. Nos'hy (n.d.) 'What caused the liquidity crisis in Egypt', www.mafhoum.com/press7/200E14.pdf.

IMF (2010) 'Regional economic outlook: Middle East and Central Asia', www.imf.org/external/pubs/ft/reo/2010/mcd/eng/mreo0510.htm.

— (2011) 'Regional economic outlook: Middle East and Central Asia', www.imf.org/external/pubs/ft/reo/2011/mcd/eng/pdf/mreo1011.pdf.

— (2012) 'Regional economic outlook: Middle East and Central Asia', www.imf.org/external/pubs/ft/reo/2012/mcd/eng/mreo0412.htm.

International Crisis Group (2011) 'Popular protest in North Africa and the Middle East VI: The Syrian people's slow-motion revolution', www.crisisgroup.org/en/regions/middle-east-north-africa/egypt-syria-lebanon/syria/108-popular-protest-in-north-africa-and-the-middle-east-vi-the-syrian-peoples-slow-motion-revolution.aspx, 6 July.

— (2012a) 'Syria's mutating conflict', www.crisisgroup.org/en/regions/middle-east-north-africa/egypt-syria-lebanon/syria/128-syrias-mutating-conflict.aspx.

— (2012b) 'Tentative jihad: Syria's fundamentalist opposition', www.crisisgroup.org/en/publication-type/media-releases/2012/mena/syria-tentative-jihad-syria-s-fundamentalist-opposition.aspx.

Joffe, G. (2011) 'Libya: past and future?', english.aljazeera.net/indepth/opinion/ 2011/02/201122412934486492.html, 24 February.

Jones, T. (2012) 'Embracing crisis in the Gulf', www.merip.org/mer/mer264/embracing-crisis-gulf.

Kaletsky, A. (2010) *Capitalism 4.0: The Birth of a New Economy*, London: Bloomsbury.

Kenner, D. (2013) 'Lebanon's government comes toppling down', blog.foreignpolicy.com/posts/2013/03/22/lebanons_government_comes_toppling_down, 22 March.

Kerr, S. (2011) 'UAE revokes citizenship of seven Islamists', www.ft.com/intl/cms/s/0/1b8b4e84-2bf0-11e1-b194-00144feabdc0.html#axzz2Q4aUx8gH, 21 December.

Khalaf, R. and A. Allam (2011) 'Club of monarchs to extend Gulf reach', www.ft.com/intl/cms/s/0/bbd079cc-7bf7-11e0-9b16-00144feabdc0.html#axzz2Q4aUx8gH, 11 May.

Kiely, R. (2007) *The New Political Economy of Development: Globalization, Imperialism, Hegemony*, Basingstoke: Palgrave Macmillan.

Kim, S. (2011) 'Egypt's Mubarak likely to retain vast wealth', abcnews.go.com/Business/egypt-mubarak-family-accumulated-wealth-days-military/story?id=12821073#.UWVnwM3fKkI, 2 February.

Kinzer, S. (2003) *All the Shah's Men: An American Coup and the Roots of Middle East Terror*, New Jersey: John Wiley.

Kotsev, V. (2013) 'Syrianization of Syria rolls on', www.atimes.com/atimes/Middle_East/MID-03-280313.html.

Kovalyova, S. (2011) 'FAP food price index hits record high', www.trust.org/alertnet/news/fao-food-price-index-hits-record-high/, February.

Krugman, P. (2008) *The Return of Depression Economics and the Crisis of 2008*, New York: W. W. Norton.

Kumar, N. (2005) 'Performance requirements as tools of development policy: lessons from developed and developing countries', in K. Gallagher (ed.), *Putting Development First: The Importance of Policy Space in the WTO and International Financial Institutions*, London: Zed Books.

Kurlantzick, J. (2013) 'One step forward, two steps back', www.foreignpolicy.com/articles/2013/03/04/one_step_forward_two_steps_back, 14 March.

Kurzman, C. (2003) 'Liberal Islam: prospects and challenges', in R. Barry (ed.), *Revolutionaries and Reformers: Contemporary Islamist Movements in the Middle East*, New York: State University of New York Press.

Lagi, M., K. Bertrand and Y. Bar-Yam (2011) 'The food crises and political instability in North Africa and the Middle East', necsi.edu/research/social/food_crises.pdf, 28 September.

Lall, S. (2004) 'Reinventing industrial strategy: the role of government policy in building industrial competitiveness', www.unctad.org/en/docs/gdsmdpbg2420044_en.pdf, April.

Landler, M. and S. Myers (2011) 'With $30 billion arms deal, U.S. bolsters Saudi ties', www.nytimes.com/2011/12/30/world/middleeast/with-30-billion-arms-deal-united-states-bolsters-ties-to-saudi-arabia.html, 29 December.

Lee, C. and I. Yamazawa (eds) (1990) *The Economic Development of Japan and Korea: A Parallel with Lessons*, New York: Greenwood Press.

Levy, E. (2011) 'Hamas ready for peace talks with Israel', www.ynetnews.com/articles/0,7340,L-4062868,00.html, 5 January.

Lobe, J. (2011) 'Saudi counter-revolution cools Arab spring', www.aljazeera.com/indepth/opinion/2011/04/2011 424133930880573.html, 24 April.

Lubold, G. (2013) 'Is anyone in charge of U.S. Syria policy?', www.foreignpolicy.com/articles/2013/06/20/who_is_in_charge_of_us_syria_policy, 20 June.

Lynch, C. and A. Gearan (2012) 'At U.N., Qatar emir calls on Arab nations to intervene in Syria', articles.washingtonpost.com/2012-09-25/world/35496045_1_syrian-opposition-syrian-people-syrian-forces-and-rebels, 25 September.

Lynch, M. (2009) 'Grading places', www.thenational.ae/news/world/grading-places, 31 July.

— (2011) 'The big think behind the Arab Spring', www.foreignpolicy.com/articles/2011/11/28/the_big_think, 28 November.

— (2013) 'Twitter devolutions', www.foreignpolicy.com/articles/2013/02/07/twitter_devolutions_arab_spring_social_media?page=full, 7 February.

Malik, A. and B. Awadallah (2011) 'The economics of the Arab Spring', www.csae.ox.ac.uk/workingpapers/pdfs/csae-wps-2011-23.pdf, December.

Mariani, D. (2013) 'Not a question of money but of dignity', www.

swissinfo.ch/eng/detail/content.html?cid=35363544, 1 April.
Mashal, A. (2012) 'The financial crisis 2008–2009 and the Arab states' economies', dx.doi.org/10.5539/ijbm.v7n4p96, 1 July.
Mayer, A. (2002) *The Furies: Violence and Terror in the French and Russian Revolutions*, Princeton, NJ: Princeton University Press.
McCants, W. (2012) 'The sources of Salafi conduct', www.foreignaffairs.com/articles/138129/william-mccants/the-sources-of-salafi-conduct, 19 September.
— (2013) 'Joining the fray', www.worldpoliticsreview.com/articles/12655/joining-the-fray-salafi-politics-after-the-arab-spring, 22 January.
Meyer, T. and L. Hinchman (2007) *The Theory of Social Democracy*, Cambridge: Polity.
Miles, H. (2011) 'The Aljazeera effect', www.foreignpolicy.com/articles/2011/02/08/the_al_jazeera_effect, 8 February.
Mirza, H. (2008) *World Investment Report 2008: Transnational Corporations and the Infrastructure Challenge*, www.oecd.org/dataoecd/30/59/41865366.pdf, March.
Moore, B. (1966) *The Social Origins of Dictatorship and Democracy*, Boston, MA: Beacon.
Murphy, C. (2011) 'GCC to set up $20bn bailout fund for Bahrain and Oman', www.thenational.ae/news/world/middle-east/gcc-to-set-up-20bn-bailout-fund-for-bahrain-and-oman, 11 March.
Murphy, D. (2013) 'Iraq attacks show coordination, planning, and numbers', www.csmonitor.com/World/Backchannels/2013/0314/Iraq-attack-shows-coordination-planning-and-numbers, 20 March.
Narli, N. (2003) 'The rise of the Islamist movement in Turkey', in R. Barry (ed.), *Revolutionaries and Reformers: Contemporary Islamist Movements in the Middle East*, New York: State University of New York Press.
Nasar, S. (2011) *Grand Pursuit: The Story of Economic Genius*, New York: Simon and Schuster.
Nasr, V. (2009) *Forces of Fortune: The Rise of the New Muslim Middle Class and What It Will Mean for Our World*, New York: Free Press.
— (2011) 'Dangers lurking in the Arab Spring', www.nytimes.com/2011/08/28/opinion/sunday/the-dangers-lurking-in-the-arab-spring.html?pagewanted=all, 27 August.
Nixon, R. (2011) 'US groups helped nurture Arab uprisings', www.nytimes.com/2011/04/15/world/15aid.html?pagewanted=all&_r=0, 14 April.
O'Bagy, E. (2013) 'The Free Syrian Army', www.understandingwar.org/sites/default/files/The-Free-Syrian-Army-24MAR.pdf.
O'Brien, R. et al. (2000) *Contesting Global Governance: Multilateral Economic Institutions and Global Social Movements*, Cambridge: Cambridge University Press.
OECD (2013) *Research and Development Statistics*, www.oecd.org/innovation/inno/researchanddevelopmentstatisticsrds.htm.
Orozco, O. and J. Lesaca (2009) 'Impact of the global economic crisis in Arab countries: a first assessment', www.clubmadrid.org/img/secciones/Background_Doc_ArabWorld_Eng.pdf, 28 October.
Pioppi, D. (2007) 'Privatization of social services as a regime strategy: the revival of Islamic endowments (Awqaf) in Egypt', in O. Schlumberger (ed.), *Debating Arab Authoritarianism: Dynamics and Durability in*

Nondemocratic Regimes, Stanford, CA: Stanford University Press.
Plato (1973) *The Republic and Other Works*, trans. B. Jowett, New York: Anchor Books.
Powers, S. and E. Gilboa (2007) 'The public diplomacy of Al Jazeera', in P. Seib (ed.), *New Media and the New Middle East*, New York: Palgrave.
Pravda (2011) 'Since Egypt became a state army', english.pravda.ru/world/africa/30-11-2011/119781-Since_Egypt_became_a_State_Army-0/.
PressTV (2013) 'Saudi prosecutor urges death penalty for Shia cleric Nimr al-Nimr: Media', www.presstv.ir/detail/2013/03/28/295506/saudi-prosecutor-wants-alnimr-executed/, 29 March.
Przeworski, A. (1996) 'A better democracy, a better economy', bostonreview.net/BR21.2/Przeworski.html, April.
Przeworski, A. et al. (2000) *Democracy and Development: Political Institutions and Political Well-being of the World 1950–1990*, Cambridge: Cambridge University Press.
Ramo, J. (2009) *The Age of the Unthinkable: Why the New World Disorder Constantly Surprises Us and What We Can Do about It*, New York: Back Bay Books.
Reuters (2009) 'Egypt may add more economic stimulus if needed: minister', www.reuters.com/article/2009/01/05/ozabs-egypt-economy-idAFJOE50400J20090105.
— (2011a) 'Factbox – Libyan investments in Africa', af.reuters.com/article/idAFLDE72723320110308?sp=true, 8 March.
— (2011b) 'Egypt sees billions in aid from Saudi, UAE soon', www.kippreport.com/2011/09/egypt-sees-billions-in-aid-from-saudi-uae-soon/, 8 September.
— (2012) 'Succession question fuels uncertainty in Oman', www.reuters.com/article/2012/05/23/oman-succession-idUSL6E8F806720120523.
— (2013a) 'Teen killed in protests on Bahrain revolt anniversary', www.reuters.com/article/2013/02/14/us-bahrain-violence-idUSBRE91DoCK20130214, 14 February.
— (2013b) 'Qatar revives proposal to send Arab force to Syria', in.reuters.com/article/2013/01/12/syria-crisis-qatar-idINDEE90B04W20130112, 12 January.
Richter, T. (2007) 'The political economic of regime maintenance in Egypt: linking external resources and domestic legitimation', in O. Schlumberger (ed.), *Debating Arab Authoritarianism: Dynamics and Durability in Nondemocratic Regimes*, Stanford, CA: Stanford University Press.
Roberts, D. (2011) 'Behind Qatar's intervention in Libya', www.foreignaffairs.com/articles/68302/david-roberts/behind-qatars-intervention-in-libya.
Robison, R. (2002) 'What sort of democracy? Predatory and neo-liberal agendas in Indonesia', in C. Kinnvall and K. Jonsson (eds), *Globalization and Democratization of Asia: The Construction of Identity in Asia*, London: Routledge.
Rodrik, D. (2008) *One Economics, Many Recipes*, Princeton, NJ: Princeton University Press.
— (2011) 'The manufacturing imperative', www.project-syndicate.org/commentary/the-manufacturing-imperative, 10 August.
Roe, G. (2003) 'The International Monetary Fund', in R. Goddard et al. (eds), *International Political Economy: State Market Relations in a Changing Global World*, Basingstoke: Palgrave Macmillan.

Rosenberg, D. (2011) 'Food and the Arab Spring', www.gloria-center.org/2011/10/food-and-the-arab-spring/, 27 October.

Roy, O. (2012) 'The new Islamists', www.foreignpolicy.com/articles/2012/04/16/the_new_islamists?page=full, 16 April.

Rubin, B. (ed.) (2003) *Revolutionaries and Reformers: Contemporary Islamist Movements in the Middle East*, New York: State University of New York Press.

Sachs, J. (2005) *The End of Poverty: Economic Possibilities for Our Time*, New York: Penguin.

— (2009) *Commonwealth: Economics for a Crowded Planet*, New York: Penguin (reprint).

— (2012) 'Government, geography, and growth: the true drivers of economic development', www.foreignaffairs.com/articles/138016/jeffrey-d-sachs/government-geography-and-growth, September/October.

Said, E. (1979) *Orientalism*, New York: Vintage.

Saif, I. (2008a) 'Egypt and Jordan: why don't the benefits of growth trickle down?', www.carnegieendowment.org/2008/08/12/egypt%2Dand%2Djordan%2Dwhy%2Ddon%2Dt%2Dbenefits%2Dof%2Dgrowth%2Dtrickle%2Ddown/us, 12 May.

— (2008b) 'The food price crisis in Arab countries: short term responses to a lasting challenge', Carnegie Endowment for International Peace, eendowment.org/files/saif_food_prices_final.pdf, June.

Sally, R. (2008) 'The WTO: what next after Doha?', www.eastasiaforum.org/2008/09/01/the-wto-what-next-after-doha/, 1 September.

Sandbrook, R. et al. (2007) *Social Democracy in the Global Periphery: Origins, Challenges, Prospects*, Cambridge: Cambridge University Press.

Santiso, C. (2004) 'The contentious Washington Consensus: reforming the reforms in emerging markets', *Review of International Political Economy*, 11(4): 828–44.

Schiller, R. (2011) 'The next market bubbles: food and farm land', english.aljazeera.net/indepth/opinion/2011/03/20113238137242847.html, 26 March.

Schlumberger, O. (2007) 'Arab authoritarianism: debating the dynamics and durability of nondemocratic regimes', in O. Schlumberger (ed.), *Debating Arab Authoritarianism: Dynamics and Durability in Non-democratic Regimes*, Stanford, CA: Stanford University Press.

— (2008) 'Structural reform, economic order, and development: patrimonial capitalism', *Review of International Political Economy*, 15(4).

Schumpeter, J. (1962) *Capitalism, Socialism, and Democracy*, New York: Harper Perennial.

Schwarz, R. (2008) 'Introduction: Resistance to globalization in the Arab Middle East', *Review of International Political Economy*, New York: Routledge.

Sharma, R. (2011) *Breakout Nations: In Pursuit of the Next Economic Miracles*, New York: W. W. Norton.

Shehata, D. (2011) 'The fall of the Pharaoh', *Foreign Affairs*, 90: 26–32.

Sick, G. (2001) *All Fall Down: America's Tragic Encounter with Iran*, Indiana: iUniverse.

SIPRI (2010) 'Military spending and arms procurement in the Gulf', books.sipri.org/files/FS/SIPRIFS1010.pdf.

Sivan, E. (2003) 'Why radical Muslims aren't taking over governments', in R. Barry (ed.), *Revolutionaries and Reformers: Contemporary Islamist*

Movements in the Middle East, New York: State University of New York Press.
Skidelsky, R. (2009) *Keynes: The Return of the Master*, London: Penguin.
Sky, E. (2013) 'Marching through the monarchies', www.foreignpolicy.com/articles/2013/02/01/marching_through_the_monarchies_middle_east_travel?page=full, 1 February.
Smith, C. (2011) 'Egypt's Facebook revolution: Wael Ghonim thanks the social network', www.huffingtonpost.com/2011/02/11/egypt-facebook-revolution-wael-ghonim_n_822078.html, 11 February.
Spiegel, P. (2011) 'University president is upbeat on democracy in Indonesia', paloalto.patch.com/articles/university-president-is-upbeat-on-democracy-in-indonesia, 21 May.
Spyer, J. (2013) 'Iran's silent war in the Gulf', www.jpost.com/Features/Front-Lines/Irans-silent-war-in-the-Gulf-308735, 6 April.
Stiglitz, J. (1999) 'Whither reform: ten years of the transition', www2.gsb.columbia.edu/faculty/jstiglitz/download/1999_4_Wither_Reform.pdf, October.
— (2002) *Globalization and Its Discontents*, London: Penguin.
Sun Tzu (2007) *The Art of War*, Massachusetts: World Publications Group.
Takeyh, T. (2006) *Hidden Iran: Paradox in the Islamic Republic*, New York: Times Books.
Taleb, N. and M. Blyth (2011) 'The Black Swan of Cairo', *Foreign Affairs*, 90: 33–9.
Terzulli, A. and R. Ascari (2009) 'The crisis in four notes', www.sace.it/GruppoSACE/content/it/consumer/research/global_market/Working_paper/WP10_The_Crisis_In_Four_Notes.html, October.
Thuman, M. and G. von Randow (2010) 'Interview with Muhammad Elbaradei on democracy in Egypt', www.ikhwanweb.com/article.php?id=25479 0, 30 June.
Time (2011) 'Time 100: Ayman Mohyeldin', www.time.com/time/specials/packages/article 0,28804,2066367_2066369_2066506,00.html.
Trager, E. (2011) 'The unbreakable Muslim Brotherhood: grim prospects for a liberal Egypt', www.foreignaffairs.com/articles/68211/eric-trager/the-unbreakable-muslim-brotherhood, September/October.
— (2013) 'In power, but not in control', www.foreignpolicy.com/articles/2013/03/21/in_power_but_not_in_control, 21 March.
Ulrichsen, K. (2012) 'Political showdown in Kuwait', mideast.foreignpolicy.com/posts/2012/06/20/political_showdown_in_kuwait, 20 June.
United Nations (2009) 'The global economic and financial crisis: regional impact, responses and solutions', www.un.org/regionalcommissions/crisispublication.pdf, May.
United Nations Development Programme (various years) *Arab Human Development*, www.arab-hdr.org/reports/regionalarab.aspx.
United Nations Statistics Division (n.d.) unstats.un.org/unsd/default.htm.
UPI (2013) 'Gulf states go big for Western hardware', www.upi.com/Business_News/Security-Industry/2013/02/22/Gulf-states-go-big-for-Western-hardware/UPI-42621361558483/, 22 February.
Wallerstein, I. (2011) 'The contradictions of the Arab Spring', www.aljazeera.com/indepth/opinion/2011/11/20111111101711539134.html, 14 November.
Wehrey, D. (2012) 'The march of Bahrain's hardliners', carnegieendowment.

org/2012/05/31/march-of-bahrain-s-hardliners/bozr, 31 March.

Went, R. (2003) 'Globalization under fire', in R. Goddard et al. (eds), *International Political Economy: State Market Relations in a Changing Global World*, Basingstoke: Palgrave Macmillan.

World Bank, Food and Agriculture Organization, and International Fund for Agricultural Development (2009) 'Improving food security in Arab countries', reliefweb.int/sites/reliefweb.int/files/resources/1F52B98A6BBC8065492575A0000B87DA-Full_Report.pdf, 20 April.

World Economic Forum (2010) *Global Competitiveness Report*, www3.weforum.org/docs/WEF_GlobalCompetitivenessReport_2009-10.pdf.

— (2011) 'Global risk 2011', opim.wharton.upenn.edu/risk/downloads/WEF_Global-Risks_2011.pdf, January.

Wright, R. (2009) 'A quiet revolution grows in the Muslim world', www.time.com/time/magazine/article/0,9171,1886539,00.html, 19 March.

Yavuz, H. (2003) *Islamic Political Identity in Turkey*, New York: Oxford University Press.

Yergin, D. (1991) *The Prize: The Epic Quest for Oil, Money and Power*, New York: Simon & Schuster.

Zizek, S. (2010) *Living in the End Times*, New York: Verso.

— (2011) 'Why fear the Arab revolutionary spirit?', www.guardian.co.uk/commentisfree/2011/feb/01/egypt-tunisia-revolt, 1 February.

— (2012) 'The revolt of the salaried bourgeoisie', www.lrb.co.uk/v34/n02/slavoj-zizek/the-revolt-of-the-salaried-bourgeoisie, 26 January.

Zurcher, E. (1993) *Turkey: A Modern History*, New York: I. B. Tauris.

INDEX